Cyber China

The CERI Series in International Relations and Political Economy

Series Editor, Christophe Jaffrelot

This series consists of works emanating from the foremost French research center in international studies, the Paris-based Centre d'Etudes et de Recherches Internationales (CERI), part of Sciences Po and associated with CNRS (Centre National de la Recherche Scientifique).

Founded in 1952, CERI has about sixty fellows drawn from different disciplines who conduct research on comparative political analysis, international relations, regionalism, transnational flows, political sociology, political economy, and on individual states.

This series focuses on the transformations of the international arena, in a world where the state, though its sovereignty is questioned, reinvents itself. The series explores the effects on international relations and the world economy of regionalization, globalization (not only of trade and finance but also of culture), and transnational flows at large. This evolution in world affairs sustains a variety of networks from the ideological to the criminal or terrorist. Besides the geopolitical transformations of the globalized planet, the new political economy of the world has a decided impact on its destiny as well, and this series hopes to uncover what that is.

Published by Palgrave Macmillan:

Politics In China: Moving Frontiers
edited by Françoise Mengin and Jean-Louis Rocca
Tropical Forests, International Jungle: The Underside of Global Ecopolitics
by Marie-Claude Smouts, translated by Cynthia Schoch
The Political Economy of Emerging Markets: Actors, Institutions and Financial Crises in Latin America
by Javier Santiso
Cyber China: Reshaping National Identities in the Age of Information
edited by Françoise Mengin

Cyber China

Reshaping National Identities in the Age of
Information

Edited by Françoise Mengin

First published in 2004 by
PALGRAVE MACMILLAN™
175 Fifth Avenue, New York, N.Y. 10010 and
Houndmills, Basingstoke, Hampshire, England RG21 6XS
Companies and representatives throughout the world

PALGRAVE MACMILLAN is the global academic imprint of the Palgrave Macmillan division of St. Martin's Press, LLC and of Palgrave Macmillan Ltd. Macmillan® is a registered trademark in the United States, United Kingdom and other countries. Palgrave is a registered trademark in the European Union and other countries.

ISBN 978-1–4039–6578–3

Library of Congress Cataloging-in-Publication Data
Cyber China : reshaping national identities in the age of information / edited by Françoise Mengin.
      p. cm.—(CERI–international relations and political economy)
    Conference held at the Centre d'Etudes et de Recherches Internationales in Paris, Dec. 16–17, 2003.
    Includes bibliographical references and index.
    ISBN 1–4039–6578–1
      1. Internet—China—Congresses. 2. China—Economic conditions—Congresses. 3. China—Politics and government—Congresses.
    I. Mengin, Françoise. II. Fondation nationale des sciences politiques. Centre d'études et de recherches internationales. III. CERI series in international relations and political economy

HM851.C92 2004
303.48′33′0951—dc22   2004044576

A catalogue record for this book is available from the British Library.

Design by Newgen Imaging Systems (P) Ltd., Chennai, India.

First edition: November 2004

CONTENTS

Acknowledgment   vii

Romanization of Chinese Names and Terms   ix

List of Acronyms   xi

Notes on the Contributors   xv

Introduction   New Information Technologies and the
Reshaping of Power Relations: An Approach
to Greater China's Political Economy   1
Françoise Mengin

Part 1   New Means, A New Polity?

Chapter One   Speaker's Corner or Virtual Panopticon:
Discursive Construction of Chinese
Identities Online   19
Karsten Giese

Chapter Two   Cyberspace and the Emerging Chinese Religious
Landscape—Preliminary Observations   37
David A. Palmer

Chapter Three   The Changing Role of the State in Greater
China in the Age of Information   51
Françoise Mengin

Part 2 Communication and Control: Sovereignty in the Age of the Internet

Chapter Four Controlling the Internet Architecture within
Greater China 71
Christopher R. Hughes
Chapter Five Government Online and Cross-Straits
Relations 91
Patricia Batto

Chapter Six The Internet and the Changing
Beijing–Taipei Relations:
Toward Unification or Fragmentation? 125
Chin-fu Hung

Part 3 Global Networking and Economic Interactions

Chapter Seven The Information Technology Industry
and Economic Interactions Between
China and Taiwan 155
Barry Naughton

Chapter Eight Global Networking and the New Division
of Labor Across the Taiwan Straits 185
Tse-Kang Leng

Chapter Nine Informational Capitalism and the Remaking
of "Greater China": Strategies of
Siliconization 205
Ngai-Ling Sum

Chapter Ten Urban Assemblages: An Ecological Sense
of the Knowledge Economy 237
Aihwa Ong

Name Index 255

Subject Index 257

ACKNOWLEDGMENT

This book is the outcome of a conference held in Paris at the CERI (Centre d'Etudes et de Recherches Internationales) on December 16–17, 2002. This conference was sponsored by the CERI and by the Chiang Ching-Kuo Foundation for International Scholarly Exchange (Taipei), both of which I want to thank here.

ROMANIZATION OF

CHINESE NAMES AND TERMS

Except for some proper nouns related to Hong Kong and Taiwan, the *pinyin* system of romanization has been followed.

LIST OF ACRONYMS

ACTA: All China Taiwanese Association
ADSL: Asymmetric Digital Subscriber Line
APEC: Asia-Pacific Economic Cooperation forum
ARATS: Association for Relations Across the Taiwan Straits
ASIC: Application Specific Integrated Circuit
AVD: Advanced Versatile Disc
BBS: Bulletin Board System
BTDF: Beijing Technology Development Fund
CCP: Chinese Communist Party
CDC: China Development Center
CDMA: Code Division Multiple Access
CIC: China Internet Company
CNNIC: China Network Information Centre
CSM: Chartered Semi-Conductor Manufacturing
CWW: China Wide Web
DPP: Democratic Progressive Party
EMS: Electronic Manufacturing Service
Fabs: Foundries
FDI: Foreign Direct Investment
GATS: General Agreement on Trade in Services
GEM: Growth Enterprise Market
GIO: Government Information Office
GMD: Guomindang
GSM: Global System for Mobile Communication
GSMC: Grace Semiconductor Manufacturing Corporation
HP: Hewlett-Packard
IC: Integrated Circuit
ICANN: Internet Corporation for Assigned Names and Numbers
ICP: Internet Content Provider

ICT:	Information and Communication Technology
IIIMIC:	Institute for Information Industry's Market Intelligence Center
IP:	Internet Protocol
IPE:	International Political Economy
IPO:	Initial Public Offering
IPR:	Intellectual Property Right
ISP:	Internet Service Provider
IT:	Information Technology
ITRI:	Industrial Technology Research Institute
ITU:	International Telecommunications Union
LCD:	Liquid Crystal Display
LMDS:	Local Multipoint Distribution Service
MAC:	Mainland Affairs Council
MII:	Ministry of Information Industry
Mm:	millimetre
MNC:	Multinational Corporation
MOEA:	Ministry of Economic Affairs
NGO:	Non Governmental Organization
NIT:	New Information Technology
Nm:	nanometer
NSC:	National Science Council
ODM:	Original Design Manufacturing
OEM:	Original Equipment Manufacturing
PDA:	Personal Digital Assistant
PDC:	Product Development Center
PLA:	People's Liberation Army
PRC:	People's Republic of China
R&D:	Research and Development
ROC:	Republic of China
SAR:	Special Administrative Region
SARFT:	State Administration of Radio, Film and Television
SEF:	Straits Exchange Foundation
SHKP:	Sun Hung Kai Properties
SMIC:	Semiconductor Manufacturing International Corporation
SNMVC:	Shanghai New Margin Venture Capital
SOE:	State-owned Enterprise
SVCC:	Shanghai Venture Capital Corporation
SVCD:	Super Video CD
TCIT:	Taoist Culture Information Centre
TDC:	Taiwan Development Center

TD-SCDMA:	Time-Division Synchronous Code-Division Multiple-Access
TFT-LCD:	Thin Film Transistor and Liquid Crystal Display
TI:	Texas Instrument
TLD:	Top Level Domain
TSMC:	Taiwan Semiconductor Manufacturing Corporation
UMC:	United Microelectronics Corporation
VC:	Venture Capital
VCD:	Video CD
WCDMA:	Wideband Code Division Multiple Access
WTO:	World Trade Organization
3G:	Third Generation

NOTES ON THE

CONTRIBUTORS

Patricia Batto holds a PhD in Chinese Studies from INALCO (Institut National des Langues et Civilisations Orientales, Paris) and is a researcher at the CEFC (French Centre for Research on Contemporary China, Hong Kong). She is mainly interested in medias and Information and Communication Technologies in contemporary China. Recent works include *L'Art de jouer au mah-jong en Chine*, Paris, éditions Philippe Picquier, 1999, and the translation, with Gao Tianhua, of the novel *L'Ecole des vers à soie,* éditions Philippe Picquier, 2002.

Karsten Giese is a research fellow at the Institute of Asian Affairs, Hamburg, Germany. Dr. Giese studies modern China studies, sociology, political science, and translation in Berlin (Germany) and Taibei (Taiwan). His research interests include social and cultural change, Internet development in Greater China, and Chinese internal and international migration, foreign politics and security politics of the PRC. Currently he is head of a German–Chinese research project on "virtual identity workshops and identity construction in the Chinese Internet." Recent publications in the field of Internet research include, in 2003, "Construction and performance of virtual identity in the Chinese Internet," in K.C. Ho, Randy Kluver, C.C.Yang (eds), *Asia Encounters the Internet* (Routledge), and "Internet growth and the digital divide: implications for spatial development" in Christopher R. Hughes, Gudrun Wacker (eds), *China and the Internet. Politics of the Digital Leap Forward* (Routledge), and in 2001, "*Big Brother* mit rechtstaatlichem Anspruch. Gesetzliche Einschränkungen des Internet in der VR China," in Benno Engels, Olaf Nielinger (eds), *Elektronischer Handel in Afrika, Asien, Lateinamerika und Nahost* (Schriften des Deutschen Übersee-Instituts).

Christopher R. Hughes is Director of the Asia Research Centre and Senior Lecturer in International Relations at the London School of Economics. He has written widely on the topic of Chinese nationalism. He has published articles in *The China Quarterly*, *Cambridge Review of International Affairs*, *New Media and Society* and *Critique internationale* on the impact of new information and communication technologies on China. He recently co-edited (with Gudrun Wacker) *China and the Internet: Politics of the Digital Leap Forward* (Routledge, 2003).

Chin-Fu Hung is a PhD candidate of Politics and International Studies at the University of Warwick, United Kingdom. He has presented various papers on the Internet and China at conferences held in France, United Kingdom, and the United States. His recent publications include: "Public Discourse and 'Virtual' Political Participation in the PRC: The Impact of the Internet" *in Issues & Studies*, 39(4) (2003) and "Internet, e-Social Capital and Public Sphere: A Study of the Qiangguo Luntan during the 16th National Congress of Communist Party of China" (November 2002) (with Peter Ferdinand) in Peter Yu and Jack Qiu (eds), *China and the Internet: Policy Issues and Cultural Formations* (provisional title), published by Blackwell, to appear in 2004. His PhD dissertation is entitled "Politics and Public Opinion in China: The Impact of the Internet, 1993–2003."

Tse-Kang Leng is Professor of Political Science, National Chengchi University, Taipei. He also teaches courses at the Business School of National Chengchi University. Dr. Leng has served as Secretary General of Chinese Association of Political Science (Taipei) since 2003. Dr. Leng received a PhD from the University of Virginia in 1995. His researches focus on cross-Taiwan Straits relations, political economy of globalization, and world city studies. His recent publications include: "Securing Cross-Straits Economic Relations: New Challenges and Opportunities" (*Journal of Contemporary China*, May 2002), "Economic Globalization and Talent Flows between Taiwan and Mainland China" (*Asian Survey*, March/April, 2002), *A Political Analysis of Information Technology Industries: Shanghai in Global Perspective* (Taipei: INK, 2002) (in Chinese), *The Taiwan–China Connection: Democracy and Development Across the Taiwan Straits* (Boulder: Westview Press, 1996) and others.

Françoise Mengin, Political Scientist, is Senior Research Fellow at the Centre for International Studies and Research (Sciences Po, Paris). Her most recent works focus on the remapping of the Greater China space in the context of globalization. She is the author of *Trajectoires chinoises: Taiwan,*

Hong Kong et Pékin (Paris: Karthala, 1998), and has co-edited with Jean-Louis Rocca *Politics in China: Moving Frontiers* (New York: Palgrave, 2002).

Barry Naughton, an economist who specializes on China, is the So Kuanlok Professor of Chinese and International Affairs at the Graduate School of International Relations and Pacific Studies of the University of California at San Diego. He has published extensively on the Chinese economic transition, industry and trade in China and Chinese political economy. His study of Chinese economic reform, *Growing Out of the Plan: Chinese Economic Reform, 1978–1993* (New York: Cambridge University Press, 1995) won the Masayoshi Ohira Memorial Prize. His newest book, co-edited with Dali Yang, is *Holding China Together: Diversity and National Integration in the Post-Deng Era* (New York: Cambridge University Press, 2004).

Aihwa Ong is Professor of Anthropology and of Southeast Asian Studies at the University of California, Berkeley. She has written on gender and Islam; Chinese transnationalism; sovereignty, governmentality, and citizenship. Her books include *Flexible Citizenship* (1999), *Ungrounded Empires* (1997), and *Buddha is Hiding: Refugees, Citizenship, the New America* (2003). She is co-editor, with Stephen J. Collier of *Global Assemblages: Technology, Politics and Ethics as Anthropological Problems* (Blackwell, 2005).

David A. Palmer is Eileen Barker Fellow in Religion and Contemporary Society at the London School of Economics and Political Science. He obtained his PhD in religious studies at the Ecole Pratique des Hautes Etudes, Paris, in 2002. His research interests include religion, society, and politics in contemporary China; religious movements, modernity, and globalization; and alliances between science and religion.

Ngai-Ling Sum is a lecturer in the Department of Politics and International Relations in Lancaster University. Her most recent publications is an edited book (with Marcus Perkmann) on *Globalization, Regionalization and Cross-Border Regions* (Palgrave, 2002). She has also contributed to *Critical Asian Studies*, *Capital and Class*, *New Political Economy* and *Urban Studies*.

New Information Technologies and the Reshaping of Power Relations: An Approach to Greater China's Political Economy

FRANÇOISE MENGIN

Chinese Cross-border Spaces: Heuristical Sites

Political implications of new information technologies (NITs) have already drawn attention from scholars. Globalization trends, as well as the opening of boarders would have replaced verticality of hierarchies by horizontality of communication.[1] The Internet would be one of the main contributors to the globalization of economy and culture.

As a matter of fact, since the open-door policy has been launched in the People's Republic of China (PRC) at the end of the 1970s, and since the resuming of Sino–Taiwanese relations 10 years on, the so-called Greater China region seems to be one telling example of Kenichi Ohmae's "region-state,"[2] an ethno-economic space that crosses across national boundaries because of a primacy of economic interests over national identification, hence calling the nation-state's sovereignty into question. This process is all the more telling as it occurs within a context of interstate rivalry (the Sino–Taiwanese sovereignty dispute) or of different political systems (Hong Kong as a Special Administrative Region of the PRC).

However, far from merging nation-states into a borderless world, into one single economy, globalization is part and parcel of state formation processes. Not only are globalization's institutions interstate bodies, but globalization factors are intertwined with governmental action. Such an understanding of globalization processes assumes that transnational activities are no exception to social activities at large, on the one hand, and that a state–society dichotomy should be left aside, on the other. As far as the Greater China area is concerned, I have argued elsewhere that the issue at stake is not to focus on the forming of a hypothetical transnational society, but to understand the various processes that alter individual strategies into collective ones, on the one hand, and on the embedding of the latter in power relations, on the other.[3]

As to the development of NITs, one cannot but notice that it generates new power struggles, that it provides new accumulation opportunities of both material and symbolic nature. In so doing, new relations of domination and subordination are being instituted. With regard to interstate or interregional competition, information technologies (ITs) can be a means of economic protection and competition. An "information race" between the PRC, Hong Kong, and Taiwan is taking place, even, within the PRC, between some provincial governments. In addition, the Internet can be a conduit for the state ideological apparatus. As to the Sino–Taiwanese dispute in particular, the Web promotes Beijing's irredentist claim. Besides, at the institutional level, strategic concerns influence the shaping of the Internet governance. Therefore, the development of ITs is both strengthening traditional national borders and new regional poles. In any case, it contributes toward a fragmentation process and not only to a unification process.

This book is the outcome of a conference held in Paris in December 2002 aiming at analyzing the interaction between the development of ITs and social logic, on the one hand, unification and fragmentation processes, on the other.[4] The issue at stake was to highlight public and private actors' strategies aiming at monopolizing benefits provided by the information society—be it for private enrichment or for government regulation purposes—, and, in consequence, the new power poles that are emerging.

Integration processes due to globalization that can be witnessed in "Greater China" are legion, and NITs are certainly one of the main means. Barry Naughton in this volume lays stress on the fact that Taiwan's economic interactions with mainland China are important in virtually every sector, but nowhere more than in electronics, while China's IT industry is developing rapidly into a world-class IT hardware industry. Ngai-Ling Sum states that Greater China is becoming the home of the "next Silicon Valley." Tse-Kang Leng, for his part, clearly shows how, facing a rising and globalizing China, Taiwan's competitive edge is rooted on its advantages in deepening international networking and incorporating China into a grand strategy of globalization. In so doing, these Taiwanese firms have made substantial contribution to China's global share of the IT market. In other words, IT networking across the Taiwan Straits is the reflection of new forces of globalization and localization. More, Leng demonstrates that U.S.-trained advanced work forces have become a catalyst of manpower integration across the strait; instead of bilateral interaction, this integrative mechanism is global-oriented.

Therefore, when organizing this conference, "Greater China" was not taken as an already shaped region taking over from specific local and national societies that it encompasses. It was only chosen as a heuristical space offering both important unification and fragmentation trends allowing more thorough analysis of societal changes and of the reshaping of power relations. In so doing, the various analyses proposed in this book, should shed light both on state formation process and on international relations theory.

As a matter of fact, no definition, nor even delimitation, of "Greater China" has been sought after in this volume.[5] Each author has chosen to focus on the space that is relevant to his/her research. Tse-Kang Leng clearly specifies that "Greater China" in his chapter refers to Taiwan, mainland China, and Hong Kong/Macao region. Ngai-Ling Sum makes clear that she uses the term "Greater China" as convenient shorthand to indicate the cross-border urban economic space of Hong Kong, Pearl River Delta, Taiwan and Yangtze Delta, and in order to remind readers that Greater China is a controversial expression, she writes it with inverted commas. Aihwa Ong extends her research to Malaysia and even gives us telling examples taken from the cyberhubs in Hyderabad and Bangalore. Patricia Batto and Chin-fu Hung focus on Sino–Taiwanese relations, while Karsten Giese looks at mainland Chinese netizens.

Thus as far as the controversial term "Greater China" is concerned, this book will not bring any decisive conclusion. Quite the contrary, as will be stressed later, the development of the knowledge economy contributes to both unification and fragmentation processes on very different scales. More, Aihwa Ong invites us to rethink the assumption according to which informational technologies will follow the networks already shaped by trade and manufacturing in configuring Greater China.

As to Chinese religious landscape, David Palmer challenges the assumption according to which NITs would bring greater integration of Chinese communities on the mainland and overseas, as well as between Chinese and non-Chinese communities. He notes a strong discrepancy (at least in the field of Daoism) between online religion in Hong Kong and Taiwan, on the one hand, and mainland China, on the other. Overall, the Hong Kong and Taiwanese sites can be said to be an extension into cyberspace of the traditional temple-based configuration of Chinese religion. The mainland sites, on the contrary, reflect a more individual, idiosyncratic, and interactive exploration of China's spiritual traditions, and a greater degree of commercialization (providing fortune-telling or feng-shui services).

Different Approaches

The chapters gathered in the first part—*New Means, A New Polity?*—offer various analyses of the impact of the Internet on the political order. Within a context of social diversification, Karsten Giese notes from the outset that, in the PRC, modern mass media have increasingly taken on a role as a framework for interpersonal reference, offering models for identification traditional social institutions of the Chinese socialist state, the *danwei* above all, previously offered. Despite the relatively short history of the Chinese Internet, usage of this medium already represents an integrated leisure activity of urban middle classes, of the younger generation in particular. Giese focuses on public discourses within Chinese language Bulletin Board Systems (BBS)—he has monitored five major ones of three well-known Chinese Internet content providers formally covering lifestyle, love and partnership as well as social and political issues—and he raises the question: is this segment of the Internet a virtual speaker's corner or, as Bentham and Foucault would put it, a super panopticon? While his answer is far from definite, he shows how identities are constructed online in many fields.

As a virtual panopticon closely monitored by the state, but at the same time as a space allowing freedom of expression and access to information, the Internet cannot but change the form of religion in China. Focusing on two case studies—Daoism and Falun Gong—David Palmer's chapter begins with three initial hypothesis: (1) the emergence of a new space for religious expression, characterized by an autonomous quest for meaning rather than collective rituals; (2) a further undermining of orthodoxies accompanied by the emergence of new centers of religious influence; and (3) greater integration of Chinese communities on the mainland and overseas, as well as between Chinese and non-Chinese communities. So far, while the data seems to support the first two hypotheses, Palmer shows that the third one needs to be reformulated: a clear difference appears between online religion in mainland China, on the one hand, and Hong Kong–Taiwan, on the other, with, surprisingly, the potentialities of the Web being more fully exploited in the former than in the latter.

Finally, Mengin's chapter aims at highlighting some of the main challenges state's action is confronted to by the development of ITs. In this respect, she distinguishes between the state as a controller, compelled to manage the undermining of its sovereignty, and the state as an arbiter of contending social interests, be they public or private, central or local. In so doing, she insists on the necessity to go away from the Weberian ideal-type of the state, and to pinpoint the various processes according to which individual and collective strategies are embedded in power relations.

Though no chapter addresses the issue of security per se, the second part of the volume—*Communication and Control: Sovereignty in the Age of the Internet*—explores the impact of NIT on interstate relations. When studying the Internet architecture in China, Christopher Hughes stresses the fact that the state-centric nature of the international system seems to provide little incentive for addressing political concerns at the global level. There is certainly awareness amongst Chinese policy-makers that the choice of information and communication technology (ICT) architecture is not politically neutral, especially when it comes to considerations of national security. Therefore, Hughes' chapter calls into question the assumption whereby the impact of the global telecommunications market in China will make ICTs into an effective tool for political transformation along liberal-democratic lines.

If information warfare per se is not tackled in this volume, Hughes' chapter gives us some insights on the waves of hacking attacks ongoing in the region. As a matter of fact, the interstate rivalry between the two sides of the Taiwan Straits is studied in this book on the basis of a comparison made by Patricia Batto between governmental sites run by Beijing and by Taipei. In her chapter, she seeks to establish whether Taiwan, taking advantage of its greater modernity, has been able to use the Internet to enhance the international visibility of the country. She then compares the two governments' communication and information policies, in particular with respect to cross-straits relations. Finally, she looks at how economic and trade links between the two sides of the Taiwan Straits are perceptible on the Internet and what one can conclude from this.

For his part, Chin-fu Hung aims at showing that although the Internet will strengthen Greater China in terms of increasingly integrated economics and socioculture, it seems unlikely to facilitate the political integration process while eroding the sovereignty claims from both sides of the Taiwan Straits, as some Internet pundits claim.

Finally, the impact of ITs on the region is examined from the starting
point of market strategies in the third part of the volume *Global Networking
and Economic Interactions*. The pace of investment in China's integrated
circuit (IC) industry has accelerated dramatically since about 1999, and
the pace of technology transfer has shown impressive results since 2001.
What are the most important sources of the dynamism of China's IT
hardware industry? In particular, how should the inter-relationship
between market forces and government policy be assessed? To what extent
are recent developments under the control of Chinese domestic actors,
and to what extent do they reflect the impact on China of international
market forces? Barry Naughton's chapter attempts to shed light on these
questions by describing some of the main economic and political forces at
work on the industry. Among economic factors, he examines the roleof
Taiwan investors in the Chinese industry, then the broader context
of IT industry development, and turning to policy factors, he examines
technology policy in China and then in Taiwan.

Among his various analysis and observations, Naughton underlines
that the progress from IC fabrication to IC design occurs under different
economic principles: it is a progression to a more labor-intensive activity,
albeit one which relies on highly skilled professional labor. Therefore,
interaction of human capital between China and Taiwan will be driving
forces of consolidating global IT networks across the Straits. Global
networking and the new division of labor across the Straits is precisely
Tse-Kang Leng's contribution in this book. His chapter first introduces
the role of "hybrid" Taiwanese semiconductor company in forming new
global and local networks of IT production. Leng also discusses the
political aspects of network formation as the Taiwanese government
intends to use both restrictive and encouraging policies to balance
national security and economic globalization and he shows how this
leads to hesitation and contradiction in the policy-making process.

The starting point of Ngai-Ling Sum's chapter is the "Silicon Wave"
vision that is very influential among public and private institutions and
actors, be they policy-makers, state technocrats, think tanks, or business
journalists, in the East-Asian region since the Asian crisis. According to
Sum, as it is unfolding in "Greater China," this Siliconization strategy
involves three elements: (1) privileging the "Silicon Valley" model in particular and "high-tech development" discourses promoted by diverse
private and public actors; (2) using these discourses to reconfigure
techno-economic subjectivities in the hope of stabilizing emerging
economic practices favorable to their particular insertions into the global
informational capitalism; and (3) consolidating and mediating this

regional mode of growth via the co-presence of cooperation–competition and integration–fragmentation.

For her part, Aihwa Ong starts her contribution with assessing that the rise of information economy calls for a refinement of the global network idea for too little attention has been focused on the disparate actors and institutions that have come together in space-making activities. She uses the Deleuzian term "assemblage" to describe this analytical problem-space that is an intersection of disparate elements, of the old and the new, and of territorialization and deterritorialization. Ong's chapter puts the stress on the fact that Asian states have shifted away from a focus on the technical aspects of development toward the problematization of the population as the key factor in achieving wealth.

The Ideological Apparatus of the State and the Knowledge Economy

David Lyon aptly reminds that "(w)hatever freedom and fun may be generated in cyberspace, the reality is that the Internet does not create a 'space apart', a realm of technologically enabled liberty. Rather, as the Internet is increasingly integrated with every day life in Asia as elsewhere, so it provides some new ways of engaging in old practices."[6] Thus, notwithstanding the fact that the Internet reinforces surveillance and social control,[7] when tackling the issue of a possible "demise" of the state due to the development of NITs, the authors of this book bring to the fore that, quite the contrary, the latter are additional means to strengthen Althusser's ideological state apparatus.[8] First, Karsten Giese puts the stress on the fact that in order "to exert the highest possible degree of control, the Internet architecture in China does not follow the familiar decentralized network pattern. To the contrary, the structure of the network is designed in a strictly hierarchical manner, with the individual user at the bottom line." Next, not only does the PRC government carry many actions in order to control the Chinese cyberspace—preventive regulations as well as repressive actions (see, for instance Mengin's chapter)—, but many authors recall the basic fact that, because of commercial interests, firms, be they Chinese or foreign, comply with government requirements.

More, Christopher Hughes notes that concepts such as "public interest" and "national security" are not clearly defined by the World Trade Organisation (WTO). Therefore, the national security caveat is given considerable scope. When examining the problem of global ICT governance,

Hughes shows that the issue of self-interests of states is likely to have far more support from governments around the world than is the advocation of human rights and liberal democracy. And he concludes that "(i)n a world system that remains state-centric despite the globalisation of ICTs, taking concerns over security as the starting point from which to address broader social issues may be a feasible project for those concerned about the promotion of international human rights standards. It is certainly a more effective way of addressing the real political problems that have to be faced in the Information Age than is starting out from assumptions that the social values of any particular society will inevitably be disseminated throughout the world."[9]

An interesting example of how the Internet is a means to spread the Chinese state policy and ideology can be found in the religious field. David Palmer shows that though state control on religion is indeed weakened by the Internet, it can continue to assert itself in manners both direct and indirect. If blocking access to websites (Falun Gong websites for instance) is an instance of direct intervention, state influence continues to be exercised in a more subtle fashion toward those sites that are accessible. Palmer brings to the fore the Taoist Culture and Information Centre (TCIC), which is based in Hong Kong, that is outside mainland China, but which is directed at mainlanders. Since the authors of the articles on the TCIC's site are for the most part academic scholars from the mainland, and since database commission makes a conscious effort to avoid content that would be politically sensitive on the mainland, the Chinese state influence on religious discourse spreads beyond Chinese borders.

Even in the field of communication per se, the Internet does not necessarily stand on the side of the country that most requires to communicate with the rest of the world. After carefully analyzing the PRC's and the Republic of China's (ROC's) governmental websites, Patricia Batto concludes that "Beijing is very visible on the Web, when it is Taiwan that has the greater need for international support."

Finally, as far as economic logic is concerned, the various trends that contribute to forming cross-border economic sites are first and foremost the result of governmental action. Ngai-Ling Sum recalls that Taiwan's Hsinchu Science-Based Industrial Park—a pioneer in the region—was built in the late 1970s thanks to the then minister of Economic Affairs— Li Kuo-ting—and narrated as a nation-building project. Barry Naughton states that, today, "the Chinese government has no intention to take a 'hands off' attitude toward technological development: they will continue to aggressively support favored firms and industries." And, if Tse-Kang Leng rightly recalls that the business community in Taiwan receives minimum supports from the state to expand its activity in mainland China, one should not conclude that the state is collapsing. If one leaves aside reasoning in terms of zero sum game, transnational trends have to be understood as part of state formation processes. This, in turn, is not without methodological consequences as shall be mentioned later.

Modernization and the Reshaping of Identities

Certainly, growing transnational flows and the formation of cross-border economic sites result in new transnational identities. One of the most prominent example is that of the Taiwanese settled in Shanghai referred to as *Shang-Tai-nese* (*Shang Tai Ren*) a term coined to encompass a double meaning as Ngai-Ling Sum recalls in her chapter: "Taiwanese in Shanghai," but also "Powerful Taiwanese." More generally, Sum draws our attention on techno-economic identities that are constructed, in various sites in Greater China, in and through high-tech symbols such as "Silicon Valley," "clustering," "entrepreneurship," "information technology," "knowledge-based economy," and "biotechnology."

But this should not lead to underestimate a concomitant trend toward the reshaping of national identities. The insightful research carried by Karsten Giese on the Chinese Internet, and more particularly on BBSs, informs us both on state formation processes and domestic political changes. With potentially omnipresent surveillance and opacity of rules for legitimate behavior or content, Giese shows that a virtual panopticon is in place, but does not function as such. Certainly, far from being speaker's corners, BBSs act however as "public spaces for experimenting with alternative identities, be they negotiated alongside ethnic, regional or local divisions, gender or sexual orientation, shared biographical experiences or political opinions." In so doing, a highly ambivalent process is at work, for beside individualized or gendered dimensions, BBS users, in a relatively abstract way, identify themselves as Chinese: "identities that are constructed here are 'indigenous' PRC-identities, not Greater China, not Overseas Chinese nor globalised identities"; but national identity is not "linked to the leading role of the Communist Party and certainly provides an alternative model competing with CCP orthodoxy."

Modernization is often apprehended in a normative way. Modernity partakes in an evolutionist conception of social change,[10] and though definitions defer from one author to the other, they all put the stress on the generalization of the state and the bureaucracy, that is a rationalization of the structures of authority,[11] and at the same time the calling into question of holistic societies by growing individualism. In other words modernization theories are based on linear models that postulate a universal set of norms and values—in fact "Western" ones, hence an ethnocentrist view—, on the one hand, and a clear cut between tradition and modernity, on the other. The point here is not to recall that such theories have already demonstrated their limits,[12] but to lay stress on the fact that as a process, modernization implies adjusting tactics; it thus produces junctions undermining any linear vision of history. As such, it can be highly ambivalent.

The religious field provides an interesting case of a "modernization" process due to the development of the Internet. In this volume, David Palmer analyses the redistribution of influence among religious organizations brought by the Internet in China: there is a shift in emphasis from a local community, ritual-based practice of religion to an individualistic approach characterized by the search for more information content, while religious organizations with a strong presence in cyberspace can acquire new influence extending much farther than their original local sphere of activities. Palmer notes that, ironically for sure, state restrictions on offline religious activity may have given the Internet a greater role in the evolution of religious culture in China than in other countries.

In this case, the ambivalent nature of modernization processes can be witnessed for the Internet reveals a more "modern" religiosity in Communist China than in Hong Kong and Taiwan, though more "advanced" societies according to modernization theories. As Palmer's research shows, Hong Kong and Taiwan sites can be said to be extensions into cyberspace of the traditional temple-based configuration of Chinese religion, while the mainland ones reflect a more individual and idiosyncratic approach of religiosity, and, last but not least, a greater degree of commercialization.

Reshaping Power: Toward Cybercolonization?

As far as economic position is concerned, the following chapters document the reshaping of power among the leading poles in the region. For instance, when contrasting the situation in Hong Kong with that in Taiwan, Barry Naughton shows that the former may well prosper in the future, but it will never be able to maintain the dominant position with respect to China's interactions with the world that it once had. Taiwan's position is quite different, as it will be pulled into increasingly close involvement with mainland industries. More generally, when studying cyber-capitalism in Greater China, Sum clearly identifies integration/ fragmentation processes: the Siliconization strategy consolidates intensified integration that may create a deepening division of labor, but also leads to fragmentation in that the different "Silicon Valleys" compete with each other for global capital, technology transfer and knowledge-based workers. In some cases, this competition can lead to interpretations in terms of "colonial" hierarchy, as does Shenzhen mayor about the Hong Kong–Shenzhen relationship.

In terms of power struggles, another interesting development documented in this book by Ngai-Ling Sum is related to the piracy issue. Well known is the fact that Intellectual Property Right (IPR) Laws are under constant challenges by piracy of softwares and media products.[13] It is practiced by consumers (businesses, nonprofit organizations, high school and college students, etc.) and by producers (especially petty capitalists). And Sum shows how piracy is becoming in the region a "way of life" in Michel de Certeau's sense. Counter-IPR narratives and practices are developing, ranging from ethical justification—information and knowledge-based products are part of a "global intellectual commons"—to purely commercial justification. Certainly, such justifications bring to the fore the false polarization in terms of legal versus illegal to understand emerging positions of power and accumulation.

But beyond trans-local or trans-regional competition, achieving wealth brings new modes of subject making, new kinds of valorized subjectivity that are produced by market competitiveness. This issue has already been documented by Aihwa Ong's book *Flexible Citizenship*.[14] In this volume, she shows how the information economy contributes to reshaping social rights in relation to skill profiles, and more generally how Asian states are shifting away from a focus on the technical aspects of development toward managing the economy indirectly through the micromanagement of the population. Hence, an undermining of the sociopolitical basis of citizenship and the creation of a new moral economy of *globalized intellectual citizenship*. "Partnerships between states and global companies created spaces of 'graduated sovereignties' whereby social rights for different segments of the population depend to a large extent on their capacity to engage global market forces."[15] She gives various examples of such processes—biopolitics in Foucault's words— leading individuals and populations to become explicit objects of government policies. For instance, the aim of Hong Kong to become "the Manhattan of Asia" is linked, according to Ong, to technologies for progressively excluding working-class families long supported by massive public housing. "The losers in this new intellectual game are poor, less educated Chinese who have less of a claim to the city." Likewise, Singaporeans, who have long felt superior to Malays in Malaysia and in Singapore itself, now feel themselves to be second-class citizens in relation to Asian expatriates. The latter seem to be preferred by the government-led corporations and private industry. More generally, Ong shows that expatriates are enjoying a transnational intellectual citizenship that cuts across different political domains of social rights. "There is the perception that the stress on intellectual advance in the sciences is a form of cybercolonization, of being discriminated against when the wealth of the country (. . .) does not necessitate the rise of a knowledge society. (. . .) Thus the new regime valorizing knowledge has induced a sense of being re-nativized in the colonial sense."

The reshaping of power carried, among other factor, by the Internet in an area composed by ethno-economic spaces crossing across national boundaries cannot but bring back to the fore Foucault's writings when he says: "(a) society is not a unitary body over which one and only one power would be exercised, but it is in reality a juxtaposition, a connection, a coordination, a hierarchy too, of different powers that remain nevertheless within their specificity.":[16] "Society is an archipelago of different powers."[17] In other words, "power relations take root in the whole of the social network."[18] Though Foucault's research is not tackling the issue of networks' internationalization, not to speak of their globalization, his definition is still relevant as long as one admits that transnational activities are no exception to social activities at large.

Methodological Learnings

First of all, the various analysis proposed in this volume bring to the fore the absolute necessity to contextualize each and every processes. In this volume no deepening of the concept of globalization per se is proposed.[19] However, the analyses meet Jean-François Bayart's methodological requirement when he states that the more globalization appears as a compound and contingent event, the more should it be interpreted in relation to its historicity.[20] In this book, Christopher Hughes insists on the fact that the impact of ICTs is not only determined by the nature of the technology itself but also by the political and cultural contexts within which they are embedded. The Chinese case certainly provides ample evidence to this. Likewise, the historical overview of the Chinese religious landscape offered by Palmer in this volume shows that prior to the advent of the Internet, the traditional religious ordering of bodies through ritual had already largely disappeared in the cities. Because temple-centered religiosity had become a pale shadow of what it used to be, many religious and spiritual groups and seekers lacked a formal, fixed location in physical space.

In addition to historical contingency, chapters of this volume show how irrelevant the cleavage between state and society may be. The entwining between private and public strategies, between state and transnational actors comes to the forefront at each crucial point of analysis. For instance, as to the impossibility of drawing a clear cut between public and private actors, Barry Naughton, Tse-Kang Leng, as well as Christopher Hughes lay stress on the prominent figure of Jiang Mianheng—son of Jiang Zemin, first secretary of the Chinese Communist Party (CCP) until 2002—who holds directorships in important Internet firms and has been appointed vice-president of the Chinese Academy of Sciences. And Naughton recalls the case of the firm Grace that is spear-headed both by Jiang Mianheng and Winston Wong—son of Wang Yung-ching, Taiwan plastics tycoon. More generally, Ngai-Ling Sum argues that there is a global-regional-local epistemic community that promotes the "Silicon Wave." This epistemic community expresses a common high-tech voice in the region and comprises state officials and government departments, university academics, Silicon Valley returnees, business journalists, industrial and trade associations, local-regional capitalists, and global capitalists with major regional interests.

For her part, Mengin reminds us that the difficulty to draw a clear cut between private and public actors that characterizes the new information economy in China is linked not only to the Chinese regulation on telecommunication but also to the fact that in the reform era the largest private firms cannot do without bureaucratic patronage. More fundamentally, authors such as Margaret Pearson[21] or Yves Chevrier[22] have demonstrated that the straddling between the state and the market is rooted in the historical trajectory—one is confronted with historical contingency once again—of the Chinese merchant elite. As early as the sixteenth century Ming, the so-called public sphere (*gong*) developed thanks to a participation of some members of the merchant elite to the official sphere (*guan*). The former is thus an intermediary zone of interaction between the state and the society, straddling the private sphere (*si*) and the official one (*guan*). Even if the relationships between the merchant sphere and the official sphere have been fluid, a "Janus-faced pattern" (in Pearson's words) has prevailed: "a pattern in which the merchant elite was neither wholly autonomous nor state-dominated but instead sat, Janus-like, between state and society, and at times even blended socially with the official class and carried out 'public' (*gong*) works."[23]

Hence, besides the very historicity of each and every process, any study of globalization processes should be carried by some basic assumptions. If one takes into account the core propositions of historical sociology[24] and of economic sociology,[25] than one has the methodological apparatus to better understand the straddling between public and private spheres,[26] politics and economics, state and society, what is legal and what is not. Thus, before studying Chinese webs, it might be useful to remind Mark Granovetter's and Richard Swedberg's central propositions of economic sociology: "1—Economic action is a form of social action; 2—economic action is socially situated; and 3—economic institutions are social constructions."[27]

The issue of shaping identities is no exception. As the imaginary projection of power relations, they too are above all flexible as witnessed by the way they are constantly reshaping, including by means of the cyberspace.

However, it could be misleading to leave the reader on the impression that because power relations are continuously reshaped, transnational actors are, by and large, escaping from hierarchical ordering; in other words, that the verticality of hierarchies would be replaced by the horizontality of communication to go back to the very initial assumption.[28] Quite the contrary; and chapters in this volume provide more than one example of the persisting hierarchical organization of powers due to struggles for controlling political and economic wealth. Hence, once again, the relevance of Foucault when he posits that power relations take root in the whole of the social network,[29] and when, through the concept of "governmentality," he lays stress on the "specific albeit complex form of power whose principal target is population, its principal form of knowledge political economy, its principal technical means apparatuses of security." [30]

Notes

1. Manuel Castells, *The Information Age: Economy, Society and Culture, Vol 1: The Rise of the Network Society* (Oxford: Blackwell, 1996).
2. Ohmae, Kenichi, "The Rise of the Region State," *Foreign Affairs*, 72, 2 (Spring 1993): 78–87; also: *The End of the Nation-State: the Rise of Regional Economies* (London: Harper Collins, 1996); *The Borderless World: Power and Strategy in the Global Marketplace*, 2nd edn. (London: Harper Collins, 1994).
3. Françoise Mengin, "Taiwanese Politics and the Chinese Market: Business's Part in the Formation of a State, or the Border as a Stake of Negotiations," in *Politics in China: Moving Frontiers*, Françoise Mengin and Jean-Louis Rocca (eds.) (New York: Palgrave Macmillan, 2002): 232-257.

4. *New Information Technologies and the Reshaping of Power Relations: an Approach to Greater China Political Economy*, CERI (Centre d'Etudes et de Recherches Internationales), Sciences Po Paris, 16–17 December 2002.

5. On Greater China, see in particular, *The China Quarterly*, 136 (December 1993).

6. David Lyon, "Cyberspace, Surveillance, and Social Control: The Hidden Face of the Internet in Asia," in *Digital Democracy: Discourse and Decision Making in the Information Age*, K.C. Ho, Randolph Kluver and Kenneth C.C. Yang (eds.) (London: Routledge, 1999): 68.

7. On this issue, ibid.: 67–82.

8. Louis Althusser, "Ideology and Ideological State Apparatuses," in *Lenin and Philosophy, and Other Essays* (London: NLB, 1971).

9. On this issue see also: Lawrence Lessig, *Code and Other Laws of Cyberspace* (New York: Basic Book, 1999).

10. Among an important literature, see Seymour M. Lipset, "Some Social Prerequisites of Democracy and Political Legitimacy," *American Political Science Review*, 53, 1 (March 1959): 69–105; Gabriel A. Almond and James S. Coleman (eds.), *The Politics of Developing Areas* (Princeton, NJ: Princeton University Press, 1960); Barrington Moore, *Social Origins of Dictatorship and Democracy: Lord and Peasant in the Making of the Modern World* (Boston: Beacon Press, 1966); and Shmuel Noah Eisenstadt, *Patterns of Modernity* (London: Pinter, 1987).

11. Modern societies would be formed of clearly delineated spheres: public, private, politics, economics, religious, etc.

12. As to their application and shortcomings to/in the Chinese case in particular, see Françoise Mengin and Jean-Louis Rocca, "Analyzing Changes through Overlapping Spheres," in *Politics in China*, Mengin and Rocca (eds.): xii–xvi.

13. On this issue, see Debora Halbert, "Piracy, Open Source, and International Intellectual Property Law," in *Digital Democracy*, Ho, Kluver, and Yang (eds.): 97–110.

14. Aihwa Ong, *Flexible Citizenship: The Cultural Logics of Transnationality* (Durham and London: Duke University Press, 1999).

15. Besides Aihwa Ong's chapter in this book, see her article: "Graduated Sovereignty in Southeast Asia," *Theory, Culture, and Society*, 17, 4 (August 2000): 55–75.

16. My translation. Original: "Une société n'est pas un corps unitaire dans lequel s'exercerait un pouvoir et seulement un, mais c'est en réalité une juxtaposition, une liaison, une coordination, une hiérarchie aussi, de différents pouvoirs, qui néanmoins demeurent dans leur spécificité." Michel Foucault, *Dits et Ecrits II, 1976–1988* (Paris: Gallimard, 2001): 1006.

17. Ibid.

18. "(L)es relations de pouvoir s'enracinent dans l'ensemble du réseau social." Michel Foucault, "Le pouvoir, comment s'exerce-t-il ?" (Power, how is it exercised?), in *Michel Foucault, un parcours philosophique, (Beyond Structuralism and Hermeneutics), 1982–1983*, Hubert Dreyfus, and Paul Rabinovitch (Chicago: University of Chicago Press, 1984): 318.

19. On the concept of globalization see, among many writings: Roland Robertson, *Globalization, Social Theory and Global Culture* (London: Sage, 1993) and Jean-François Bayart, *Le Gouvernement du monde: Une critique politique de la globalization* (Paris: Fayard, 2004).

20. Ibid.

21. Margaret M. Pearson, *China's New Business Elite: The Political Consequences of Economic Reform* (Berkeley: University of California Press, 1997).

22. See in particular, Yves Chevrier, "L'empire distendu: esquisse du politique en Chine des qing à Deng Xiaoping," (The loose state: an outline of Chinese politics from the Qing to Deng Xiaoping) in *La greffe de l'Etat* (The graft of the state), Jean-François Bayart (ed.) (Paris: Karthala, 1996): 263–395.

23. Pearson, *China's New Business Elite*: 45.

24. See in particular, Theda Skocpol (ed.), *Vision and Method in Historical Sociology* (Cambridge: Cambridge University Press, 1984).

25. See the seminal work of Mark Granovetter and Richard Swedberg (eds.), *The Sociology of Economic Life* (Boulder, Co.: Westview Press, 1992). For the relevance of historical sociology's and economic sociology's propositions to the case of China, see Françoise Mengin and Jean-Louis Rocca, "Analyzing Changes," in *Politics in China*, Mengin and Rocca (eds.) xvii–xix.

26. On the issue of the privatization of the state—that is not only the privatization of public firms and public services, but also the privatization of state activities such as redistribution or security—see Béatrice Hibou (ed.), *La privatisation de l'Etat* (Paris: Karthala, 1999), and the English version *Privatizing the State* (London: Hurst, 2004, and New York: Columbia University Press: 2004). This book shows how the public/private dichotomy is not relevant in as much as the issue at stake is different modes of government that can be carried by direct, as well as by indirect forms.

27. Granovetter and Swedberg (eds.), *The Sociology of Economic Life*: 6.

28. See earlier, note 1. However, it is not doing justice to Manuel Castell's work to limit it here to this one proposition. The embeddedness of cultural constructs into power relations is taken into account by Castells who postulates "new styles of governmentality, in which different categories of citizens are treated according to their ability to serve market competitiveness." Castells, *The Rise of the Network Society*: 416.

29. See earlier, note 14.

30. Foucault, *Dits et Ecrits II*: 655. My translation.

Original and complete quotation: «Par ce mot de «gouvernementalité» je veux dire trois choses. Par gouvernementalité, j' entends l' ensemble constitué par les institutions, les procédures, analyses et réflexions, les calculs et les tactiques qui permettent d'exercer cette forme bien spécifique, bien que complexe, de pouvoir, qui a pour cible principale la population, pour forme majeure de savoir, l'économie politique, pour instrument technique essentiel les dispositifs de sécurité. Deuxièmement, par «gouvernementalité», j'entends la tendance, la ligne de force qui, dans tout l'Occident, n'a pas cessé de conduire, et depuis fort longtemps, vers la prééminence de ce type de pouvoir qu'on peut appeler le «gouvernement» sur tous les autres: souveraineté, discipline; ce qui a amené, d'une part, le développement de toute une série d'appareils spécifiques de gouvernement et, d'autre part, le développement de toute une série de savoirs. Enfin, par gouvernementalité, je crois qu'il faudrait entendre le processus ou, plutôt, le résultat du processus par lequel l' Etat de justice du Moyen Age, devenu aux XVe et XVIe siècles Etat administratif, s'est trouvé petit à petit «gouvernementalisé».»

PART 1

New Means, A New Polity?

CHAPTER ONE

Speaker's Corner or Virtual Panopticon: Discursive Construction of Chinese Identities Online[1]

KARSTEN GIESE

Change and Stability

Rapid socioeconomic changes undoubtedly have been taking place in China in the last 20 years. During this process, though still claiming absolute political power, the Chinese Communist Party (CCP) had to give way to new social—and political—actors. As a result, the capacity of the CCP to enforce social and political compliance decreased. Without any competitor in China for decades, communist ideology now has also lost much of its former attractiveness. Furthermore, the CCP lost much of its former integrative capacity and has to face the necessity to strive for the loyalty of the Chinese citizens. By creating a self-image as the leading force in the struggle for national unity and strength, the CCP discovered the construct "national identity" as a new power tool for achieving social and political integration under the leadership of the CCP. Consequently, the term "identity" has continuously gained importance, at both social and personal level, and political power now is directly linked to the ability to control relevant discourses.

The intellectual debate on cultural modernity of the 1980s[2] and the heated controversy regarding Chinese identities triggered by the TV series "*Heshang*"[3] provide two early examples of the highly political nature of the term identity in contemporary China. But it is not only political debate that dominates the quest for identity. Social change, globalization and the general uncertainty of possible outcomes of these processes all have created a strong desire for common features, acceptance, mutual understanding, and the emotional security of shared identities. The resulting widespread search for the individual and collective "self" does—almost unnecessary to say—seldom follow the Party line.

Having said this, in this chapter I will discuss recent social and technological developments that facilitated individualization, diversification, and privatization. I then will identify the Internet as a major innovation that, set against the background of the struggle for political hegemony in the field of identification, calls for government regulation and thought control. Focusing on public discourses within Chinese language Bulletin Board Systems (BBS), the question arises: Is this segment of the Internet a virtual speaker's corner or a super panopticon. Challenges to CCP rule, strategies, and counterstrategies will be discussed and evaluated.

The Setting: The Propaganda State at a Loss

Socioeconomic Change and the Individual

As a result of the economic reforms initiated by the Chinese government some 20 years ago rapid economic, social, and last but not least cultural changes undoubtedly have been taking place in China. The growing integration into the world market, influences of globalization and technological innovations all have had a great impact on the changing Chinese life spheres—most visible among today's younger generation in the modern urban conglomerations.

Politically this process has, besides anything else, produced tension between the CCP's claim of absolute political power and moral leadership on the one hand and the growing autonomy of smaller social units and particularly the individual on the other. The result is of rather dialectical nature: positively speaking, the more the Party and the central government encourage—economic—initiatives, the greater the power these groups or individuals gain versus the Party state, and the larger the number of actors that the CCP has to deal with; the more social tasks the Party state, and its basic organizational units depart from, the weaker the basis becomes for agenda setting and integration; and last but not least, the fewer the functions that traditional social institutions like the *danwei* are able to fulfill, and the smaller the number of their members, the narrower becomes the ground for political or moral guidance, identification, and sanctioning that these institutions may exert.

In other words, the number of individuals, particularly young urban individuals, who find themselves beyond the reach of traditional social institutions of the Chinese socialist state has been constantly growing. On the one hand this lack of affiliation equals a loss of the once dominating models for identification, but on the other hand it results in unprecedented individual freedom to choose from a growing variety of lifestyles and value orientations. What we see here is the typical process of individualization.

Reaching the Hearts of the Masses

Within this context of social diversification, modern mass media have increasingly taken on a role as a framework for interpersonal reference, offering models for identification the *danwei* had previously offered. Chinese television, in particular, is outstanding in its role as mouthpiece of Party orthodoxy and provider of models for orientation.

For decades, the Chinese mass media served the Party state as means to accomplish ideological and moral hegemony by providing every individual in every possible aspect of life with official interpretations of reality.[4] Electronical mass media and particularly the nationwide victory of television thus enabled the Chinese state to reach almost every—at least urban—citizen, affiliated to traditional social institutions or not. Already in 1987 when TV sets in private households were not as numerous as they are today,[5] more than half of the surveyed population of Greater Shanghai admitted their most important family activity was watching TV.[6]

Within the top-down media system directly controlled by the CCP censorship body nowadays called "Publicity Department" the few national TV stations then offered almost uniform models for identification. During the 1990s, however, Chinese TV and its role within the propaganda system has changed dramatically. Commercialization and liberalization of the media sector made way for a growing number of economic actors as well as for an increasing variety of programmes—not least foreign media products.[7] Representations of alternative lifestyles like widely watched soaps from Taiwan or Hong Kong style game and music shows provide new perspectives on Chinese national identity beyond the borders of the PRC. Unnecessary to say that lifestyles and models for individual identification presented in these programmes often do not at all conform with Party orthodoxy, and bans, as a helpless reaction, even increased the attractiveness of these undesireable contents.[8] Furthermore, with the

growing influence of commercial, regional, and local TV stations broadcasting in local dialects, distinct regional, local, ethnic, or cultural identities can be expected to develop alongside, or even in place of, dominating
national identities. The Party perspective, once dominating all spheres
of life without any serious challenge, now seems to be at a loss and diversification from the general pattern.

Technological Revolution and Privatization

In addition to individualization of life and diversification of models for
identification, privatization can be identified as the third major development of the 1990s. Even television can be characterized as a medium
that serves the acquisition of culture and models for identification in an
individualized private setting.[9] Viewed from a wider perspective, however, it is certainly the telecommunication revolution in Chinese cities
that has essentially contributed to this process of privatization.

In 1990 only six out of 1,000 citizens even of the modern metropolis
Shanghai owned a telephone,[10] and *private* calls were only to be made at
public phone booths observed and controlled by block leaders and street
committees. Only 10 years later, by the end of 2001, 35 out of 100 urban
dwellers had direct private access to a fixed line telephone,[11] and the
number of mobile phones exceeded 144 million nationwide.[12] As a
result, today private phone calls really have become a *private matter*, well out
of the reach of easily controlling "when," "with whom," "how often," and
"what topic." In this way the Chinese telecommunication revolution has
created a private communication space, which—viewed from the perspective of identity construction—provides ample opportunities for
confirmation and consolidation of shared identities, a process that originally was confined to direct communication face to face within existing social institutions and possibly listened in by moral and ideological
watchdogs.

Technological Revolution and New Public Spaces for Discourse

As telecommunication has contributed to the creation of peer-to-peer
private spaces for communication, the introduction of Internet services
to China may, besides others, be interpreted as the creation of multiple
symbolic spaces for public communication and discourse, thus bridging
individuals and groups independent of space and time.

Despite the relatively short history of the Chinese Internet, usage of
this medium already represents an integrated leisure activity of urban

middle classes, the younger generation in particular.[13] The CNNIC survey of mid-2002—as well as earlier and later ones—showed that interpersonal communication clearly dominates the usage patterns of the estimated 45 million Chinese netizens. For 45.5 percent of users, socializing in chat rooms represents the most frequent online activity, while almost 19 percent use BBSs most often.[14]

As this usage pattern demonstrates, the Internet does not only serve as alternative source of information to the monopolized and strictly controlled state media,[15] so often discussed and probably highly over-exaggerated by Western authors. More important, it also facilitates the widespread exchange of opinions and public discourse.

Identity Construction and Public Discourse

By subdivision into particular fields of interest and topics, the fragmented nature of this highly commercialized network in China provides individuals with ample space for self-realization: thousands of BBSs serve as what can be called virtual Good Places or Third Places in cyberspace.[16] In this way, this part of the Chinese Internet provides a huge variety of spaces facilitating the discursive construction of identities. Furthermore and most important, here, in contrast to past decades in China, this process now is self-organized and takes place in public.

Mutual anonymity of the actors as one of the main features of BBS communication obviously contributes to tearing down traditional barriers of public moral, Confucian values and behavioral rules, striving for harmony, the conception of face, the sense of shame, or political repression, which usually limit such discourses within offline social institutions like the *danwei* or the family. BBSs in this way act as public spaces for experimenting with alternative identities, be they negotiated alongside ethnic, regional or local divisions, gender or sexual orientation, shared biographical experiences or political opinions. Both anonymity and the very limited severeness of potential sanctions by the virtual community for one's words contribute to a much more open and controversial discussion and a much more courageous positioning of individuals than in traditional offline social settings. Large numbers of users are frequent guests in these numerous virtual Good Places and, as I will show, many of them, indeed, make use of the new freedom of expression. In my opinion, these public discourses, mainly engaging in negotiating identities, represent the real subversive potential of the Internet in China, because it is mainly the educated urban elites who make use of the Internet in this way. Consequently, in the long run it is this feature that will pose one of the greatest challenges to the ideological and moral leadership, and, among other factors, possibly also to the political rule, of the Party as it appears today.

Building a Virtual Panopticon

The CCP Perspective: Challenges and Policies

Much has been writtten on Internet censorship and the Great Fire Wall of China. All authors have identified information as well as interpretations of reality alternative to the dominating view of the CCP as the major challenge to the CCP's claim of absolute power. Most of the scholarly discussions focused on policing undesirable content, mainly provided from outside the PRC. These discussions on the blocking of—mainly foreign—websites and the use of proxy servers as one feasible counterstrategy, important as they might still be from the perspective of certain groups in China and abroad, nevertheless may be misleading. In the same way the CCP used to censor traditional media, the Internet has been subjected to censorship of information.[17] In the early stages of Internet development in China, the blocking of websites may have been a central question, because users had to rely on foreign, and on English language contents in particular, due to the lack of Chinese content provided within the PRC. Today, the picture looks different; more than 126,000 domains and 293,000 websites—eductional sites not counted—registered under the national top-level domain.cn[18] give ample evidence of the huge supply, custom-taylored for the Chinese market mainly by providers, who, because of commercial interests, basically comply with government requirements.

Against this background, in regard to the results of user surveys and the latest technological developments, it seems, that the battle to control the contents of webpages has already been fought and won by the Chinese censors. Besides language and code barriers, often underestimated in relevant discussions in the West, that prevent PRC users from accessing information from foreign as well as from Hong Kong or Taiwan servers, the government initiated drive to provide suitable Chinese language content probably decided this battle in favor of the Party.

However, this success might prove a Pyrrhic victory for the CCP. Competition between Chinese Internet Content Providers (ICPs) increasingly leads to the dissemination of information and interpretations of facts labeled not desirable by authorities at various levels, as a number of well-known examples show.[19] While enforcing compliance of online journalists affiliated to formal institutions by direct sanctions can be regarded a relatively easy task, thousands of online communication forums with millions of simultaneously participating individuals definitely call for a different approach.

Hierarchical Network Architecture, Vertical Responsibility System, and Multilayered Policing

In order to exert the highest possible degree of control, the Internet architecture in China does not follow the familiar decentralized network pattern. To the contrary, the structure of the network is designed in a strictly hierarchical manner, with the individual user at the bottom line. Top-down, on the highest level we find, under the direct control of the Ministry of Information Industry (MII), only a handful of international gateways that connect the Chinese network to the World Wide Web. Below, there are ten so-called *interconnected networks* that interlink the so-called *connected networks* of Chinese Internet Service Providers with each other and function as interfaces to the international gateways. The whole architecture is centrally controlled by the MII and additional authorities at various levels, including the CCP Publicity Department.[20]

All institutional or economic actors of each level within this hierarchy hold responsible to ensure compliance with the relevant laws and regulations policing the Chinese Internet and can be sanctioned for any failure to comply. Besides physical control of networks, the whole system of policing is focusing on content. Insofar, a number of laws and regulations have been enacted in order to police undesirable contents and to sanction noncompliance. Following the relevant regulations on mass media, these rules leave ample space for interpretation of what kind of content has to be regarded unlawful. Theoretically, all institutions maintaining interconnected networks can, for example, be severely sanctioned for any portion of unlawful content an individual publishes in the Internet, while directly or indirectly using their network services. The same applies to the lower levels of the network structure including ICPs and those who physically provide access—everyone operating an Internet café, for example. As a result, a multilayered system of surveillance and censorship has been established that is potentially omnipresent by making use of sophisticated surveillance technologies and human censors—so-called *Big Mamas* or, more neutral, *banzhu* or operators—in the case of BBSs.[21]

Regarding network structure and the reports on successful implementation of the latest technological achievements in screening and packet-sniffing devices in China,[22] many observers conclude that not a single byte of information disseminated via the Chinese part of the Internet will eventually evade the eyes of the censor and the long arm of the state—at least potentially, as public reports on arrests of individuals and revoking of licenses for economic actors as sanctions for noncompliance seem to prove.[23]

The Panopticon is Built

What does this mean for the individual user of the Chinese Internet and for the BBS user and participant in identity-related discourses in particular? Although theoretically registration with the local Public Security Bureau was required from every individual user, this policy has never been enforced on a larger scale, as it proved unrealistic.[24] As a result, until very recently individuals were able to evade surveillance and the risk of being sanctioned by simply accessing the Internet from Internet cafés. A number of postings from different BBSs give evidence of a probably quite common practice to participate in discussions on politically sensitive topics only from Internet cafés, although they had access to the Internet at home as well. This example shows two things: (1) users usually were well aware of the political limits imposed on free speech, but (2) nevertheless decided for noncompliance, because they also knew too well how to evade state control and potential sanctions. However, this strategy also shows that the panoptic principle prevalent in the whole Chinese society for decades was successfully transplanted to the Internet, or, more accurate at this point, the Internet has been incorporated into the imperfect panoptic system of the social and political reality of the PRC.

This situation reflected the status quo for a couple of years, but recently things have changed. Not only have technological achievements perfected the system of electronic surveillance, but evasion of state control now also does not seem to offer a realistic option any longer for participants at least of major Chinese BBSs. Afraid of possible state sanctions, all major providers of Internet-based communication forums now require active participants to register. While this had been obligatory in the past as well, this requirement was often met only formally, and individuals were able to evade potential personal identification by simply registering fictitious names and addresses. Now, in the majority of cases an existing mobile phone number and/or the ID number is required for registration as an individual identifier that will be checked by the provider before assigning the necessary password.[25] Because no provider wants to be held responsible for the deviant behavior of individual BBS users, the panoptic system is now reaching down to this level of the network hierarchy and, one is inclined to conclude, this has been successfully implemented. Under these circumstances, probably no individual will voluntarily provide his identity for others to hide.

Panopticon at Work? Discursive Identity Construction in BBSs as Reality Check

With potentially omnipresent surveillance, opacity of rules for legitimate behavior or content, actors isolated by individualization, intimidation by erratic sanctioning and arbitrary persecution, the virtual panopticon seems to be fully functional by now.[26] Nonetheless, after monitoring the communication of five major BBSs and analyzing patterns of the contruction of multiple and fragmented identities via online discourses in our research project for almost a year now, serious doubts arise that this system is really operational.

The Stage: BBS Communication and Identity Formation

Most discussions on Chinese BBS are based on the observation of only one of the many thousands of such communication forums in China—the Strong Country Forum (*Qiangguo Luntan*) provided by the Party newspaper People's Daily (*Renmin Rinbao*). Because this BBS is exceptional in many ways and does not at all reflect the reality of all the other Chinese BBSs, I decided not to include it into our ongoing study. The majority of Chinese BBSs does not at all focus on political issues. On the contrary, most of them have to be regarded communication platforms for exchanging news and views on lifestyle and pop culture issues. BBSs subdivided by larger topics are serving virtually all aspects of mainstream modern urban lifestyles: partnership, marriage, sexuality, parenthood, girls' and women's issues, education, studying abroad, software, sports, fashion, food, entertainment, cars, pop music, movies, travel, literature, finances, or military and foreign policy issues, and so on.

In this way, these communication forums facilitate interpersonal exchange in a wide range of topics, based on individual preferences or dislikings, subjective perspectives, shared experiences and beliefs as well as collective orientations and values. In other words:

> [By communicating] with each other, members display their group identity and their personal identity at the same time. (. . .) Not only

subjective identities are tested and created, but identity of the group whilst defining boundaries and rules. Simultaneously continuous public discourses about these processes are taking place. (. . .)

In those virtual public platforms an experimental construction of identities is happening, and it comes to (. . . .) complex interactions between fictional-virtual and real life sphere related identities. In this regard normative-practical discussions develop in the sense of a political public: Subjective identities and public opinions perform in mutual dependence at this place.[27]

Online organic construction of alternative individual and collective identities therefore definetely poses a severe challenge to Party hegemony and orthodoxy, as these discourses are potentially undermining the Communist Party's offline efforts to build a unified Chinese national identity.

The Play: Constructing Multiple Identities Online

In our study, we have monitored five major BBSs of three well-known Chinese ICPs, formally covering lifestyle, love and partnership as well as social and political issues.[28] Although large variations exist both over time and between individual BBSs, traffic on average amounts to a total of roughly 8,000 individual messages posted by more than 2,000 active participants every month. Our study shows that, although formally each BBS is assigned a topic, the content of communication is (1) not confined to this topic at all, and (2) offline events and major discussions are picked up in all the BBSs at roughly the same time. This is reflected by the fact that, besides a small minority of users who, in MUD-like manner, create avatars as *ludic identities* for online role play not related to offline reality,[29] all content of communication and the actors themselves are deeply rooted in their offline settings. Terms of reference are clearly the social and political reality of the PRC. Insofar, and in regard to registration requirements, identities that are constructed here are "indigenuous" PRC identities, not Greater China, not overseas Chinese nor globalized identities.

Although the range of identity-related topics is huge, spanning from very personal questions over social matters and religious beliefs to moral issues and politics, only a few dimensions can be touched in this chapter. Individual perspectives, for example, freedom to choose individual ways of life alternative to traditional role models and standardized biographies, struggles for privacy and freedom to develop as an independent individual without interferences by relatives, superiors, teachers or the state,

omnipresent in the offline world, and the various limitations the participants are subjected to in their social settings, are some of the topics most
prevalent in all the BBSs we study, regardless of the topics formally
assigned to them. Self-realization and a good deal of narcissism and
weariness are central issues. Self-centered as many of the participants
obviously are, this fact, in regard to society offline, nonetheless attracts a
lot of criticism. Selfishness and irresponsibility are the most criticized
features of modern Chinese society and individuals. The majority of the
obviously younger participants in this kind of discussions definitely
yearns for wealth, luxuries, and power. They identify themselves with
representatives of respective lifestyles but do not—or not yet—possess
the necessary material means. Many, as a matter of fact, believe to be
underprivileged and deprived of the fulfillment of their material desires
without their own fault. As members of the educated urban elites, however, they feel to be even more qualified for these material privileges
than other social groups or individuals. This feeling of relative depriva-
tion more than egalitarian romanticism or any sense of social justice,
obviously makes a good breeding ground for numerous utterances
of discontent against the rich and the powerful who are suspected of
generally abusing their privileges and status. Not surprisingly, individual
figures within administration, government and Party are often targeted
directly. Usually verbal attacks are mostly confined to those already fallen
out of favor with the political nomenclature and widely criticized as
scapegoats of, for example, anticorruption campaigns by state media.
Nonetheless, relevant discourses tend to develop their own logic and
dynamism, and the moderators or *banzhu* of the BBSs sometimes find it
hard to maintain political correctness of such heated debates.

Departing from the peaks of politically sensitive debates and returning
to the lowlands of the struggle for individual happiness, there are outstanding characters who seem rather obsessed with the idea to reform or
revolutionize gender or sexual relationships and identities in particular.
Polygamy, concubinage, and faithfulness are hot topics for widespread controversial discussion, and online love affairs seem to be both a particularly
attractive option and a somewhat theoretical issue. Gender roles and identities are both reconstructed and deconstructed, and a gender gap seems to
materialize in this context. Self-perceptions and qualities assigned to male
or female identities by participants representing the opposite sex often
show huge differences and contradictions. Following traditional orientations many males demand sexual freedom and promiscuity for themselves,
whereas females should generally be denied these "privileges." More and
more females, on the other hand identify themselves as sexual beings with

their own wills demanding equal treatment and freedom. While some participants, regardless of their gender, view family and childrearing as fulfillment of their lives, a growing number of others, and obviously more females than males, regard themselves as perfect entity and identify with the romantic image of a modern urban single presented mainly in foreign movies. Although many users seem to be convinced to present their own individual and unique perspectives and models, comparison shows that the majority of relevant statements, nonetheless, reveals a high degree of uniformity and, most striking, many parallels with traditional or conservative models in regard to gender, sexuality, partnership or family and broader moral issues of individual orientation and behavior.

Besides these individualized or gendered dimensions, BBS users, in a relatively abstract way, identify themselves as Chinese. But, as far as discussions focus on inner-Chinese issues, being members of a particular ethnic group is seldom a topic. Participants explicitly identify themselves with the PRC—in their capacity as Chinese citizens, but marked by shared culture, language, history, and traditions rather than by state borders, government, or Party politics. National identity, in this respect, is not at all linked to the leading role of the Communist Party and certainly provides an alternative model competing with CCP orthodoxy. Closely related to the topics that are discussed, other bonds to localities sometimes seem to gain the upper hand. Culturally Chinese in the first place, participants feel as Beijingers, Shanghainese, or Sichuanese and appear to be rather preoccupied with deeply rooted and long-standing prejudices against those not sharing their own regional, sub-ethnic identities. By doing so, BBS users depart from their protective anonymity, at least in part. Probably not least because of this strong regional or local affiliation and implicit acts of exclusion, grouping of participants by geographical origin for online social interaction is more widely observed than any comparable pattern. Shared geographical identities not only facilitate strong emotional bonds online, they also provide opportunities for participants to easily expand social interactions into the offline reality of the respective cities. There is ample evidence within BBS communication that this is not only a theoretical feature. Participants from Shanghai or Beijing, to give an example, or migrants living there and identifying themselves with their places of abode, have met several times, some of them regularly over longer periods of time. Social interaction based on shared geographic locations usually is not merely transplanted from the online into the offline social world as a result of offline contacts, as one might think, but rather develops in an integrated way with both online and offline components.

Last but not least, identities are constructed political beings. There is one dominant common pattern for the construction of identities related to politics: opposition against and criticism of the Chinese government in general and the Communist Party or prominent members of one of these bodies in particular. Although criticism often tends to be very outspoken and directly challenging the CCP, this pattern should, however, not be mistaken for principled political opposition. Relevant discourses are always related to particular political issues and, surprisingly, in principle do not seem to draw more general conclusions. Some participants, united in their criticism of human rights policies of the CCP, share a common identity as protagonists for human rights in China. Some group around environmental issues and others around censorship and free speech. All of them share common features as opponents to government policies and identify themselves with this role. On the other hand, they are far from constructing a unified identity as political opposition or dissidents, rather confining themselves to shared critical or oppositional views on isolated political fields. Individual interests in certain issues rather than principled engagement in politics seems to be the driving force behind this widespread pattern.

The Actors: Taboos and Evasive Strategies Versus Confrontation

Our ongoing study shows that, notwithstanding the panopticon in place, discourse and discursive construction of identities online in many aspects represent features of a virtual speaker's corner rather than a jailhouse designed by Jeremy Bentham or the internalized power of the omnipresent social panopticon imagined by Michel Foucault. However, we should be careful not to be misled in our conclusions by widespread evidence of utterances of discontent and politically challenging criticism of the Chinese government and the CCP in isolated issues. Although even Falun Gong has been a topic for discussion among BBS participants during our time of observation, there certainly are taboos that even the most daring do not touch. The democracy movement of 1989, or the cases of a number of political dissidents for example, represent some of these taboos. Not a single posting touched upon these topics, neither directly nor indirectly—for good reasons, as the examples of so-called Internet activist Huang Qi[30] and a Beijing based student arrested late 2002 for posting a message in support of Huang's case to a Bulletin Board[31] clearly demonstrate.[32]

Participants in online communication seem to know very well which topic has to be left untouched and how far they may go. There is ample evidence of a number of evasive strategies cautious individuals use to apply. While homophones are useful in order to trick filtering software, this certainly is no feasable strategy to evade the eyes of Big Mamas and will certainly not provide any protection against arbitrary state persecution. A more sophisticated way to disguise one's argument is to split it into a number of headers of otherwise empty postings, leaving it to the readers to pull the strings together. This obviously often proved successful as far as software filters and *banzhu* are concerned, but probably will not protect the authors from state persecution. Therefore, the strategy most prevalent in many suspectedly politically sensitive discourses is a practice best described by the Chinese proverb "Pointing at the mulberry tree while actually addressing the acacia." By avoiding directly challenging the authority of the Party state, critical authors are, nevertheless, able to express their views easily to be understood by other participants, as this practice represents a traditional offline pattern.

Given that panopticon is at work, one might think, that this evasive behavior is clearly a result of intimidation. But such a conclusion is not backed by empirical facts as some BBS users confine themselves to this practice and others do not. Usually discussions on topics that, on first sight, do not qualify to be political, such as love and partnership issues, gender, sexual or lifestyle questions, obviously do not call for evasive strategies. Regarding political discourse, however, there also does not exist any distinct pattern as to which topics or statements evasive strategies are applied. But, daring an informed guess at this stage of our study, one pattern possibly can be identified according to our observations. There seems to be a behavioral generation gap. While older participants, probably based on their personal experiences from politically more turbulent periods, tend to make use of evasive strategies more eagerly, the younger generation generally seems to be more outspoken and critical regardless of the discussed issues.

To draw a conclusion, these findings may be interpreted as a virtual panopticon that is fully functional only for certain parts of Internet users, the older generation in this case. Internet-based communication forums are for sure far from being speaker's corners, but, to ask the decisive question: is a panopticon functioning for only half of its inmates still a panopticon?

Conclusion: Identities Constructed Online— a Challenge to CCP Hegemony?

Verbal communication and social interaction in Chinese BBSs touch upon a multitude of different aspects related to individual and collective identities, and identities are constructed in many fields. The nature of these identities is aspect-related and fragmented, or multidimensional. Different dimensions of individual and collective identities constructed via online discourse do not compete with each other, but rather supplement each other creating an eternally incomplete patchwork-identity.

On the other hand, these identities do, in a number of ways, pose a potential threat to identification models propagated by CCP orthodoxy. Communist hegemonism in this field, however, is not yet seriously challenged by complete sets of distinct collective identities competing with the CCP political construct of unified national identity. In this regard, although the national components of identities that are constructed online in parts greatly differ from the CCP model or are even opposed to it, participants in online discussions have neither created a complete mindset nor do they pick distinct existing alternative models for identification like the Taiwanese or the Hong Kong model.

Observers of Chinese political and social reality sometimes have been surprised how open and critical political discussions sometimes tend to be in face-to-face settings. The CCP has long adopted a very economic approach, on the one hand allowing an astonishing degree of individual freedom for voicing political discontent as long as those utterances are isolated and private, and supressing all forms of opposition as soon as they take steps for self-organization or try to go public on the other. This principle applied to BBSs may explain the large freedom for alternative and oppositional online statements directly targeted at the Chinese government and Party. From the CCP perspective, online communication forums only provide very limited and highly fragmented public spaces, and no organizational efforts related to political topics has been spotted yet. BBSs, therefore, do not pose a serious challenge to the Party's monopoly over political power, as long as they only provide opportunities for individualized utterances of discontent that may well serve the desirable function as online safety valves for offline social and political reality.

The younger generations of urban Chinese in particular, much less intimidated as their online representatives show, do not yet pose a greater threat to CCP rule, as well. Although much more outspoken and confrontational in discourse, they, on the other hand, represent the most individualized and self-centered segment of society today. But challenges may arise in the future, because of the potentially far-reaching subversive power of changing lifestyles and value orientations that develop among the younger generation as relevant online discourses show. While this potential, if at all, probably will materialize only in the long run, two more aspects of the discursive construction of identities in BBSs seem to have the potential to challenge the political status quo. These discourses from time to time produce charismatic characters and opinion leaders who may create groups of loyal followers posing a serious threat to the Chinese government at least potentially. Empirical evidence shows that the CCP is well aware of this, and applies a two-tiered counterstrategy. In some cases the traditional arsenal of intimidation and persecution is made use of, but other cases show that individuals also are successfully wooed by the Party for enlisting them on its own payroll. Evidence of the second strategy at work can be found in a number of politically oriented BBSs, which generally are under closer surveillance. Manipulation of discourses is a well tried and tasted means of thought control.

Last but not least, the development of online communities reaching out into offline reality as a growing number of real world meetings of participants shows, probably receives a lot of attention on the government side. Today, this reaching out from online to offline settings seems to be confined to groups of shared geographical background. But what if political identification will add a new dimension to this pattern of affiliation?

Notes

1. This essay draws on findings from a larger ongoing study on the discursive construction of Chinese identities in the Internet involving a survey of four major Chinese BBSs. This qualitative research has been funded by the Volkswagen Foundation and is due to be finished by mid-2004. In the meantime research progress will be documented on the project's website: http://www.chinaBBSresearch.de.
2. Beate Geist, *Die Modernisierung der chinesischen Kultur*, Mitteilungen des Instituts für Asienkunde Nr. 263 (Hamburg: 1996).
3. Cui, Wenhua (ed.), *Heshang lun* (River elegy) (Beijing: 1988); Sabine Peschel (ed.), *Die Gelbe Kultur. Der Film Heshang: Traditionskritik in China* (Bad Honnef: Horlemann, 1991).
4. Cf. i.a.: Lee, Chin-Chuan (ed.), *Voices of China: The Interplay of Politics and Journalism* (New York: Guilford Press, 1990); Daniel C. Lynch, *After the Propaganda State* (Stanford: Stanford University Press, 1999); Shanthi Kalathil and Taylor C. Boas, "The Internet and State Control in Authoritarian Regimes: China, Cuba, and the Counterrevolution," *First Monday*, 6, 8 (August 2001), online available via: http://firstmonday.org/issues/issue6_8/kalathil/index.html (accessed: September 20, 2002).
5. A penetration rate of 100 percent is said to be achieved at least in the 30 largest Chinese cities. Cf. Shanti Kalathil, "Chinese Media and the Information Revolution," *Harvard Asia Quarterly*, VI, 1 (Winter 2002), online available via: http://www.ceip.org/files/publications/kalathil_harvardasia.asp (accessed: November 25, 2002).
6. Godwin C. Chu and Ju, Yanan, *The Great Wall in Ruins. Communication and Cultural Change in China* (New York: State University of New York, 1993).
7. Dong, Qingwen, Alexis Tan, and Cao, Xiaobing, "Socialization Effects of American Television and Movies in China," in *Communication and Culture: China and the World Entering the 21st Century*, D. Ray Heisey, and Gong, Wenxiang (eds.) (Amsterdam, Atlanta GA: Editions Rodopi B.V.: 1998): 31–327; Guan, Shijie, "The Prospects for Cross-Cultural Communication between China and the West in the 21st Century," in ibid.: 15–38.

8. The most prominent example probably is the 2002 banning of the Taiwanese soap opera *Meteor Garden* from Chinese television, which right away resulted in an unprecedented demand for video tapes, VCDs and web broadcasts among the Chinese urban youth. Furthermore, it was reported that within 24 hours after the ban more than 70,000 web users logged on to forums hosted by netease.com only in order to utter their complaints against the ban. Cf. i.a.: Jasper Becker, "A Soap Opera, China's Teens, and a Cyber-revolt," *The Christian Science Monitor* (May 24, 2002), online available via: http://www.csmonitor.com/2002/0524/p01s04-woap.html (accessed: November 20, 2002); Tsai, Ting-I, "Local Officials in a Lather Over Soap Opera Ban in China," *Taipei Times* (March 18, 2002), online available via: http://www.taipeitimes.com/News/archives/2002/03/18/0000128169 (accessed: October 20, 2002).

9. See Walter Prigge, "Medialisierung—die Rolle der neuen Medien für die Stadtkultur," Vortrag im Rahmen des Symposiums Stadtkultur—Kultur der Stadt. Stadtentwicklungskonzepte in Hongkong und Berlin, Berlin, July 29–30, 2000.

10. Peng, Foo Choy, "Shanghai Races to Fore as Investment Pays Off," *South China Morning Post* (August 28, 1997), online available via: http://special.scmp.com/cbr/cbr199709/ZZZZ8NPZRKC.html (accessed: May 16, 2001).

11. The Economist Intelligence Unit, *Country Profile 2002—China* (London: The Economist Group, 2002).

12. Ministry of Information Industry (MII), "2001 nian 12 yue zhuyao tongxin zhibiao zhaiyaobiao" (Summary of Major Statistical Indicators for Telecommunications) (December 2001), online available via: http://www.mii.gov.cn/mii/hyzw/tongji/yb/tongjiziliao200112.htm (accessed: February 7, 2002).

13. China Internet Network Information Center (CNNIC), *Statistical Survey Report on the Development of Internet in China* (July 2002), online available via: http://www.cnnic.net.cn/develst/2002–7e/index.shtml (accessed: October 18, 2002); Bu, Wei and Guo, Liang, "2000 nian Beijing, Shanghai, Guangzhou, Chengdu, Changsha hulianwang shiyong zhuangkuang ji yingxiang de diaocha baogao (chengren bufen)" (Survey report on the state of usage and the impact of the Internet in Beijing, Shanghai, Guangzhou, Chengdu, and Changsha 2000 (Adults)) (April 2001), online available via: http://www.chinace.org/ce/itre/ (accessed: July 25, 2001); Bu, Wei and Guo, Liang, "2000 nian Beijing, Shanghai, Guangzhou, Chengdu, Changsha hulianwang shiyong zhuangkuang ji yingxiang de diaocha baogao" (Survey report on the state of usage and the impact of the Internet in Beijing, Shanghai, Guangzhou, Chengdu and Changsha 2000) (April 2001), online available via: http://www.chinace.org/ce/itre/index_.htm (accessed: July 26, 2001).

14. CNNIC, *Statistical Survey Report on the Development of Internet in China.*

15. Bu, and Guo, "2000 nian Beijing, Shanghai."

16. Howard Rheingold, *Virtuelle Gemeinschaft. Soziale Beziehungen im Zeitalter des Computers* (Bonn, Paris, Reading, Mass: Addison Wesley, 1994); Sherry Turkle, "Virtuality and its Discontents: Searching for Community in Cyberspace," *The American Prospect*, 24 (Winter 1996): 50–57, online available via: http://epn.org/prospect/24/24turk.html (accessed: March 15, 2000); Bernhard Debatin, "Elektronische Öffentlichkeiten. Über Informationsselektion und Identität in virtuellen Gemeinschaften" (1996), online available via: http://www.unileipzig.de/~debatin/english/Articles/Fiff.htm (accessed: October 20, 2000).

17. Karsten Giese, "Das gesetzliche Korsett für das Internet ist eng geschnürt," *China aktuell* (October 2000): 1,173–1,181.

18. CNNIC, *Statistical Survey Report on the Development of Internet in China.*

19. One of these cases was the so-called "School Blast Incident"; cf. i.a.: Joanne Lee-Young, "Beijing Cracks Down on Firecracker Scandal," *Industry Standard* (March 15, 2001); CNN.com, "Chinese Chatrooms Cleared of School Blast Critics" (March 10, 2001), online available via: http://edition.cnn.com/2001/WORLD/asiapcf/east/03/10/china.school/#2 (accessed: November 20, 2002); Agence France-Presse (AFP), *Top Chinese Website Shuts Chatroom Over School Blast Anger* (2001). The second prominent cases was the AIDS scandal in Henan province; cf. i.a.: Elisabeth Rosenthal, "China Frees AIDS Activist After Month of Outcry," *New York Times*

(September 21, 2002); Canadian HIV/AIDS Legal Network, "Detention of Dr. Wan Yanhai, Recipient of the International Award for Action on HIV/AIDS and Human Rights. Background to the Situation" (September 11, 2002), online available via: http://www.aidslaw.ca/ Media/backgrounders/e-backgr-sept1302Wan.pdf (accessed: September 26, 2002).

20. Dai, Xiudian, *The Digital Revolution and Governance* (Ashgate: Aldershot, 2000); "ICTs in China's Development Strategy," in *China and the Internet. Politics of the Digital Leap Forward*, Christopher R. Hughes and Gudrun Wacker (eds.) (London: Routledge, 2003): 8–29; Gudrun Wacker, "The Internet and Censorship in China," in ibid.: 58–82.

21. Karsten Giese, "*Big Brother* mit rechtstaatlichem Anspruch. Gesetzliche Einschränkungen des Internet in der VR China," in *Elektronischer Handel in Afrika, Asien, Lateinamerika und Nahost* 50, Benno Engels and Olaf Nielinger (eds.) (Hamburg: Schriften des Deutschen Übersee-Instituts, 2001): 127–153; Gudrun Wacker, "The Internet and Censorship in China."

22. Cf. i.a.: Geoffrey York, "China Stifling Dissent on Internet," *The Globe And Mail* (October 5, 2002), online available via: http://www.theglobeandmail.com/servlet/ArticleNews/PEstory/ TGAM/20021005/UCHINMM/International/international/international_temp/3/3/32/ (accessed: October 9, 2002); Benjamin Edelman, "When the Net Goes Dark and Silent," *South China Morning Post* (October 2, 2002); Edward Young, "Internet: Beyond the Great Firewall," *China Economic Quarterly*, 4 (2002): 50–53; Reporters Without Borders, "China, Living Dangerously on the Net" (May 12, 2003): Censorship and surveillance of Internet forums, online available via: http://www.rsf.org/article.php3?id_article=6793 (accessed: May 14, 2003); Henry Hoenig, "Beijing Goes High-tech to Block Sars Messages," *The New Zealand Herald* (June 16, 2003), online available via: http://www.nzherald.co.nz/storyprint.cfm?storyID=3507534 (accessed: June 19, 2003).

23. Gudrun Wacker, "The Internet and Censorship in China;" Reporters Without Borders, "China. Internet: a Chronicle of Repression" (August 6, 2002), online available via: http://www.rsf.org/ article.php3?id_article=1290 (accessed: November 10, 2002).

24. Karsten Giese, "*Big Brother* mit rechtstaatlichem Anspruch"; Gudrun Wacker, "The Internet and Censorship in China."

25. Such measures have been taken by all major ICPs like sina.com, sohu.com, netease.com etc. Nevertheless, there are still a few options left for those who are desperate to evade personal identification, but those shall not be disclosed here.

26. In this essay I follow the concepts of panopticon provided by Jeremy Bentham, *Panopticon* (London: Payne, 1791), and later and in a far more universal approach Michel Foucault, *Surveiller et punir. La naissance de la prison* (Paris: Gallimard, 1975).

27. Debatin, "Elektronische Öffentlichkeiten" (no page number provided, translation by the author).

28. The following paragraphs reflect some of the preliminary results of our ongoing qualitative content analysis of BBS provided by sina.com, sohu.com and cyol.com. I am indebted to my colleagues Shi Ming, Teng Chin-Feng, Britta Uihlein, and Julia Welsch for their major contributions in interpreting the raw data.

29. On this specific aspect, cf.: Karsten Giese, "Construction and Performance of Virtual Identity in the Chinese Internet," in *Asia Encounters the Internet*, Ho, K.C., Randy Kluver and Yang, C.C. (eds.) (London: Routledge, 2003): 193–210.

30. "Subversion Trial Set for Web Site Creator," *South China Morning Post* (Hong Kong: February 10, 2001); Reporters Without Borders, "China. Internet: A Chronicle of Repression."

31. Yahoo! Inc., "China Nabs Student for Internet Use," in *Yahoo! Headlines* (December 8, 2002), online available via: http://uk.news.yahoo.com/021208/80/dgad3.html (accessed: December 10, 2002); Reporters Without Borders, "China. Internet: A Chronicle of Repression."

32. The number of people arrested and/or sentenced for disseminating "unlawful messages" in Internet forums has grown constantly. Cf. i.a.: Reporters Without Borders, "China. Internet: A Chronicle of Repression"; Reporters Without Borders, "China, Living Dangerously on the Net."

CHAPTER TWO

Cyberspace and the Emerging Chinese Religious Landscape—Preliminary Observations

DAVID A. PALMER

It is still too early to assess the full impact of the Internet on China's rapidly evolving religious landscape. The effectiveness of Falun Gong's cyber-militancy has, however, underscored the role new information technologies (NITs) are playing in the shifting relations of power between a classic repressive state apparatus and deterritorialized religious or sectarian movements. While the impact of the development of the Internet and other information technologies (ITs) on the economy and politics of the Chinese world has been amply commented upon, to my knowledge no in-depth research has yet been conducted on how the Internet is changing the form of religion in China. And yet, religious changes represent an important dimension of the cultural recomposition and transformation of the Chinese-speaking world. This chapter proposes some initial hypotheses and observations on these issues, a preliminary report on what will, I hope, become a full-fledged study on the expansion of religion in Chinese cyberspace and its impact on religious practices, communities, and state–religion relations in contemporary China. I will begin with some general considerations on the relationship between IT and religion; briefly present the types of religious information available on the Chinese Internet; and consider the cases of Daoism and of Falun Gong. In these case studies, we will see how, as a "virtual panopticon" closely monitored by the state while at the same time a space allowing unprecedented freedom of expression and access to information, the

Internet is becoming a new zone of tension in the age-old agonistic relationship between religion and state in China.

I began this study with three hypotheses. It was assumed that NITs would have three effects on the Chinese religious landscape: (1) the emergence of a new space for religious expression, characterized by an autonomous quest for meaning rather than collective rituals; (2) a further undermining of orthodoxies accompanied by the emergence of new centers of religious influence; and (3) greater integration of Chinese communities on the mainland and overseas, as well as between Chinese and non-Chinese communities. So far, while the data seems to support the first two hypotheses, the third needs to be reformulated: a clear difference appears between online religion in mainland China and Hong Kong–Taiwan, with, surprisingly, the potentialities of the Web being more fully exploited on the mainland than in Hong Kong and Taiwan. This discrepancy will be described and explained in our case study of Daoism.

General Considerations

Religion can be considered as the transmission of a specific type of memory or information. On this basis, the invention of NITs has had a profound impact on the transformations of religion throughout history, and can shed light on current trends of religious modernity, notably the globalization of religion on the one hand, and the increasing autonomy of the religious subject on the other. One way to see religion is as a system for creating, maintaining, developing, and controlling the individual or collective consciousness of belonging to a specific line of belief,[1] by linking individuals to a body of memory. As such, one of the overriding concerns of religion is the perpetuation and diffusion of this body of memory. The social forms of religion will to a large extent reflect the technical means by which religious teachings and practices are transmitted. For instance, the role of religious specialists, whose duty is to hold, protect, and transmit sacred traditions, will be different in entirely oral cultures, in societies in which there exists a small class of scribes, and in literate civilizations in which all people have access to religious scriptures. The impact of the printing press on the emergence of Protestantism is well known: the mass production of the Bible and its distribution outside of clerical circles to lay believers, helped to popularize the notion of the individual's direct and unmediated relation to God. The gradual trend, throughout history, of the "modernization" of religiosity expressed by the increasing autonomy of the individual in religious experience and belief, can be linked to the evolution of ITs from orality to writing, printing, electronic media, and now the Internet. Each of these advances have permitted the dissemination of religious information on an increasingly global scale, at an increasingly rapid pace, to an ever larger number of people, with an ever increasing diversity of content. Seen from a broad perspective, the evolution of religion in modern times has seen a tendency toward globalization on the one hand, and individualization on the other. In this context, spiritually "free" individuals, whose religious identity is no longer merely inherited, can create new communities of choice out of a limitless, worldwide range of religious possibilities. More specifically, the Internet challenges the traditional grounding of religion in bodies, territories, and institutions. For oral cultures, the primary means for the reproduction and transmission of religious memory has been through the disposition of bodies and objects in ritual performance. Scriptures reduced but did not eliminate the importance of ritual in literate cultures, often becoming central to the ritual manipulation of sacred books. Digital culture, however, dematerializes religious texts. The gestures of manipulation are the same, making no distinctions between the Word of God, gossip, or smut, all transmitted through the same wires and flashed onto the same screen. Polarities in space and time between the sacred and the profane are corroded; the ritual coordination and movement of bodies gives way to the solitary clicking of electronic mice. The physical congregation of worshipers in a single spot—the temple, church or sacred ground, often with its own territory marking the limits of a community—can be replaced by online networks of individuals with common affinities, seeking the same information and communicating directly with each other. The foundations of religious (and, in the Chinese case, political) institutions—bureaucratized channels for the generation, processing, and control of religious information—are eroded in a virtual marketplace where nothing is easier than mixing and matching the itinerary of one's own spiritual journey. Disembodiment, deterritorialization, and disinstitutionalization are processes that could be triggered or accelerated by the Internet in relation to religion.[2]

Such are some of the ways in which we can assume that the form of cyberspace will modify the flows of spiritual information. But the "on-line world" does not eliminate and replace offline reality; rather, the interpenetration of the two is what is creating new religious formations.[3] A rapid overview of the pre-digital configuration of Chinese religion will allow us to better understand the results of this interpenetration in the Chinese case.

The Chinese Case

New information technologies can be said to be accelerating the "institutional deregulation of belief,"[4] which is a global characteristic of modernity, a phenomenon that has affected the Chinese religious landscape as much as in the West, albeit as a result of a different historical process. Since the Song dynasty (960–1279), by attempting to control and limit the expansion of the institutionalized religions (Buddhism and Daoism), the state has contributed to the gradual weakening of "orthodox" religions, creating the conditions for the flourishing of popular religion and sectarianism.[5] The only centralized institution comparable to the "Church" as we know it in the West was the Imperial state itself, with its Son of Heaven embodied by the Emperor, its ritual system of governance, and its "clergy" of Confucian administrators trained in the art of virtues. Locally, religious life centered around the temple, which was the focus of all community life. Temples and their festivals structured the space and time of families, lineages, villages, guilds, and the state. Temples were usually autonomous organizations governed by local associations, which hired clergy to conduct rituals.[6] However, the role of temples in Chinese community life has steadily declined since the beginning of the twentieth century, particularly in the cities. During this period, waves of war and modernizing revolutions have largely eliminated the concrete and visible forms of religious life centered around neighborhood temples and festivals in the cities. The destruction of family and local cults, through which Chinese peoples' religious identity was expressed,[7] has created atomized bodies, "modern" individuals cut off from their ancestral filiations. The weakening and destruction of traditional religious institutions has accelerated the emergence of a modern religiosity characterized by individual, voluntary engagement. In the 1980s and 1990s, body cultivation practices known as *qigong*, owing to the simplicity of their transmission and their indeterminate status between health practice and religion, were one of the few forms of religious transmission and practice to survive in urban areas. After the Cultural Revolution, while the spread of other forms of religious practice and community was still difficult, *qigong* could rapidly propagate and integrate itself into the urban fabric of society. Parks, sidewals and public spaces had become, through *qigong*, alternative spaces for the expression of a modern religiosity. But since the late 1990s, the militancy of Falun Gong, with its roots in the *qigong* movement, and the repression it has provoked, have led to most *qigong* groups dissolving or going underground.[8]

It is in this context that cyberspace has emerged as a new frontier for the dissemination of religious ideas and for the expression of the spiritual search. Our historical overview shows that prior to the advent of the Internet, the traditional religious ordering of bodies through ritual had already largely disappeared in the cities. The meditation and gymnastic traditions of *qigong*, however, could adapt to an industrial organization of homogenized individuals gathering daily for mass exercise sessions. As we will discuss further, Falun Gong was able to connect this movement to digital communication technologies, facilitating the spontaneous organization of large public demonstrations. Many religious and spiritual groups and seekers, however, at a time when temple-centered religiosity has become a pale shadow of what it used to be, and when *qigong*-style group practice in parks has been banned or discouraged, now lack a formal, fixed location in physical space. It is in this context that the Internet has opened a new virtual space for the development of religion.

Portals to Religion

A foray into the world of online religion can begin with one of the main Chinese language Web portals, such as Chinese yahoo.com and sohu.com. These provide links to religious sites summarized in tables 2.1 and 2.2. The first thing we notice from these tables is how a "denominational" classification of religion has imposed itself on the internet portals—even though the Chinese-designed portal, *sohu*, mixes denominational categories with others: organizations, institutes, religious problems, news, etc. Superficially, the portals may be reinforcing the "denominationalization" of Chinese

Table 2.1 Religious sites listed in cn.yahoo.com[9]

Category	Total number of sites	Number of sites listed as related to mainland China
Protestantism	607	140
Buddhism	352	109
Catholicism	38	8
Divination	34	7
Islam	33	12
Daoism	23	13
New age	10	1
Yiguandao	8	—
Popular religion[10]	4	—

Table 2.2 Religious sites listed in sohu.com[11]

Category	Total number of sites
Buddhism	1,186
Christianity	1,049
Islam	75
Daoism	69
Judaism	25
News and media	24
Other religions	18
Religious organizations	12
Religious institutes and schools	10
Resources for research	8
Religion and the times	8
Religious problems	8
Chan	6
Baha'i	3
Hinduism	3

religion, a process that has been going on since the twentieth century and especially since the founding of the Peoples' Republic, which, importing Western theories of religion, undertook to identify Chinese religious "believers" and classify them according to institutional affiliations. Indeed, prior to the twentieth century, although the "Three Doctrines" of Confucianism, Daoism, and Buddhism, each with its own clergy and scripture, had an independent existence, most local temples and religious communities were not explicitly associated with one or the other of the main traditions. Whether Internet users remain loyal to one "religion" or freely surf from one tradition to the other is a question that merits further investigation. A second, evident observation is the overwhelming predominance of Christianity and Buddhism. Compared to the indigenous tradition of Daoism, which has always been closely tied to the liturgical structures of local communities, Christianity and Buddhism were already, prior to the Internet, globalized religions, less embedded in local territories and ritual, with a greater focus on textual doctrine, and a strong commitment to the universal propagation of sacred text: orientations that could more easily translate into the colonization of cyberspace. Within Christianity, the weak presence of Catholicism is also striking compared with Protestantism: the horizontal, fragmented configuration of Protestant communities seems to have penetrated the Internet faster than the monolithic, hierarchical institutions of the Catholic Church.

It should be noted that sites classified under "religion" represent only part of the online world devoted to the spiritual and religious search. *Sohu*, for instance, lists a further 1263 sites under "mysterious culture"— mostly devoted to various forms of divination and ghost stories; 492 sites under "myth and folklore," which include sites on popular cults such as Mazu, Bulletin Board System forums on the *Book of Changes*, etc. Under "sports and recreation," one finds 77 sites devoted to *qigong* and 714 to martial arts.

Online Daoism

A deeper exploration of the ocean of online data can begin with a look into the sites listed under "Daoism." Choosing the most "Chinese" of the religions allows us to see what is happening online in the tradition that we would assume to be the least influenced by international networks. Getting a comprehensive picture is also facilitated by the small number of sites in this category.

A survey of 29 Chinese-language websites listed under "Daoism" in the portals in March 2003 found 14 sites based in mainland China, eight in Taiwan, six in Hong Kong and one in Germany. A significant difference can be seen between the mainland and Hong Kong/Taiwan sites: the latter are all run by temples or by established organizations, while most of the mainland sites are maintained by individuals or businesses. Almost all of the Hong Kong and Taiwan sites publicize temple or organization activities, while only two of the mainland sites (also maintained by temples) do so. The mainland sites are more likely to contain general information on Daoism, offer scriptures for download, provide online forums or chat services, and post opinions and editorials. The Taiwanese sites are more likely to offer specific information, notably on temple divinities. Few of the Hong Kong sites contain opinion pieces or content pertaining to temple divinities. Overall, the Hong Kong and Taiwanese sites can be said to be an extension into cyberspace of the traditional temple-based configuration of Chinese religion. The mainland sites, however, reflect a more eclectic mix, where one finds sites created by individuals impassioned by Daoism (see http://a863.xiloo.com) and others who claim to be masters (see www.jingxiantianshi.com), and by various types of groups promoting Chinese culture. Overall, the mainland sites reflect a more individual, idiosyncratic and interactive exploration of China's spiritual traditions, and a greater degree of commercialization (providing fortune-telling or feng-shui services).

The Internet thus reveals a more "modern" religiosity in Communist China, detached from organized institutions, more centered on the individual, and in which the separation between online and offline realities is greater than for the more traditional configuration of religion in Taiwan and Hong Kong. It would appear that in the mainland, Communist control has not prevented a greater degree of individual initiative and entrepreneurship from emerging than in the temple-dominated religious landscape of Taiwan and Hong Kong. On the mainland, the Internet is reinforcing what was previously a minority trend in Chinese religion, in which individual study of religious writings and content becomes more important than participation in temple rituals. While there has always been a current of "lettered," more mystical, and individualistic religion pursued by Chinese literati and scholars, traditionally, ritual practice has been more important than doctrine in Chinese religion. Religious surfing on the Internet, however, changes the emphasis from practice to content.

The Political and Geographic Dynamics of a Daoist Website

An interesting case in point is the Taoist Culture & Information Centre (TCIC) (www.taoism.org.hk), one of the largest websites on Daoism, produced by a Hong Kong Taoist temple, the Feng Ying Seen Koon.[12] This project began in 1998, after some members of the Hong Kong Daoist community noticed the lack of information on Daoism on the Internet in comparison with Buddhism and Christianity. The temple then decided to sponsor a major Chinese–English online database as a contribution to the propagation of the religion. Several challenges were encountered in the course of this project. The first was how to produce large quantities of text on Daoism that would be accessible to lay readers. In the absence of practicing Daoists able to write at length on the history, major figures, and major concepts of the religion, the temple had to hire academic scholars from mainland universities, including Qing Xitai, Li Gang, and Jiang Sheng, whose contributions were often based on Marxist and materialist theory. At the end of the first phase of the project in 2002, over 400 articles had been posted in three versions: traditional Chinese, simplified Chinese and English. By all accounts, the project was very successful: by June 2002, the traditional Chinese version of the site was registering approximately 1.1 million hits per month, the simplified had over 400,000 hits with a monthly increase of approximately 25,000 visits since the beginning of the year; and the English version was visited by over 320,000 surfers.[13]

In its discussions on the kind of additional content that should be added to the website, the database commission, composed of prominent members of the Hong Kong Daoist community and academic scholars of Daoism from the mainland and Hong Kong, was then confronted with a new problem: it was noted that while Christian and Buddhist websites contain simple and precise explanations of their respective religions' doctrines and positions on current social problems, this aspect was weak in the case of the Daoist website. After much discussion, it was decided to write up the "Daoist position" on current events and social issues such as terrorism and the environment. But this decision was not made without debate, some commission members raising the issue of the absence of any commonly recognized authority to come up with these positions. Gradually, however, the website has come to acquire an authority of its own, to such degree that the London Museum once addressed a request to the database commission to resolve an enigmatic interpretation of a Chinese Daoist painting in the museum.

The success of the Feng Ying Seen Koon's TCIC was not without creating some jealousies among other Daoist temples in Hong Kong, some of which are reported to be considering developing their own large-scale websites. Through its website, the Feng Ying Seen Koon, which was previously a relatively minor local temple in Hong Kong, has suddenly risen to global prominence in Daoist circles and now exercises a global influence in the dissemination and interpretation of information on Daoism.

The case of the TCIC thus illustrates two trends which are accelerated by the introduction of the Internet into religious life: the first is a shift in emphasis from a local community, ritual-based practice of religion to an individualistic approach characterized by the search for more information content. The second is a shift in the relative influence of different religious organizations: those with a strong presence in cyberspace can acquire new influence extending much farther than their original local sphere of activities.

Such a redistribution of influence among religious organizations can further undermine institutionalized religion, which has always been relatively weak in China. Informal and non-orthodox organizations can be as easily accessible online as state-supported institutions. However, though state control on religion is indeed weakened by the Internet, it can continue to assert itself in manners both direct and subtle. If blocking access to websites is an instance of direct intervention, state influence continues to be exercised in a more subtle fashion toward those sites that are accessible. The TCIC, for instance, is very careful to present content that is acceptable in the context of current Chinese ideology and political tendencies.

The TCIC is based outside of mainland China, but directed at mainlanders, a strategy that seems to be tolerated by the Chinese authorities. Such a site acts as a hub for the building of religious networks and common discourse throughout the Chinese world and beyond. While the majority of visits are to the traditional Chinese version (likely coming from Hong Kong and Taiwan), sizeable minorities are from mainland China (readers of the simplified Chinese version) and from other countries (English version). The content of all three versions is identical. Since the authors of the articles are for the most part academic scholars from the mainland, and since the database commission makes a conscious effort to avoid content, which would be politically sensitive on the mainland, we can see how, indirectly, Chinese state policy and ideology on religion exercises itself not only on sites based in the mainland, but also on a site based in Hong Kong, which has become an important provider of online information on Daoism for the whole Chinese world. Interpenetration and mutual influence characterize this strategy, where an outside organization can penetrate into Chinese cyberspace, but, at the same time and indirectly, Chinese state influence on religious discourse spreads beyond Chinese borders.

The Online Militancy of Falun Gong

An alternative strategy is one of direct confrontation, the best-known example of which is Falun Gong. NITs had become central to the organization's functioning by 1997–98, when its founder, Li Hongzhi, settled in the United States and created an international communication system allowing him to lead, from a distance, his millions of followers in China. Beginning in the 1980s, the *qigong* movement—of which Falun Gong was one school—had developed an organizational model based on the systematic tramsmission of exercise routines from a central association down to thousands of local parcs and practice sites around China and the world. This setup, based on loose networks of volunteer trainers and requiring almost no property or resources, allowed for the rapid creation of mass organizations by hundreds of *qigong* masters. Li Hongzhi was the first of these to make full use of the Internet, allowing him and his key disciples to send directives from anywhere in the world, spreading through electronic means and then word of mouth (not only e-mail but also telephone and fax—the Internet had not yet become a mass phenomenon in 1999) to millions of disciples. *Qigong* transmission networks, which until then had been devoted to the propagation of simple, repetitive exercise routines, could now instantly activate millions of people to trigger spectacular events, without needing a rigidly structured organization. Through the informal circulation of news and directives between practitioners, "spontaneous" but perfectly organized mass demonstrations were held in dozens of localities around China between 1997 and 1999, usually to protest government or media organs critical of Falun Gong, sometimes attracting over 10,000 practitioners. It was such a protest, surrounding the Party leadership's compound at Zhongnanhai on April 24, 1999, with the heavy symbolism which it evoked, that triggered the Chinese state's ruthless anti-Falun Gong campaign.

Against Falun Gong, the state deployed the classic repressive apparatus: mobilizing the Party and government-controlled mass organizations; lauching a propaganda campaign through all media; punishing leaders and hard-core practitioners with torture and internment in prisons, psychiatric hospitals, and work camps. But the enemy was not a typical dissident organization. Its leader lives abroad; Falun Gong's virtual organization can easily set up new nodes at points anywhere on Earth. No longer a strictly Chinese organization, it has rapidly adopted the best techniques of the American art of public relations and online militancy. An all-out propaganda war is being waged between Falun Gong and the Chinese state, and cyberspace has become one of the key battlefields.

The Chinese government's position has largely been defensive: all Falun Gong websites have been blocked in China, and practitioners have been arrested for disseminating Falun Gong e-mails.[14] A dozen anti-Falun Gong websites have been created by various government agencies. Some of them are available in English and can be accessed from Chinese embassy websites.[15] Interestingly, one mainland Chinese-language anti-Falun Gong website contains a point-by-point refutation of Falun Gong claims that the supposed self-immolation by practitioners on Tiananmen Square on January 23, 2001, was a government-staged hoax—implicitly acknowledging that the Falun Gong version is widely known on the mainland.[16] Indeed, in spite of state attempts to block mass e-mailings, Falun Gong "spam" tracts do reach the electronic mailboxes of ordinary Chinese e-mail users.

Outside China, Falun Gong and its practitioners have established dozens of websites, most of which are based in the United States and Canada, but also in Europe, Iran, Turkey, India, Israel, Brazil, etc. Most

local sites carry information diffused by eight official Falun Gong sites.[17]
One of these, www.falundafa.org, contains downloadable Falun Gong
scriptures, instructions for practice, and contact information for practice
sites; another, www.pureinsight.org, contains articles on scientific and
cultural subjects related to Falun Gong. The other six sites are almost
exclusively devoted to the campaign to defend Falun Gong against Jiang
Zemin and the Chinese government. An online TV station (fgmtv.net)
provides videos of practice methods, testimonies, and news programmes
in several languages. A twice-weekly e-newsletter and daily press releases
disseminate the latest news on the repression in China, lawsuits launched
against Jiang Zemin and other officials before courts in dozens of countries, expressions of support from legislators, etc. Falun Gong is continually publishing staggering amounts of information online. Dozens of
human rights reports can be downloaded. One example is a 91-page
report, which contains the names, photographs, and biographies of victims
of psychiatric internment; the exact addresses and telephone numbers of
the departments involved; the names, titles, and ages of the perpetrators;
and detailed accounts of incidents of torture.[18] Elsewhere online, the
names and contact details of scores of persons involved in the persecution in China, including minor officials, were posted, as targets of letter-
writing, fax, and telephone campaigns. Misfortunes that had occurred to
these individuals, such as illnesses, accidents or death, were described as
signs of karmic justice. How Falun Gong was able to obtain such
detailed information in dozens of small Chinese localities was not clear.
Even natural disasters and bad weather hitting various parts of China
were reported as signs of dharmic retribution.[19] All manner of bad social
and economic news on China were also given as proof of the moral
depravity of the regime and the calamities it is bringing on the country.
Overall, Falun Gong has been thoroughly systematic in its use of the
Internet to propagate its message and to organize its campaigns. This has
allowed for the growth of a loosely organized worldwide movement able
to respond instantly to information, campaigns, and spiritual guidance
disseminated through both a centralized hierarchy of websites and
through the horizontal spread of electronic communications between
practitioners. Online access to the Master's pronouncements makes it
possible to eliminate intermediate formal structures of authority within
the movement, even though Li Hongzhi's public appearances—the only
times his disciples can enter his physical presence—are rare and brief.
Cyberspace becomes a medium through which the master's charismatic
power can be exercised by establishing a direct virtual connection
between himself and each individual practitioner.[20]

Concluding Remarks

These pages have only touched on the surface of what is becoming an essential dimension of the Chinese religious landscape. In spite of the "panopticon effect" of a cyberspace through which the Chinese state can easily monitor its subjects, the Internet has allowed the emergence of new networks of seekers and providers, and for the exploration of forms of religiosity that are difficult to express in other public spaces in China. Ironically, then, state restrictions on offline religious activity may have given the Internet a greater role in the evolution of religious culture than in other countries. And if the militancy of Falun Gong has led the state to impose an almost complete blackout of nongovernmental information on Falun Gong in China, a different dynamic is prevailing in the rest of the online religious world in mainland China: creation, exploration, and ambiguity are daringly pursued under Big Brother's nose.

Further inquiry on Chinese religion in cyberspace should include a systematic analysis of the content of religion on the Chinese Internet, the differences between online and print content, and the relative dissemination of information originating from the mainland, from overseas Chinese sources, and from non-Chinese sources, with particular attention to discussions in online forums. Is there a specific online religious discourse which is different from other forms of religious discourse? Key websites representative of various religious and spiritual traditions should be analyzed in depth, detailed statistics on their users obtained, and their sponsors and authors interviewed. Links between websites should be mapped, in order to trace the existence of affinity networks which may (or may not) reveal the emergence of new currents. Online religious seekers should be contacted and interviewed, and typical profiles drawn up, so as to understand the sociological makeup of religious surfers. The relationship between using online information and other forms of religious practice and community should also be elucidated: is the internet a complement to other forms of religious practice and community? Does it direct seekers away from other forms or, on the contrary, is it a conduit that leads them to join religious communities? Does the Internet have an impact on other forms of religious practice? Another area deserving of investigation is the link between religion and civil society as expressed in the Internet. Are virtual religious networks on the Internet self-contained in a closed circuit, or are they linked to other groups and other social concerns? Will the proliferation of religious content on the Internet lead to a relaxing of state policy toward religious and other popular groups, or will it, on the contrary, provoke even harsher measures of control?

Notes

1. Cf. Danièle Hervieu-Léger, *La Religion pour mémoire* (Paris: Editions du Cerf, 1993): 119.
2. For a bibliography of general works on religion and the Internet, see Stephen O'Leary, "Suggested Readings in Online Religion," in *Online Journalism Review*, http://www.ojr.org/ojr/business/1017965578.php.
3. Cf. Daniel Miller and Don Slater, *The Internet: An Ethnographic Approach* (Oxford: Berg, 2000), Chapter 1.
4. Danièle Hervieu-Léger, *La religion en miettes ou la question des sectes* (Paris: Calmann-Lévy, 2001): 126.
5. David Ownby, "A History for Falun Gong: Popular Religion and the Chinese State since the Ming Dynasty," *Nova Religio*, 6, 2 (2003): 223–243.
6. On the role of temples in Chinese religious life, see Vincent Goossaert, *Dans les temples de la Chine. Histoire des cultes, vie des communautés* (Paris: Albin Michel, 2000).
7. See Kristofer Schipper, "Rediscovering Religion in China," communication at the symposium Modern Society and the Science of Religion, 1997; Prasenjit Duara, *Rescuing History from the Nation. Questioning Narratives of Modern China* (Chicago: University of Chicago Press, 1995): 85–110. Many of these cults have been reconstituted in the countryside after the end of the Cultural Revolution (see Kenneth Dean, *Taoist Ritual and Popular Cults of Southeast China* (Princeton: Princeton University Press, 1993)), but this phenomenon has not occurred in the cities.
8. On the *qigong* movement in China, see David A. Palmer, *La fièvre du qigong. Guérison, religion et politique en Chine contemporaine* (Paris: Editions de l'Ecole des Hautes Etudes en Sciences Sociales, forthcoming). English edition (*Qigong Fever: Body, Science, and Politics in Modern Chinese Religion*), forthcoming at Hurst.
9. Data accessed on October 10, 2003.
10. Includes two sites devoted to the god Guangong and the sites of two other temples (Lingjianmiao and Xingtiangong).
11. Data accessed on October 10, 2003. The *sohu* index includes some English-language sites: most of the sites listed under Judaism are in English. For most categories, however, almost all of the listings are for Chinese-language sites.
12. The author of these lines is the copy editor of the site's English version.
13. The average time for each visit was 15 minutes for the traditional Chinese version, 13 minutes for the simplified Chinese version, and 21 minutes for the English version. Source: internal statistical report, TCIC.
14. Stephen O'Leary, "Falun Gong and the Internet," *Online Journalism Review*, http://www.ojr.org/ojr/ethics/1017964337 (accessed: October 10, 2003).
15. For example, see http://www.chinaembassycanada.org/eng/c3161.html, http://211.99.196.218/fanduixiejiao/eng/index.htm.
16. http://ppflg.my163.com/ (accessed: October 10, 2003).
17. See www.falundafa.org, www.faluninfo.net, www.clearwisdom.net, www.clearharmony.net, www.pureawakening.net, www.pureinsight.org, www.fofg.org, www.flgjustice.org.
18. Falun Gong Human Rights Working Group, "Falun Gong Practitioners Tortured in Mental Hospitals Throughout China," downloaded in March 2003 from www.clearwisdom.net.
19. www.minghui.cc/mh, accessed in November 2001.
20. For further analysis on Falun Gong and the Internet, see Mark R. Bell and Taylor C. Boas, "Falun Gong and the Internet: Evangelism, Community, and Struggle for Survival," *Nova Religio*, 6, 2 (2003): 277–293.

CHAPTER THREE

The Changing Role of the State in Greater China in the Age of Information

FRANÇOISE MENGIN

The World Bank has recently released a report prepared at the request of the Chinese government on the knowledge and innovation perspectives for China's development strategy. The authors consider that the building of the foundations of the knowledge economy consists of three elements:

(1) "An improved economic incentive and institutional regime, requiring actions, among other areas, in the legal, regulatory, and competition framework, and the labor and financial markets;

(2) "A well educated population, equipped with skills needed to cope efficiently with the challenges and opportunities of the knowledge revolution: new efforts and reforms required for the adaptation of the Chinese education system;

(3) "A massive investment in information and telecommunications infrastructure, key infrastructure of the knowledge economy and information society"[1]

Certainly, rational administrative policies should require such actions. However, when assessing the role of the state, one cannot but take into account not only the political and economic constraints which it is confronted to, but also the fact that government action is embedded in a whole set of power relations, conflicting interests, which implies constant arbitration. At the national level, the People's Republic of China (PRC) and Taiwan are both caught into intertwining processes, that of economic globalization and market reform, for the former, and that of economic globalization and national security concerns triggered by the cross-straits sovereignty dispute, for the latter. In addition, and very roughly speaking, economic activity does not only rely on rational objective criteria but also, among many elements, on personal relationships between individuals, while the state–society relationship is in perpetual reshaping.[2] As perfectly put by Mark Granovetter and Richard Swedberg, economic action is socially situated in the sense that it "is embedded in ongoing networks of personal relationships rather than being carried out by atomized actors."[3]

As far as the development of information technologies (ITs) is concerned, governmental action in the PRC as well as in Taiwan is confronted to contending issues. In order to develop its indigenous IT industry, China can easily seek technology from the rest of the world—including Taiwan— as many foreign firms are eager to get access to the Chinese market. However, this growing liberalization of economic relations goes hand in hand with the threat under which the legitimacy of the Chinese Communist Party (CCP) is because of Internet development within China. Taiwan industry, for its part, needs to keep its competitive edge, which is not only a requirement in terms of national economy, but also in terms of national security, because the country's integration in the international arena depends, first and foremost, on its economic relations, for lack of de jure sovereignty. In addition, further cross-straits liberalization is continually on the agenda, not only in terms of relocating Taiwan plants on the mainland, but also, and this is more recent, in terms of opening the Taiwan environment to mainland elite.[4]

By setting a kind of framework, this chapter aims at highlighting some of the various contending issues with which governmental action must deal when faced with the development of ITs both as a communication means and as a key industry.

The State as a Controller: Managing the Undermining of its Sovereignty

The Net in China: A Threat to the Communist Party's Legitimacy?

For the mainstream view, the development of ITs would gradually undermine the nation-state's sovereignty in a way that can be presented as a threefold process. First of all, as far as international relations are concerned, informational flows are part of those transnational flows that are calling into question the sovereignty of nation-states by reducing their capacity to govern effectively. In Krasner's words: "(. . .) technological change has made it very difficult, or perhaps impossible, for states to control movements across their borders of all kinds of material things (from coffee to cocaine) and not-so-material things (from Hollywood movies to capital flows)."[5] Part of this process is the fact that the Internet could be a conduit for disseminating state secrets. Next, as national economies are integrating within the global economy, while governments are striving to increase growth rates, a too strong dependence upon foreign technologies may call into question national security. In the Chinese case in particular, economic development is the main leadership's legitimizing tool since the policy of reforms and overture was launched in the late 1970s. Finally, the Net would be the best weapon of "peaceful change" in the PRC, of pluralization first, democratization next. This trend could be further accelerated by foreign governments' action.[6] At least, the Net can be a means to enhance individualization processes. As put by Karsten Giese: "(. . .) tension between the individual and the virtual group does exist. However, the individual has the upper hand in the virtual world, since membership is more likely to be based on the free personal decision to be a member of a given virtual group than in the real-world setting. (. . .) Chinese virtual communities have the potential to support individualization and fragmentation of the social linkages of modern Chinese individuals."[7]

As a matter of fact, the PRC government has striven to control the Chinese cyberspace.[8] These actions are well known, and can be summarized into three categories. First, "preventive" regulation has been set. It has to be noted that in China, one of the few countries to have set such a regulation, there is a separation[9] between Internet content providers and Internet service providers for the latter are seen less sensitive than the former.[10] In addition, websites have been brought under strict control. In addition to "firewalls" that block out harmful foreign websites (such as CNN or Time), websites have been more and more brought on under the rule of law: while government control was for long limited to the tracking of individual cases of transgression, laws are now passed that strictly regulate the dissemination of online information.[11] Bulletin boards, talk sites, news sites and users are all being checked. Second, "repressive" actions are carried on. "Internet police" teams to fight Internet crime and illegal behavior have successively been established in various provinces.[12] In 1999, there was the well-known case of computer businessman Lin Hai who has been sentenced to 2 years in prison for providing e-mail addresses to overseas media. This was the first case of Internet user being tried as a political crime. In 2000, other people were tried for similar crimes, such as Huang Qi because his "*Tian wang xun ren*" site carried reports of cases of breaches of human rights and corruption. Besides, after a deadly fire in an Internet café in Beijing in 2002, the authorities closed thousands of Internet cafés, and required from those allowed to reopen that they install suveillance and firewalls software to block "subversive" websites.[13] Third, the Chinese authorities are regulating the Internet by implementing their own sites. As early as 1996, was a controlled intranet—the China Wide Web (CWW)—launched by the China Internet Company (CIC).[14] Moreover, the Chinese authorities are actively developing five central-government managed news websites,[15] and do not hesitate to display governmental action—be it in the field of corruption or developing projects—on the Net,[16] not to speak of instrumentalizing the latter for nationalist purpose as witnessed during the 1998 riots targeting ethnic Chinese in Indonesia, or the 1999 U.S. bombing of the Chinese embassy in Belgrade.[17]

However, whatever successful the Chinese government is in controlling the Internet, there shall always be hackers developing programmes to defeat this censorship. Above all, I shall not discuss here the issue whether, in spite of stops and goes in the control exerted on Chinese cyberspace, the latter will not, in the long run, contribute to the development of dissident movements.[18] As a matter of fact, if one refuses the functionalist/evolutionist paradigm, modernization models set as linear models,[19] the issue at stake is not a speculation about the hypothetical mechanical impact dissident movements could have, notwithstanding their intrinsic importance. The point I want to make here is that the political and sociological landscape within which Internet is developing in China should downplay the threat the latter is hanging over the regime, and not only because the media, in China, are closely linked to the CCP.

First of all, market logics cannot but compel foreign companies to abide by the Chinese regulations. As already pinpointed by some scholars, Christopher R. Hughes in particular, under the World Trade Organization's (WTO) rules, the state will retain considerable leverage over the behavior of foreign firms and, because they will be subjected to the same pressures as their indigenous partners, one should not expect foreign Internet operators to risk legal sanctions in the PRC by promoting human rights and democracy.[20] Likewise, though the Taipei government may be resisting Beijing's sovereignty claims over Taiwan by developing government sponsored websites,[21] the "struggle" takes place at an interstate level—where noninterference in other states' domestic affairs remains the principle—and in no way at the transnational one. In other words, as far as politics are concerned, the sovereignty dispute forbids any active commitment of Taiwan's political forces to put pressure on the Chinese government so as to initiate a democratization process on the mainland, or to be actively involved alongside Chinese dissidents. Quite the contrary, protecting Taiwan's democracy, that is protecting the autonomy of the Republic of China on Taiwan, for lack of its de jure independence, requires a low-profile attitude in this field.[22] If the room for manoeuvre of any Western democracy to pressurize Beijing as far as human rights are concerned is narrow, it is even more for Taiwan. This applies in particular to Taiwanese investors on the mainland.[23]

Second, ITs are developing in mainland China at a time when the working class is lacking a political dimension, as is revealed by its inability to launch and develop collective actions at a general level.[24] More, the mentality and behaviors of the new "working class" are characterized by the importance of local networks, "during recruitment as well as within the labor process."[25] In the process of working class transition in China, Ching Kwan Lee shows that "management power reigns supreme, often making use of preexisting localistic, paternalistic, and patriarchal authorities. (. . .) Localism also implies a strategy of divide and rule inside (the) firms, diluting class opposition between employers and workers by introducing regional division among them."[26] Concerning high-tech companies, this is all the more true. As pinpointed by Rocca, "(. . .) in the new modern capitalist sector, the fact that it is dominated by technology-oriented strategy and service-oriented activities contributes to marginalize labor in the economic realm (. . .) The question at stake seems to be less the one of transition between an old working class and a new capitalist class than the one of the decay of labor as it was defined in industrial states."[27]

The fact that ITs are developing in China at a time when class opposition is diluting (which does not mean that class inequalities are decreasing, quite the contrary), partakes in a more general trend, as noticed by some: "In the new world, informational labour is the prime creator of wealth, while the working class is in terminal decline because (. . .) it lacks flexibility. As a result, politics is shifting away from class (. . .) towards social movements such as feminism, ethnic nationalism and environmentalism. These movements reach far beyond traditional class allegiances and appeal to the lifestyles and identities of supporters."[28] The issue at stake here is not whether the development, in China, of IT play a leading part in the process—certainly we are facing a chicken and

egg situation—but to stress the fact that, as far as the Internet may be
a technology of control for the political leadership, the current mutation
of labor in China cannot but favor such control.[29] As pinpointed by Jens
Damm: "it is unlikely that the vast majority of Chinese internet users are
critical of the current regime: the average user is young, highly educated
(more than 75 percent have a senior high school degree or higher),
belongs to the new urban middle class, and is without any doubt the
beneficiary of the economic and, to some degree, political reforms
which gained pace after Deng Xiaoping's historical southern trip
(*nanxun*) in 1992. (. . .) These users have a highly pragmatic approach
towards the government and the CCP. In their view political discourse
aimed at overthrowing the current regime would probably lead to political instability (i.e. chaos or *luan*) and they therefore support the regime's
efforts to establish the internet as part of a modern economy and society
and to control 'sensitive issues'."[30]

In addition, for the 46 million Internet users in the PRC, the Net is
closely related to entertainment purposes. Therefore, as long as people
use the Internet for leisure activity, the part played by IT in the so-called
"peaceful evolution" of China will remain marginal. Moreover, among
the sensitive issues closely monitored by the Chinese leadership, some do
not find an echo among the vast majority of the Chinese population,
such as the Tibet and the Taiwan issues.

By and large, one cannot but view that the control exerted on the
cyberspace in China should lead us to the well-known analysis of power
by Foucault. Such is the purpose of some works that use the concept of
the Panopticon prison[31] as a metaphor to demonstrate that the Chinese
government, by way of the Internet, can further enforce control of the
internet.[32] In other words, normalization of behavior is achieved by
surveillance practices, where the subjects are at the same time implicated
as both the bearers and the effects of disciplinary power. In so doing,
China comes into line with other states, the difference being more a
question of severity than of nature.[33]

Cross-Straits Interaction: A Threat to Taiwan's National Security

As for Taiwan, the issue at stake is not so much censoring the content of
the Net, than controlling IT industries' investments on the mainland.
Taiwan's most salient feature is that its economy is outward oriented, and
this since the 1960s. Generally speaking, globalization has, for each and
every state, reduced their room for maneuvre, in particular in terms of
national economic policy. This is all the more true in the case of Taiwan

as, on the one hand, its economy is highly dependent on relocation strategies, and, on the other, the sovereignty dispute with the PRC is far from being settled. In recent years, Taiwan's medium and large enterprises' investments across the Straits have shifted from traditional industries to IT and high-tech sectors. In so doing, these firms have invested in the PRC as part of their international division-of-labor deployment. Besides, this investment tide has been accelerated by China's entry into the WTO, as Taiwanese firms wanted to take advantage of their dual status as "foreign investors" and "special domestic investors," a special treatment the PRC can no longer accord under the principles of the most favored nation status. In addition, Taiwanese companies will be more and more put on equal footing with foreign ones, as there will be a gradual harmonization of preferential policies at the central and local government levels.

As to the sociology of international relations, Taiwanese investments in mainland China seem an apposite case of transnational relations,[34] and of territorial divisions—termed "Natural Economic Territories" by Robert A. Scalapino,[35] or "Region-State" by Kenichi Ohmae—that transcend contending interstate relations. Hence, an undermining of national sovereignty, and a progressive remapping of the world, that, in the context of globalization, is based on functional criteria. Therefore, the issue at stake is that an over-concentration of investment across the Strait can, in the future, pose a security risk to Taiwan. The Taipei government is facing a constant dilemma: giving priority to national security at the risk of slowing down economic growth, or enhancing the latter at the expense of the former. Since Taiwan's economy began to slow down in the fourth quarter of 2000, this dilemma is all the more strong. As a matter of fact, in the long run, Taipei's mainland policy appears as an ex post legalization of the breaches opened by firms. Yet, the government's regulation lags far behind the current situation. With regard to the investment policy, the motto "patience over haste" (*jieji yongren*) has been replaced in 2001 by "active opening and effective management" (*jiji kaifang, youxiao guanli*). Though indirect investment (i.e. via a third country or territory, usually Hong Kong) is still the rule, investments below US$1 million do not necessitate the setting up of a special firm in the third country or territory.[36]

The information industry—which accounts for more than 40 percent of Taiwan's GNP[37]—has heavily invested in mainland China in recent years. Yet, semiconductors are on a government list of industries deemed strategic to Taiwan's interests, for which investments in China are strictly monitored. Thus, the Taipei government blocked, in late 2001, both Taiwan Semiconductor Manufacturing Corp. (TSMC) and

United Microeletronics Corp. (UMC)—the world's two largest foundry operators—from investing in China. So, while huge amounts of private capital from Taiwan has gone into building Chinese fabs for ventures like the Shanghai-based venture called Semiconductor Manufacturing International Corp. (SMIC) and Grace Semiconductor, big-listed companies like TSMC and UMC are still hampered.

Besides, in terms of talent flow, Leng Tse-Kang has shown that the real brain drain does not occur between Taiwan and China, but between the Greater China area and the United States. This brain drain is the result of rational choices of talented individuals. States on both sides of Taiwan Straits have limited instruments to regulate this talent flow.[38] In addition, in order to avoid restrictive regulations limiting Chinese talent flows in Taiwan, many Taiwanese firms prefer to establish their own R&D teams on the mainland.[39]

However, when assessing Sino–Taiwanese flows in regards of the nation-state sovereignty's undermining, two elements must be borne in mind that qualify this trend. First of all, though this chapter will not elaborate on Taiwan's economic competitive edge, the latter must be assessed by taking into account not only the national (i.e. Taiwanese) industry, but also the Chinese one. As far as ITs are concerned, the stress should be put on the fact that not only has the PRC bypassed Taiwan in 2000 when it became the world's third largest IT producer, but also on the fact that Taiwanese companies accounted, the same year, for half of the mainland IT industry's hardware production.[40]

In political terms, I have recently argued[41] that Sino–Taiwanese links, though an apposite case of transnational relations, are still participating in the formation of the state (i.e. Taiwan). I use here the distinction drawn by John Lonsdale between *state-building* and *state formation*. In Lonsdale's words:

> [There is] a key distinction between *state-building*, as a conscious effort at creating an apparatus of control, and *state-formation*, as an historical process whose outcome is a largely unconscious and contradictory process of conflicts, negotiations and compromises between diverse groups whose self-serving actions and trade-offs constitute the "vulgarization" of power.[42]

Growing transnational relations go hand in hand with a state-building process because of the interweaving of transnational factors and governmental action. Taiwanese investors on the mainland support the (Taiwan) state, benefit from it, and use it for their own ends. Therefore, if one does not focus on mutually exclusive sovereignties' vision of the world—object of governmental agreements or disagreements—but on the borders of power as the stake of negotiations, both for producing and controlling wealth between transnational and governmental actors, one is still witnessing a process of state formation according to Lonsdale's concept.

Therefore, when analyzing the transformation of the state in the era of globalization, one has to move away from the Weberian ideal-type of the sate, from a sharp opposition between state and society, and look closely to the interweaving between state and non-state logics; in other words, one has to pinpoint the various processes according to which individual and collective strategies are embedded in power relations.

The State as an Arbiter: The Embeddedness of Economic and Social Relations in Power Relations

For the Chinese government, IT—both in terms of building a competitive industry and in terms of business applications linked to IT—plays an important part in the country's economic modernization, hence on the legitimacy of the former. It is expected that China will build an indigenous IT industry, competitive on the global scale. The formation of a "Super Minister of Telecommunications and New Technologies" in March 1998 bears witness, among other things, to this priority.

Critics of Castells' works have pinpointed to the fact that although Castells is not a strict proponent of technological determinism, he tends to downplay the social processes of innovation and deployment. "Technology, along with knowledge (information), is often treated as a black box: that is, as stable and robust entities or processes whose embeddedness into the circumstances of their production and use are hidden. (. . .) However, technology needs to be examined not from a 'disembodied' perspective but from one that is cognizant of the social conditions within which it emerges and is employed."[43] In addition, and as far as China is concerned, Jean-Louis Rocca puts the stress in his most recent work on the fact that the model of modernity China is confronted with is not the ideal type of politics as the locus where communally life is determined, but the very real locus of the confrontation of social interests and of technocracy. Though the Chinese administration still lacks power to arbitrate between social interests, technocracy is gaining weight in leadership groups; both think tanks and research centers put stress on the rationalization of public policies.[44] Yet, as Charles Lindblom has demonstrated, in a market-oriented system, not only does the government have to collaborate with business, but it must often defer to business leadership to make the system work.[45]

The Straddling Between Public and Private Sectors

Since the early 1980s, through a state-led industrial policy, China has attempted to restructure the country's large state-owned enterprises (SOEs) and develop a globally competitive economy. In 1997, the Party Congress further acknowledged the necessity of modernizing the public sector in order to make it profitable. The official discourse insists on the necessity to "leave the small ones and grasp the big ones" (*fangxiao zhuada*).[46] However, in this process, the legacy of the pre-reform era should not be underestimated. In particular, as far as the information economy is concerned, the current underdevelopment of the service sector must be ascribed to the paradigm of the soviet economy where only material production mattered.[47] Besides, one must also not forget that some sectors such as the construction industry, the infrastructure management, the production and supply of water and electricity are still out of bounds to private entrepreneurs.[48]

In addition, Leng Tse-Kang notes that "China's development in the IT industry is different from the Silicon Valley model of the bottom–up dynamism of innovation. As a late-comer in the high-tech field, the state plays a crucial role by initiating top-down investment policies in such key IT industries as telecommunication and semiconductor."[49] Among many examples, one can think of the National Informationalization Leading Group, which is headed by Zhu Rongji himself, and which is spearheading the drive to upgrade information systems in government departments and to develop the nation's IT industry as a whole.[50]

Organically speaking, the line between public and private spheres is difficult to set clearly. The category of the so-called "privately managed" companies (*minying qiye*) is linked, as Gilles Guiheux has shown, to the development of high-tech industries and the authorization given during the 1980s to universities and research institutes to set up units, at the time of their being established, selling services and seeking profit.[51] Today, the expression *minying qiye* designates companies with differing legal status, which is the case of most companies in the IT sector: they enjoy a very high degree of autonomy and have only been registered as public or collective enterprises because private enterprises were not allowed before 1988.[52] In addition, "(s)ome companies became shareholder companies listed on the Shanghai stock exchange (the case of Start), for some of their subsidiaries in Hong Kong (the case of Legend and Stone), a part of the shares being distributed among the staff. (. . .) That said, the state may still control a majority of the capital and remain in fact the principal owner."[53] Besides, because of China's joining the WTO, the market is certainly more and more competitive. However, the September 2000 regulation on Telecommunication stipulates that the state must keep the majority in any company operating in this sector.[54]

Generally speaking, the largest private firms cannot do without bureaucratic patronage. More specially, the entwining between private and public strategies has been well brought to light by David Wank's study of power conversion in the making of China's rentier entrepreneur elite: he has demonstrated that it is not the private ownership of productive means that determines such an elite, but wealth accumulation that itself relies on access to state agents, that is state resources.[55]

Balancing the Interests Between the Central and Local Authorities

Superposed to the entwining between public and private spheres is that between central and local players. The main part of China's economic prosperity has come from the dynamism of local authorities, which have systematically favored growth and employment on the territory they are in charge of. From then on, it is difficult to find any kind of autonomization process on the part of the economic elite from the local political authorities.[56] The economic levers belong to networks that control a territory and/or some economic sectors. When these networks strive to become more autonomous, it is vis-à-vis the central authorities, by diversifying their activities and by trying to escape from state regulations, particularly in terms of taxation. Part of this trend, is the strategy of some leading IT groups to establish software parks around the country, and establishing the group as a local company in each place.[57] All in all, it can be said that the economic reforms in China have resulted less in a privatization of the economy, than in a decentralization process from central authorities to local authorities, be it at the provincial, township, or village level.

However, if relatively autonomous local governments have created a strong basis of regional support for emerging large firms, in the long run this can impede China's large firms to compete directly on the global level playing field, and they might be constrained to confine themselves to the domestic market. Indeed, globalization trends make it very difficult for a country to support several major players inside each sector. In this respect, Peter Nolan[58] has shown that one salient features of China's industrial reform is that there has been no process of merging large

strong enterprises into large multiplant companies, as it has occurred in
Western countries since the beginning of the 1980s. The merging or the
acquisition of large SOEs with/of other large state enterprises in
the same sector has been opposed both by central and local authorities.
The central ministry of holding company has frequently opposed mergers because the resulting powerful entities could undermine their
authority. On their part, local governments have strongly resisted the
merger of large local firms based elsewhere in the country: "There has
been persistant local resistance to cross-regional mergers due to fears of
downsizing and loss of control of a 'local asset'."[59]

The issue at stake, is not so much of favoring a "top-down" policy, but
of finding a balance between the interests of the central and the local
governments, as testified by the Taiwan experience. In terms of talent
flows, Leng Tse-kang concludes that "(i)n order to help 'grow' an ideal
location of talent interaction, cooperative mechanisms have been gradually developed between central authorities, local governments, and civil
society."[60]

Coping with Democracy

In any democracy, policies are the outcomes of conflicting interest
groups. Democratization in Taiwan has resulted in a remodeling of the
state–business relationship. It went hand in hand with growing interactions between business and politics that can be witnessed on two different grounds: partisan conflicts, on the one hand, individual commitments
of businessmen to domestic politics on the other hand.

As far as Taiwan is concerned, there is no need to insist on the fact that
the development of its industry at large, and of its IT industry in particular, is heavily dependent upon the management of cross-straits relations.
Regulations concerning relocation on the mainland, as well as the integration of mainland talent in the Taiwan market must constantly be
revised. And, as said previously, the national security issue always stand in
the picture. So, far from shifting the balance of power away from politics
and toward private interests, ending hypothetically in a demise of the
state, cross-straits relations are politicizing the whole realm of economics.
It could appear that economic policies are less politicized than they were
in the authoritarian period in the sense that it is no longer the
Guomindang that is dominating the whole decision-making process. But,
at the same time, because of growing cross-straits relations, no decision
is free from national security concern. The fact that, since the election of
Chen Shuibian at the presidency in 2000, the government has not

enjoyed the support of a majority in the Legislative Yuan first, and can only rely on a very short one since December 2001 elections, makes the legislative process all the more intricate. Apart from partisan cleavages, the picture is further complicated by the high factionalism that has always characterized the Minjindang.

More, the progressive implementation of popular sovereignty on Taiwan has deprived the technocratic elite from a monopoly in the decision-making process. The process at work, here, is quite the contrary of that of the so-called strong state, insofar as decisions are no longer those of a coherent bureaucracy. Indeed, democratization has offered multiple opportunities to businessmen wishing to weigh on the elaboration of policies, which can be assessed as a bottom-top process. Political change in Taiwan, in particular the regular renewal since 1992 of the legislative body by the whole electorate, has resulted in growing interaction between political and business interests at the legislative level. In short, electoral campaigns rely heavily on business donations,[61] while firms can now put pressure on legislators to protect their interests. Within this trend, firms investing in China are no exception. Direct participation in electoral politics is increasing as some big businessmen have been elected at the Legislative Yuan. As far as the deliberation field is concerned, one should also mention the participation of businessmen in the main political parties' ruling institutions, be it the Guomindang or the Minjindang,[62] as well as, upstream, in the scholar field through the various foundations and research institutes they have established.[63]

Generally speaking, one should remind what some authors such as Mark Granovetter[64] have clearly shown, that the motivating forces of economics are not confined to merchant interests rationally determined, that economics does not stand apart from other social activities, politics in particular.[65] With regard to Taiwanese businessmen, Gilles Guiheux[66] has demonstrated that the employer's legitimacy is not based exclusively on the profession of individual values, but also on that of collective ones. The growing involvement of big firms in politics is all the more strong as there exist some collective authorities within which big businessmen are closely associated with the decision-making process.

In Hong Kong, the issue at stake is not, for the time being at least, deadlocks democratic institutions can bring in terms of rational industrial policy, but the conflicting interests of business groups and the calling into question of the Tung administration's willingness, or capacity, to impartially arbitrate between them. Not only does the basic law provide strict safeguards against popular sector pressure within the Legislative Council, but big businessmen and pro-Beijing activists have become the new power interlocutors.[67] But, though the business community has maintained its influence and position as the central force in Hong Kong politics, the legitimacy of Chief Executive Tung Chee-hwa has been called into question by the very business elite. In a recent work, Tak Wing-Ngo has shown that Tung is suspected of not having arbitrated the conflicting interests of Hong Kong's businessmen. As a prominent example, he gives the unusual confrontation staged by the largest property developers against government decisions over the multibillion HK$ cyberport project announced during the budget speech of March 1999. "What was surprising for the business tycoons, who all have a stake in property development, was that such a huge project was decided without any public planning sessions, open land auctions, or invitations for tender. The development of the cyberport was entrusted to the Pacific Century Group, a company set up in 1993. The company is owned by Richard Li, the 32-year-old son of Li Ka-shing. According to the government's calculations, the cyberport project will cost HK$13 billion, with the Pacific Century Group investing HK$7 billion while the Hong Kong government provides the land at an estimated cost of HK$6 billion."[68] Consequently, "(i)n an unprecedented move, the territory's ten largest land developers—with the exception of Li Ka-shing's company—through a legal adviser issued a joint statement to the government challenging the whole project."[69]

Not only does the power of the state not shrink but instead transforms in the age of information, but a detour via domestic processes indicates that far from replacing the verticality of hierarchies by the horizontality of communication, globalization trends cannot but comfort conflicts of interests, and therefore power relations, within each jurisdiction, not to speak of interstate rivalry.

Notes

1. Carl J. Dahlman, and Jean-Eric Aubert, *China and the Knowledge Economy: Seizing the 21st Century*, WBI Development Studies, (Washington DC: The World Bank, 2002): 49.
2. Here, one cannot but mention Foucault's work showing that power relations take root in the whole of the social network. See, in particular, Michel Foucault, "Le pouvoir, comment s'exerce-t-il ?" (Power, how is it exercised?), in *Michel Foucault, un parcours philosophique*, (*Beyond Structuralism and Hermeneutics*), *1982–1983*, Hubert Dreyfus, and Paul Rabinovitch (Chicago: University of Chicago Press, 1984): 318.
3. Mark Granovetter and Richard Swedberg (eds.) *The Sociology of Economic Life* (Boulder, Co: Westview Press, 1992): 9. See also the Introduction in this volume.
4. See Leng, Tse-Kang, "Economic Globalization and IT Talent Flows across the Taiwan Straits: the Taipei/Shanghai/Silicon Valley Triangle," *Asian Survey*, 42, 2 (2002): 20–21.

5. Stephen D. Krasner, "Sovereignty," *Foreign Policy* (January/February 2001): 21.
6. In early October 2002, the Republican from California, Christopher Cox, introduced a legislation in order to create an Office of Global Internet Freedom, and spend U.S.$100 million over 2 years to fund efforts to develop censorhip-busting technology. Some Asian countries are the main targets—Vietnam, Burma, Laos, and North Korea—, and particularly the PRC. See *Far Eastern Economic Review* (hereafter: *FEER*) (November 7, 2002).
7. Karsten Giese, "Construction and Performance of Virtual Identity in the Chinese Internet," in *Asia.com, Asia Encounters the Internet*, K. C. Ho, Randolph Kluver, and Kenneth C. C. Yang (eds.) (London and New York: Routledge, 2003): 205.
8. For historical overview of the development of the Internet in China, see Shanthi Kalathil and Taylor C. Boas, *Open Networks Closed Regimes: The Impact of the Internet an Authoritarian Rule* (Washington, DC: Carnegie Endowment for International Peace, 2003): 21–23.
9. In particular in terms of foreign ownership limits under the WTO.
10. See Kalathil and Boas, *Open Networks Closed Regimes*: 18 and 158 (note 12). For an overview of Internet content regulations in China, see Carolyn Penford, "Global Technology Meets Local Environment: State Attempts to Control Internet Content," in *Asia.com*, Ho, Kluver, and Yang (eds.): 92–93.
11. See in particular, *Jiaoliu* (Exchange) 55 (February 2001).
12. Ibid.
13. Internet cafés have to keep records of all users for a 90-day period (*FEER*, September 26, 2002).
14. Lokman Tsui, "The Panopticon as the Antithesis of a Space of Freedom: Control and Regulation of the Internet in China," *China Information*, VII (2)(2003): 65–82 and Karsten Giese's chapter in this volume.
15. People's Daily, Xinhua News Agency, Zhongguo guoji guangbo diantai, China Daily and Guoji hulian wangluo xinwen zhongxin. *Jiaoliu*, 55 (February 2001).
16. Kalathil and Boas, *Open Networks Closed Regimes*: 14.
17. See Christopher Rene Hughes, "Nationalism in Chinese Cyberspace," *Cambridge Review of International Affairs*, 13, 2 (Spring-Summer 2000): 195–209.
18. Michael S. Chase and James C. Mulvenon argue that the remarkable feature of the Internet, is that dissidents (Falun Gong practitioners in particular) can "pursue their activities in some instances without attracting the attention of the authorities,": in *You've Got Dissent: Chinese Dissident Use of the Internet and Beijing's Counter-strategies*, The Rand Corp. According to Mulvenon, "(. . .) in the long term, it is not difficult to imagine a situation in which the spread of information technology . . . contributes to gradual pluralization of the system" (quoted in *FEER*, November 7, 2002).
19. See the introduction "New Information Technologies and the Reshaping of Power Relations: An Approach to Greater China's Political Economy" in this volume.
20. See Hughes's chapter in this volume.
21. See Batto's chapter in this volume.
22. See Françoise Mengin, "Taiwanese Politics and the Chinese Market: Business's Part in the Formation of a State, or the Border as a Stake of Negotiation," in *Politics in China: Moving Frontiers*, Françoise Mengin and Jean-Louis Rocca (eds.) (New York: Palgrave-Macmillan, 2002): 250.
23. Ibid.; and Françoise Mengin, "Freezing or Stalling the Status Quo in the Taiwan Strait?" *China Information*, XIV (1) (2000): 87–88.
24. See Jean-Louis Rocca, " 'Three at Once': the Multidimensional Scope of Labor Crisis in China," in *Politics in China*, Mengin and Rocca (eds.): 9.
25. Ibid.: 21.
26. Ching Kwan Lee, "Three Patterns of Working-Class Transitions in China," in *Politics in China*, Mengin and Rocca (eds.): 65.
27. Rocca, " 'Three at Once': the Multidimensional Scope of Labor Crisis in China": 22.

28. Abigail Halci and Frank Webster, "Inequality and Mobilization in *The Information Age*," *European Journal of Social Theory*, 3 (1) (February 2000): 69.

29. On the transformation of Chinese labor force see Rocca " 'Three at Once': the Multidimensional Scope of Labor Crisis in China," and Lee, "Three Patterns of Working-Class Transitions in China."

30. Jens Damm, "Internet and the Fragmented Political Community," *IIAS Newsletter* 33 (March 2003): 10.

31. See Jeremy Bentham and Michel Foucault, *Le Panoptique* (Paris: Belfond, 1977) and Michel Foucault, *Surveiller et Punir: Naissance de la prison* (Paris: Gallimard, 1975).

32. Tsui, "The Panopticon as the Antithesis of Space and Freedom," and Giese's chapter in this volume. See also David Lyon, *Surveillance Society: Monitoring Every Day Life* (Buckingham, Philadelphia: Open University Press, 2001), *The Electronic Eye: The Rise of Surveillance Society* (Cambridge: Polity Press, 1994) and "Cyberspace, Surveillance, and Social Control. The Hidden Face of the Internet in Asia" in *Asia.com*, Ho, Kluver, and Yang (eds.): 67–82.

33. See case studies on China, but also Cuba, Singapore, Vietnam, Burma, the United Arab Emirates, Saudi Arabia, and Egypt in Kalathil and Boas, *Open Networks Closed Regimes*.

34. Transnational relations have been defined, among others, by Robert O. Keohane and Joseph S. Nye as "the movement of tangible or intangible items across state boundaries when at least one actor is not an agent of a government or an intergovernmental organization," in Robert O. Keohane and Joseph N. Nye Jr (eds.), *Transnational Relations and World Politics* (Cambridge, Mass.: Harvard University Press, 1972): xii.

35. In Jane Khana (ed.), *Southern China, Hong Kong, and Taiwan: Evolution of a Subregional Economy*, The Center for Strategic and International Studies, Significant Issues Series, XVII, 7 (Washington, 1995): viii.

36. See current regulations on the Ministry of Economic Affairs site: www.moea.gov.tw

37. Estimation given by Kao Charng, Chung-Hua Institution for Economic Research, personal interview, Taipei, December 2001.

38. Leng, "Economic Globalization and IT Talent Flows across the Taiwan Straits": 6.

39. Ibid.: 21.

40. Interview Kao.

41. Françoise Mengin, "Taiwanese Politics and the Chinese Market": 232–257.

42. Bruce Berman and John Lonsdale, *Unhappy Valley, Conflict in Kenya and Africa* (London: James Currey, Nairobi: Heinemann Kenya, Athens (Ohio): Ohio University Press,1992): 5. Underlined in the original. See also chapter 2 by John Lonsdale:"The Conquest State of Kenya, 1895–1905": 13–44.

43. Nico Stehr,"Deciphering Information Technologies: Modern Societies as Networks," *European Journal of Social Theory*, 3 (1) (February 2000): 83.

44. Jean-Louis Rocca, *La Condition de la Chine* (forthcoming).

45. Charles E. Lindblom, *Politics and Markets: The World's Political-Economic Systems* (New York: Basic Books, 1977).

46. Jean-François Huchet, "Concentration and the Emergence of Corporate Group in Chinese Industry," *China Perspectives*, 23 (May–June 1999): 5–17.

47. François Gipouloux, "Hong Kong, Taiwan and Shanghai: Rival Logistic Hubs along the East Asian Maritime Corridor," *China Perspectives*, 33(January–February 2001): 6.

48. See Gilles Guiheux, "The Incomplete Crystallisation of the Private Sector," *China Perspectives*, 42 (July–August 2002): 27.

49. Leng, "Economic Globalization and IT Talent Flows across the Taiwan Straits": 18.

50. *FEER* (September 19, 2002).

51. Guiheux,"The Incomplete Crystallisation . . . ": 28.

52. "Thus the firm Stone (*Sitong xinxing chanye gongsi*) was created in 1984 thanks to a loan of 20,000 yuan from a local council, the municipality of Sijiqing in the Haidian district of Peking." Ibid.

53. Ibid.: 29.

54. See Eric Sautedé, "Telecommunications in China: Towards a Post-WTO Shock Therapy?" *China Perspectives*, 41 (May–June 2002): 33–45.

55. David Wank, "The Making of China's Rentier Entrepreneur Elite: State, Clientelism, and Power Conversion, 1978–1995," in *Politics in China*, Mengin and Rocca (eds.): 118–139.

56. Jean Oi, in particular, has shed light on the entrepreneurial role of local bureaucrats. In her works, "local state corporatism" refers to the symbiotic nature of relations between the private sector and the local bureaucracies. Jean C. Oi, *Rural China Takes Off, Institutional Foundations of Economic Reform* (Berkeley: University of California Press, 1999). See also David L. Wank, *Commodifying Communism, Business, Trust and Politics in a Chinese City* (Cambridge: Cambridge University Press, 1999).

57. For instance, Top Group has established 23 software parks in China: "Explains Fang Ye, the group's chief operating officer: 'Our taxes go to the local government. As far as they are concerned, we are investing there, and we are registered locally, so they treat us as a local company.' The result, he says, is that 'local governments will give us benefits compared to other companies.' " (*FEER*, September 19, 2002).

58. Peter Nolan, *China and the Global Business Revolution* (Basinkstoke: Palgrave, 2001), and *China at the Crossroads* (Cambridge: Polity Press, 2004): 18–27.

59. Ibid.:21.

60. Leng, "Economic Globalization and Talent Flows across the Taiwan Straits": 23. More generally, he states that "In order to attract the best brainpower from around the world, states choose to cooperate with urban centers to promote material and culture amenities. (. . .) Such efforts include improving transportation, communication, environment and general amenities." Ibid.

61. The single nontransferable vote system according to which the majority of Taiwan's representatives are elected enhaces the part played by money in politics, even if the latest legislation has put a curb in this field.

62. See Françoise Mengin, "Taiwanese Politics and the Chinese Market": 244.

63. Ibid.: 244–245.

64. Mark Granovetter, "Economic Action and Social Structure: the Problem of Embeddedness," in *The Sociology of Economic Life*, Granovetter, and Swedberg (eds.): 53–81.

65. In Granovetter's and Swedberg's words:"(. . .) economic action cannot, in principle, be separated from the quest for approval, status, sociability, and power." Ibid.: 7.

66. Gilles Guiheux, *Les Grands entrepreneurs privés à Taiwan: La main visible de la prospérité* (Paris: CNRS Editions, 2002): 220–227.

67. Through their appointment as members of the Basic Law Consultation Committee, Hong Kong Affairs Advisers, District Affairs Advisers, Preliminary Working Committee, and Preparatory Committee. See Tak-Wing Ngo, "Money, Power, and the Problem of Legitimacy in the Hong Kong Special Administrative Region," in *Politics in China*, Mengin and Rocca (eds.): 100.

68. Ibid.: 108.

69. Ibid.: 109.

PART 2

Communication and Control: Sovereignty in the Age of the Internet

CHAPTER FOUR

Controlling the Internet Architecture within Greater China[1]

CHRISTOPHER R. HUGHES

A Chinese Puzzle

. . . no nation has yet discovered a way to import the world's goods and services while stopping foreign ideas at the border. It is in our interests that the next generation in China be engaged by the Information Age, not isolated from global trends shaping the future.

Since U.S. Secretary of State James Baker heralded the end of the Cold War in the Asia–Pacific with the earlier mentioned statement,[2] the idea that the globalization of Information and Communication Technologies (ICTs) can transform an authoritarian state like China in harmony with American national interests has become something of a mantra for successive Washington administrations. In December 2000, U.S. President Clinton compared cracking down on the Internet in China with "trying to nail Jello to the wall."[3]

If this view of the Internet is correct, though, decision-makers in Beijing seem to be remarkably relaxed about the prospect. Not only did China announce 1999 to be the "year of on-line government" and 2000 the "year of on-line enterprise," but in concluding the U.S.–China bilateral agreement on China's accession to the World Trade Organization (WTO) on February 2, 2000, they made sweeping commitments to loosen their control over ownership of the telecommunications sector.

This chapter will attempt to evaluate the assumptions behind these opposed views over the political impact of ICTs in China and draw out some implications for international politics. As China enters the WTO, this is a worthwhile exercise not only for academic interest, but also due to the ethical considerations that are raised for the policies of foreign governments, international organizations and institutions, and investors and operators in China's telecoms market.

The WTO Effect

The requirements that China has agreed to for opening up the telecoms sector to foreign investment and services on accession to the WTO will have a sweeping effect on the provision of information-related services in that country. Central to these is the equal treatment principle included in the General Agreement on Trade in Services (GATS) and in the U.S.–China Agreement on accession that requires China to accord to services and service suppliers of other WTO members treatment no less favorable than that it accords to its own like services and service suppliers. This will mean allowing competition to the near-monopoly held so far by China Telecom, permitting significant foreign investment in indigenous enterprises, and abolishing tariff concessions and discriminatory procurement processes.[4]

Caution is called for, however, before we assume that the consequent impact of the global telecommunications market in China will make ICTs into an effective tool for political transformation along liberal-democratic lines. First of all, it should be borne in mind that the scope of the WTO regime is in fact carefully restricted by acknowledgments that states can legitimately impose regulations for reasons ranging from the protection of consumers to maintaining the overriding public interest or national security. As a report on e-commerce prepared for the WTO Secretariat puts it, "Neither the GATT nor the GATS attempts to pronounce on the legitimacy of regulatory objectives as such, as long as the objective is not the protection of domestic industry."[5]

That policy-makers in China believe this leaves enough room to impose some fairly comprehensive regulations was demonstrated quite clearly when a comprehensive raft of regulations to enhance state control over activity in cyberspace was introduced on December 25, 2000,[6] just seven months after the conclusion of the U.S.–China Agreement on accession. These regulations include, among others, measures that make Internet Service Providers (ISPs) responsible for surveilling content and activity that passes through their servers by requiring them to keep records of all content that appears on their sites and all users who dial on to their servers for 60 days, and to hand these records to the security agencies on demand.

The long list of activities that are proscribed by the December 2000 regulations includes familiar Internet crimes, such as the dissemination of pornography, the breaching of copyright and fraud. Yet, it also includes activities that "violate the fundamental principles of the constitution," "damage national unification," "damage unity between the different ethnic groups," "damage state policy on religion by propagating 'feudal beliefs,' " and "endanger social stability." Such crimes may appear to be nothing out of the ordinary, until we realize that Article 1 of the Constitution states that China is a socialist system ruled by the people's democratic dictatorship, that the main challenges to national unification exist in Taiwan, Tibet and the mainly Islamic region of Xinjiang, and the most widespread religious movement is the Falun Gong. Threats to "social stability" is a catch-all category. The kinds of people arrested for Internet crime since Shanghai-based software engineer Lin Hai was sentenced to 2 years in prison in early 1999 for providing e-mail addresses to the U.S.-based pro-democracy organization VIP Reference, however, confirms that such categories can definitely be extended to include pro-democracy activists.

Outside legal opinion tends to agree with the view that regulations such as that mentioned earlier above do not conflict with WTO principles. As lawyer Mark Kantor puts it, "The WTO rules do not, however, mandate free speech or a free press and authoritarian Chinese policies limiting access to uncontrolled information remain legally unaffected by these developments so long as discrimination between foreign and local providers does not occur."[7] Complaints could be made by appealing to the "fair play" requirements contained in Article VI of the GATS, which stipulates that regulatory decision-making should be conducted in general "in a reasonable, objective and impartial manner."

Such a complaint would have to prove that a policy related to the "overriding public interest or national security" was an unwarranted excuse for the protection of domestic industries. Yet, the national security caveat is given considerable scope by the way in which concepts of "public interest" and "national security" are not clearly defined by the WTO. It would be a brave company that would want to mobilize their government to challenge China in the WTO on such grounds. Not only would such action mean going through the lengthy and complex procedures of the WTO dispute resolution machinery, it could also hamper

individual efforts to penetrate the Chinese market. No doubt many
CEOs in the telecommunications sector will remember the example of
Rupert Murdoch, who claimed in September 1993 that satellite TV is a
threat to totalitarian regimes the world over, only to witness the Chinese
government promptly ban the ownership of private satellite dishes. The
following April, Murdoch began the process of amelioration by dropping
the BBC from his Star TV network covering North Asia and China.

The position of firms bent on entering the Chinese telecommunications market under the WTO rules will be even more exposed than that
of Murdoch in 1993, though. This is because the U.S.–China Agreement
accepts that they must work with indigenous partners, holding a maximum stake of 49 percent, rising to 50 percent after 2 years. Domestic
Chinese regulations also stipulate that indigenous firms must gain
approval from the Ministry of Information Industries (MII) before they
are allowed to receive foreign capital, cooperate with foreign businesses
or list domestic or overseas stocks.[8] So far this policy has been applied
lightly, tolerating practices such as the listing of China-based stocks in
overseas jurisdictions like the Cayman Islands. This indicates that its
significance lies more on the political side than the economic, by providing the MII with an effective veto over which foreign investors and
businesses link up with which indigenous firms.

As the state has strong regulatory powers over the behavior of indigenous players in the Chinese telecoms market, it has, by extension, considerable leverage over their foreign partners. This is partly due to the
general lack of clarity concerning the distinction between "public" and
"private" in the Chinese economic system. At the provincial end of the
scale, this can be seen in a set-up like the Lantian Corporation, a local
government financed project established to introduce intelligent agriculture in the province of Jilin, using technology donated by IBM, of
which Shaun Breslin concludes that it "isn't exactly state-owned but nor
is it wholly private."[9] At the other end of the scale, the U.S.–China
Agreement tacitly acknowledges the problem when it accepts that the
big state-run telecoms monopolies are to be treated as "private" firms by
the WTO. While this benefits foreign competitors, because state-owned
monopolies cannot be exempted from the equal treatment provisions of
the GATS, it also means that foreign firms will be working in partnership with state-controlled firms when they claim to be working with the
"private" sector.

Links between indigenous firms and the state are also forged by
personal relationships. At one extreme is President Jiang Zemin's son,
Jiang Mianheng, who boasts a long list of directorships of Internet firms

and has been appointed vice president of the Chinese Academy of Sciences, making him something of a spokesman for the electronics industry. Or take Eastcom, a leading player in the mobile communications market that is now developing Internet services as a top-level domain registrar under Internet Corporation for Assigned Names and Numbers (ICANN). This "private" firm actually grew out of the Equipment Supply Office of the Posts and Telecommunications Bureau of Zhejiang province. A look at Eastcom's board of directors dispels any illusions that Internet startups are the preserve of the young, and confirms that control is still in the hands of personnel who staffed the old state-owned enterprises (SOEs). Seven are over 50 years of age, four over 45, and only two below the age of 35, and 58-year-old chairman and CEO has been distinguished with the Model Worker Medal for Zhejiang Province.[10]

It is important to note this close relationship between the "private" sector and the state in China when we consider what kind of partnerships are being forged as foreign investors enter the market under the supervision of the MII. Of more political concern is a key partnership like that established in 2001 between Legend Holdings and AOL-Time Warner. Although Legend is not a SOE, it has been cultivated by the government to be part of a "national team" of very large enterprises that should be able to compete in the global economy. Since its foundation in 1984 with a $24,000 loan, it has become China's largest personal computer manufacturer, thanks largely to its merger with the Computing Institute of the Chinese Academy of Sciences and financing that derives largely from close ties with the Bank of China.[11]

Part of the appeal of this partnership to AOL-Time Warner is that it will allow AOL to "bundle" its Internet services software on PC desktops, using the marketing strategy that has worked well in the United States. But this is not the only advantage. As the *International Herald Tribune* put it, "Legend enjoys cordial relations with China's regulators and a strong reputation among Chinese consumers—assets that could help offset AOL's lack of operating experience in China and ease apprehensions among Chinese officials and consumers that the company will use its services to download U.S. culture into China."[12]

With the convergence of interactive digital services and cable television, it is also worth noting that AOL-Time Warner and Rupert Murdoch's News Corporation are also making inroads into the Chinese cable television market. In April 2001, the minister of the State Administration of Radio, Film and TV, Xu Guangchun, announced that these firms would be permitted to broadcast via cable directly to a part of Guangdong Province. At the same time, Xu announced that overseas companies (including those listed in Hong Kong and Taiwan) would be forbidden from taking direct equity stakes in mainland cable TV concerns, unless they confined themselves to just leasing equipment to local companies. It did not go unnoticed that the way had been paved for the triumphs of AOL and the Murdoch empire through the building of personal links between their top managers and the Chinese Communist Party (CCP) elite, with the head of Star TV, James Murdoch (son of Rupert) describing the banned Falun Gong movement as "dangerous" and an "apocalyptic cult," and AOL-Time Warner CEO Gerald Levin introducing the CCP leader as "my good friend Jiang Zemin" and "a man of honour, dedicated to the best interests of his people" at a dinner in Hong Kong.[13] It might also be remarked that one of the conditions for granting permission to AOL-Time Warner and News Corporation to broadcast into China was that they should support efforts by China Central Television to broadcast its English-language channel to the United States, standing the globalization of liberalism thesis on its head somewhat.[14]

Commercialization and the Question of Architecture

That the state will retain considerable leverage over the behavior of foreign firms and investors in China's telecoms market under WTO rules has significant political implications that arise from the way in which ICT architecture will develop under market mechanisms. There is certainly awareness among Chinese policy-makers that the choice of ICT architecture is not politically neutral, especially when it comes to considerations of national security. The mass of regulations introduced since 1994 stipulates that computers carrying sensitive information must be separated from the Internet, and puts in place fire walls and machinery to permit surveillance of information flows between domestic and foreign computers. Efforts to develop indigenous architecture and code are also under way, with much attention focused on attempts to make Red Flag Linux an alternative to Microsoft products. Much defensive technical work is also carried out under the auspices of military research and development, with the People's Liberation Army (PLA) claiming to have made breakthroughs in areas such as the manufacture of routers capable of resisting information warfare attacks.[15]

Such attempts to adapt the architecture of ICTs in ways that can be used to maintain state security should not be sneered at. China overtook Taiwan in the volume of its hardware production in the middle of 2000, and has joined India in supplying software engineers and services to the world. However, the fact remains that China is entering a global market in which 35 out of the world's top 36 hardware companies (ranked by R&D expenditure) are based in the United States. In 1998 Cisco and Lucent, both American corporations, accounted for 52 percent of the world market capitalization in the telecoms hardware sector. Their combined market capiliztion was a staggering U.S.$300 bn. Development of the Internet in China has relied heavily on such foreign expertise and investment. The upgrading of the fixed-line network for Internet use has relied largely on buying equipment from Cisco. The fiber-optic transmission trunk that was built in the 1990s was constructed by firms like Lucent, Alcatel, Nortel, and Ericsson.[16]

The MII and security agencies are of course painfully aware of the technological lead enjoyed by foreign firms. Lacking ways to close the gap, they have to try to ensure that a combination of regulation and market mechanisms can harness the expertise possessed by foreign entrants into the domestic market in ways that strengthen the power of the state, and not the reverse. An extensive investigation by Greg Walton for the Montreal-based International Centre for Human Rights and Democratic Development,[17] thus details how leading North American and European firms take part in annual "Security China" trade exhibitions and are supplying crucial assistance for converting the Internet into a massive surveillance system, known as the "Golden Shield." Leading foreign firms, he explains, are lured by lucrative contracts with central and local governments into helping with the construction of a "massive, ubiquitous architecture of surveillance," the ultimate aim of which is "to integrate a gigantic online database with an all-encompassing surveillance network." This will include linking up cutting-edge technologies such as speech and face recognition, closed-circuit television, smart cards, credit records and Internet surveillance technologies.

As Walton points out, the sheer volume of data that is now flowing across ICTs, fueled by the move toward broadband, means that the technology to control communications is now moving away from old-style firewalls in favor of dispersing monitoring and censorship architecture throughout the system, down to the level of individual PC platforms. It is somewhat ironic that the kind of cooperation between foreign firms and the Chinese state that this requires bears out the argument developed by commentators on the impact of ICTs in the United States who see that the commercialization of architecture is having a detrimental impact on civil liberties.[18]

Whereas the Internet may well have once been a network for the open exchange of information among scientists who believe that knowledge

would flourish under conditions of unfettered communication,[19] fundamental changes had to occur when the ban imposed on commercial
activity by the National Science Foundation of the United States was
lifted in 1991. While the massive private investment that this stimulated,
certainly, spread access to the Internet and encouraged the design of
more user-friendly technology, new functions also had to be installed in
the architecture if the Internet was to be used for business purposes.
At a minimum, these facilities include the ability to efficiently collect
and process data about users and their activities, usually without them
knowing it.

Chinese observers of the commercialization of the Internet are just
as aware as their foreign counterparts are of developments such as the ability of Microsoft software to transmit information to the Microsoft website
without the knowledge of users.[20] Such functions are of course indispensable if commercial organizations are to be able to build customer
databases of immense size and sophistication. As the Internet develops in
China largely for the purposes of e-commerce, the same kind of data-
collecting architecture is being adopted there as a matter of course.

In fact, Internet firms wanting to perform functions such as the
registering of domain names under ICANN, can even be required to
install certain kinds of data collecting and processing technology in order
to meet international standards. Eastcom, an ICANN accredited, thus
uses network architecture mostly provided by Cisco and an IBM DB2
Enterprise Extended Edition 7.1 for its database. This is due to the database's ability to "support business intelligence applications such as data
warehousing and on-line analytical processing," and its "proven ability to
help customers find competitive advantage, better customer service or
reduced costs by mining their data for the knowledge required to make
better decisions."

The degree to which data collection, processing, and censorship of
content is now developing into an architecture for the surveillance state
appears to come into conflict with elements of international human
rights standards. Article 19 of the *Universal Declararation of Human Rights*
declares: "Everyone has the right to freedom of expression; this right
includes freedom to hold opinions without interference and to seek,
receive and impart information and ideas through any media and regardless of frontiers." The right to receive and impart information and ideas
regardless of frontiers is enshrined in the *International Covenant on Civil
and Political Rights*, to which China signed up in 1998.

It is more than likely, however, that human rights may be a poor foundation upon which to appeal against measures taken to control ICTs

under the rubric of maintaining national security. Just as with the WTO, both the Declaration and the Covenant also legitimate sweeping powers for states to maintain "morality, public order, general welfare in a democratic society" (Declaration, Art. 29) and when the protection of national security or public order, or of public health or morals is at stake (Covenant, Art. 19). The kinds of activities that are outlawed in Chinese cyberspace, such as publishing content that is "subversive," "supports cults," "harms the reputation" of China or hurts efforts to "unify" Taiwan with the PRC, can be seen as lying entirely within this list of exceptions. Perhaps Perry Keller sums up the overall situation at present when he points out that the intersnational regimes developed so far to underpin a Global Information Society have been established by economic law, leaving the "other foundational leg" of international human rights law less well developed.[21]

Global Governance?

If the global regimes established to govern international trade and human rights are too weak to have a significant impact on the ways that states use ICTs to surveil their citizens, the types of international organization established to oversee their technological standardization cannot be expected to play much of a role either. In fact, these are carefully designed in ways that deliberately prevent them being able to intervene in domestic politics. Take the case of ICANN. As the organization charged with overseeing the allocation of Internet Protocol (IP) number blocks, maintaining the Internet root server system, determining the policy for adding new Top Level Domains (TLDs), and coordinating the assignment of technological parameters, ICANN has enormous potential power to shape the architecture of the Internet. Yet, while ICANN expects accredited registrars like Eastcom to install powerful data collecting and processing architecture, it has no power to constrain national security agencies from mining the data that is collected.

A look at the structure of ICANN reveals how it is an organization carefully crafted so as to be too weak to ever mount a challenge to the authority of states, or to be "captured" by any one state. It is precisely to ensure this that the Clinton administration established ICANN as a private, nonprofit-making organization. Granted, a token gesture of democratic governance has been lent to ICANN by making nine of its nineteen directors "at large" representatives of five "world regions," elected by an online ballot that was conducted in October 2000. The lucky winner for the "at large" directorship to represent all Internet users in the Middle East, Pakistan, India, China, Japan, Australia, Afghanistan, and "countries to the East," including the East Indian Ocean islands and Antarctica, (but excluding United States and Latin American possessions) was the Maryland-based Japanese employee of Fujitsu, Masanobu Katoh, who polled no less than 13,913 votes! That China finds this type of democracy acceptable is clear from the fact that it supported the establishment of ICANN and endorsed its principles when it joined the inaugural meeting of ICANN's Governmental Advisory Committee on March 2, 1999.

While international organizations dedicated to the economic and technological governance of ICTs are depoliticized, however, the state-centric nature of the international system seems to provide little incentive for addressing political concerns at the global level. Perhaps the greatest pressure mitigating against such cooperation is the need to maintain international security. This is quite simply because, if the porosity of borders heralded by the globalization of ICTs really poses a threat to the Chinese state, it poses a threat to all other states as well. Schneier neatly sums up the situation when he points out: "Any organised crime syndicate with enough money to launch a large-scale attack against a financial system would do well to find a country with poor computer crime laws, easily bribable police officers, and no extradition treaties."[22] The implication of this is that the greater the threat posed to state jurisdiction and international order by interconnectivity, the stronger will be the countermeasures that have to be taken by states to protect their sovereignty and maintain order.

This is not a new phenomenon. As Frederick points out: "Throughout history, one clear pattern is apparent. Every time a new innovation in communication technology appears, sooner or later international law arises to regulate it."[23] But the degree of interconnectivity presented by a technology like the Internet means that all states have an increased stake in ensuring that it is regulated in less-developed economies such as China, if holes are not to be created through which the "Four Horsmen of the Information Apocalypse,"[24] namely terrorists, drug dealers, money launderers, and child pornographers, can ride out. This has the potential to generate a serious conflict between the principles of order and justice at the global level.

The way in which this predicament stands the liberal vision of globalization on its head, however, can be seen when states that hold very different political values have to collaborate to maintain security. In November 2000, for example, a network was cracked that involved the use of the Internet by criminals in China and the Republic of China on Taiwan to illicitly siphon off money from a South African bank. Such successful police action must have resulted from extensive cooperation between the security agencies from both sides of the Taiwan Strait, yet their governments do not even talk to each other.

The challenge that such international cooperation presents liberal democracies has become clearer since the terrorist attacks that took place against New York and Washington on September 11, 2001. When leaders of the states that make up the Asia–Pacific Economic Cooperation forum (APEC) issued a statement on counter-terrorism at Shanghai on October 21, for instance, they called for measures to counter "all forms of terrorist acts." These measures included the following: strengthening activities to protect critical sectors, including telecommunications; cooperation to develop electronic movement records systems that will enhance border security; strengthening capacity building and economic and technical cooperation to enable member economies to put into place and enforce effective counter-terrorism measures.[25] APEC, however, includes states as diverse as China, the United States, Australia, Brunei, Canada, Chile, Hong Kong, Indonesia, Japan, Malaysia, Mexico, New Zealand, Papua New Guinea, Peru, Philippines, Russia, Singapore, South Korea, Taiwan, Thailand, and Vietnam.

The context for surveillance cooperation between states with different domestic political regimes is already being put in place by the convergence of domestic legislation around the world. In the case of China, it is clear that the MII in China is looking to foreign legislation for ideas on how to exert state control over the flow of information.[26] The parallels can be quite remarkable. For example, Chinese legislation now requires ISPs to keep records of all content and all users that appear on their servers for scrutiny by the security agencies if required. In the United Kingdom, the Regulation of Investigatory Powers (RIP) Bill also requires every ISP to retain all communications data originating or terminating in the United Kingdom, or routed through U.K. networks. Employers in the United Kingdom are permitted to monitor the e-mail of their staff, and the Home Office is considering granting powers to the security agencies to have access to records of every phone call, e-mail and Internet connection made in Britain. The director general of the national criminal intelligence service, Roger Gaspar, even compared the proposed new data bank to the national DNA database under development.[27]

Yet, as Mathiesen points out with reference to the integration of European Union databases, even democratic parliaments are not equipped with sufficient knowledge and insight, or enough power, to monitor how security agencies collect and use data.[28] When data is exchanged between states, this problem is magnified. Serious questions over the implications for civil liberties that arise from exchanging data on citizens between member states of the European Union, for example, were raised when the House of Lords held an inquiry into the linking up of European Union databases. More relevant to the case of China is that the inquiry acknowledged that there was growing pressure from third countries for access to such information, and warned that this may aggravate the risk of error or misuse as it may not always be clear which data protection rules apply and which, if any, body is responsible for supervising the data flows.[29]

As the exchange of data becomes ever broader, accountability is inevitably weakened, especially when it extends to a state like China, which lacks the balancing institutions being put in place by liberal-democratic governments to protect citizens from unwarranted surveillance, such as data protection officers and legislation. Yet, the European Union, since 1999 at least, has been exploring the possibility of exchanging information on individuals accumulated on its various intelligence databases with the United States and Russia.[30] Not only are both of these states, as APEC members, now committed to collaborating with each other in the war against terrorism, but Russia is also a member of the "Shanghai Six," which brings it together with China, Uzbekistan, Kazakhstan, Kyrgyzstan, and Tajikistan to maintain security in Central Asia. The main concern for China in Central Asia has long been the secessionist movement of the Islamic Uighur population in Xinjiang under the rubric of its "strike hard" campaign. Its fight against "splittists" is of course much wider, taking in areas such as Tibet and Taiwan as well. As there is still no internationally accepted definition of "terrorism," though, it is unclear where international cooperation starts and ends on such issues.

It may be the case that the need to maintain international order gives liberal democracies a strong incentive to turn a blind eye to draconian measures adopted by a state like China to maintain security in its portion of cyberspace. At worst, as liberal democracies are faced by the threat of terrorism—let alone lorry loads of illegal immigrants appearing at their borders—they will have to give in to pressure to exchange information with the security agencies of authoritarian states and assist them in ensuring that their areas of cyberspace are well monitored. The Information Revolution, therefore, is already being followed by something of a counterrevolution, as states seek to restore order.

Or Virtual Realism?

It would be wrong, however, to conclude that the international need to exchange information between databases means that there are no ways to limit the ways in which they manipulate the shape and usage of ICTs. The most compelling case for political accountability, however, is based not on human rights concerns but on the growing awareness of the military vulnerabilities consequent upon the growing dependence on globalized ICTs for economic purposes. After all, if there is near hysteria in the United States over the prospects of information warfare,[31] the Chinese military is equally concerned over the threat to their national security posed by an overreliance on hardware and software sourced from American-based firms.[32]

This mutual concern over security provides a far stronger motivation for developing institutions to regulate ICTs at the global level than do fears over human rights abuses. Particularly pressing, for example, is the need to evolve international law in ways that can re-define the legitimate use of force in a way that keeps up with technological change. In particular, such a development implies the evolution of a new interpretation of the UN Charter and customary international law that can accommodate the definition of cyber-warfare as a form of the use of force. Without such a definition, it will be difficult to decide what constitutes legitimate self-defense against cyber-warfare. Moreover, when such definitions are decided, they will have to be made enforceable by the construction of multilateral treaties that facilitate tracking, attribution and transnational enforcement.[33]

Despite the need to evolve the laws of war to cope with cyber-attacks, however, limitations on information can already be found in agreements such as the 1947 declaration on *Measures to be Taken Against Propaganda and Inciters of a New War*, in which the UN General Assembly condemned "all forms of propaganda, in whatsoever country conducted, which is either designed or likely to provoke, or encourage any threat to the peace, breach of the peace or act of aggression."[34] Moreover, given the weaknesses of international human rights regimes, it is somewhat ironic that another body of international law that already acknowledges the need for constraints on the use of information to attack states is the *Covenant on Civil and Political Liberties*. This is because Article 20 of the *Covenant* prohibits the transmission of certain types of information that constitute propaganda advocating war, or advocating national, racial, or religious hatred that constitutes incitement to discrimination, hostility, or violence. It could also be argued that the "communication analysis"

of peace and war that can already be found in some international
institutions should be extended to cover ICTs. The most notable example of this is the preamble to UNESCO's constitution, which points
out that "since wars begin in the minds of men, it is in the minds of
men that the defences of peace must be constructed." It continues by
adding that "State parties . . . are agreed and determined to develop and
to increase the means of communication between their peoples and to
employ these means for the purposes of mutual understanding and a
truer and more perfect knowledge of each other's lives."[35]

The relevance to China of this connection in international law between
communication and peace can be illustrated by some fairly dramatic
examples: when the Chinese embassy in Belgrade was hit by Nato missiles
on May 8, 1999, the Beijing municipal authorities not only felt the need
to bus students in to besiege Western embassies, they also established a
"Sacred Sovereignty" website where people could express their outrage,
learn the e-mail addresses of Nato governments and political parties, and
study the techniques of hacking and service-denial attacks. Even the most
liberal of the Party-controlled newspapers published such addresses and
reported hacking attacks with pride.[36] Since then, waves of hacking attacks
have been launched against traditional foes in Taiwan and Japan. In
August 1999, over 7,000 attacks were made on public websites in Taiwan
following an announcement by the island's president, that was seen in
China as tantamount to a declaration of independence. Taiwanese hackers
responded with some eight waves of their own attacks until the call went
out for a ceasefire.[37] Chinese hackers have attacked Japanese sites, too, most
conspicuously when a conference was held in Osaka in January 2000 to
discuss whether the 1937 Nanjing Massacre was a fabrication. At one
point, some 1,600 strikes were launched against the Bank of Japan's computer system within the space of seven minutes. Moreover, this kind of
information warfare is becoming increasingly organized, as demonstrated
by the waves of hacking attacks launched against sites in the United States
almost exactly a month after a U.S. reconnaissance aircraft was forced to
land on Hainan Island by Chinese jet fighters on April 1, 2001.[38]

Given the linkage in international law between certain types of propaganda and warfare, it is worth asking who should be held responsible
for this burgeoning international aggression in Chinese cyberspace. The
Chinese state itself cannot avoid all culpability, when the CCP has been
using ICTs to mobilize nationalism to legitimate its own claim to power.
The foreign ministry website, for example, promotes the CCP's view of
its mission of national salvation in the international context, the "Strong
State Forum" of the *People's Daily* is a hotbed of nationalist fervor, and

the electronic version of the PLA newspaper, *Liberation Army Daily*, reminds surfers from time-to-time of the existence of China's nuclear deterrent during times of tension within foreign relations. Other sites are aimed at more specific nationalist projects, such as those used by "united front" organizations to promote Beijing's version of Tibetan identity (http://www.tibet-web.com), and to promote "unification" with Taiwan by helping Taiwanese who want to invest in the mainland (http://www.tailian.org.cn). In this respect, the Internet is being used as another example of what Althusser calls "ideological state apparatuses," along with schools, the legal system, culture, religion, and the media.[39]

The resulting activity that occurs in Chinese cyberspace indicates how difficult it is for the state to stop the nationalistic politics that it so assiduously cultivates from spilling over and threatening to destabilize foreign relations. This phenomenon can be seen unfolding since at least 1998, when the Internet was used to disseminate information inside China about atrocities committed against the ethnic Chinese community in Indonesia following the fall of the Suharto regime. A patriotic student movement soon burgeoned, and when news was posted that the Chinese foreign ministry was adopting a soft policy toward Jakarta (a sensible stance calculated not to risk reprisals against the Chinese-Indonesians), outbursts of anger in the chat rooms showed that citizens were not impressed by the failure of their government to stand up for compatriots overseas. Disappointment with the government's stance turned to disgust and patriotic condemnation when the Beijing municipal authorities refused to grant permission for a demonstration to the Indonesian embassy, organized partly by Internet.[40]

Similarly, when the *People's Daily* website tried to ameliorate soured Sino–Japanese relations by setting up a "China–Japan Forum," the result was a barrage of anti-Japanese invective. Prominent members of the government, including even Foreign Minister Tang Jiaxuan, have suffered probably the worst possible accusation possible for a Chinese citizen, being condemned as a pro-Japanese traitor. Even criticism of the failure of President Jiang Zemin's Taiwan policy appeared on the *People's Daily* website shortly after the election of the secession-orientated Chen Shuibian as the island's president in March 2000.

Seen from this angle, the impact of the Information Age is indeed having an impact on Chinese politics. A survey conducted under the auspices of the Chinese Academy of Social Sciences found that 60.8 percent of respondents believe that the Internet is giving them more opportunity to express their political views, 51 percent think it gives them more opportunities to criticize government policies, 55.9 percent think it gives them a better knowledge of politics, and 43.8 percent think it will allow high officials to have a better understanding of the views of the common people.[41] Yet there is little reason to assume that this net increase in political activity amounts to the importation of "foreign ideas" or enhances international stability in the way that James Baker had expected at the end of the Cold War. One of the first messages to appear on the "Strong State Forum" chat room after the terrorist attacks on the United States on September 11, for example, read, "Now is the best time to attack Taiwan."[42] More of the same kind of material, along with a wave of anti-American rhetoric, appeared over the following days.

Although ICTs play a role in the organization of pro-democracy campaigns, dissident activities by non-Han ethnic groups, and the organization of religious movements like the Falun Gong *outside* Chinese firewalls, there is no evidence so far of the Internet playing a significant role in such campaigns *inside* the country. This may be due in part to the way in which the state has continued its well-established tradition of stifling dissent by imposing harsh penal measures well into the Information Age. That the arrests that have taken place for pro-democracy-related activities since the imprisonment of Lin Hai in 1999 have not been very numerous, indicates the success of a traditional policy of "killing the chicken to frighten the monkeys," rather than leniency on the part of the state.[43] Some foreign observers have already noticed that a strong culture of self-censorship over Internet usage has already developed.[44] Such a pattern of behavior fits in well with a tendency for postcolonial states with an authoritarian bent to build what Zinnbauer has called "the paralyzing perception of a surveillance state."[45]

While evidence of ICTs being used for democratic activity and organization remains thin, though, nationalist activity grows by the day and by the international crisis. It is important to acknowledge the existence of such a tendency, because it draws our attention to the need to understand the political impact of ICTs as being partly determined by cultural norms that originate outside cyberspace. This observation is in line with the theoretical perspective developed by critics of the Internet such as Lawrence Lessig, who draws our attention to the importance of the manipulation of what he calls "norms" in the regulation of cyberspace.[46] Social scientists such as Castells also emphasizes the close relationship between culture and the use of ICTs, as when he reminds us that "The transition between modes of development is not independent of the historical context within which it takes place; it relies heavily on the social matrix initially framing the transition, as well as on the social conflicts and interests that shape the transformation of that matrix."[47]

It is only when we escape from deterministic mythologies about the nature of technological change and acknowledge the reality of this kind of complex political relationship between ICTs and international security, that a more realistic way of thinking about global governance can be developed. The fact that international institutions favor the actions of sovereign states to maintain domestic order, does not mean that political choices on issues of global importance are impossible regarding ICTs so long as the relationship between communication and state "security" is properly understood. As lawyers know all too well, the very existence of international law is only made possible in the present world system by the realization that states need to adhere to certain standards of behavior if they are to preserve both themselves and the overall system.[48] Approaching the problem of global ICT governance from this perspective of the self-interests of states is likely to have far more support from governments around the world than is the advocation of human rights and liberal democracy. Perhaps it is only when the nexus between communication, international security and human rights is properly understood, that the extension of global governance to the political sphere can become a feasible project.

Communications, Order, and Justice

It has been argued earlier that the advent of the "Information Age" presents a more complex picture than that of authoritarian states being transformed by waves of "foreign ideas" and "global trends shaping the future." While the case of China shows that the globalization of ICTs does have a political impact on states, this tends to reflect attempts to manipulate architecture and the collection and processing of data for the causes of strengthening the legitimacy and security of regimes, rather than the promotion of liberal-democratic transformation. The following tentative conclusions can also be drawn:

First, assumptions that the Information Age will be a benign global force for upholding human rights and enhancing social stability could be dangerously misleading if they excuse policy-makers and citizens from addressing the serious political issues that do arise from the impact of ICTs. The case of China provides ample evidence to remind us that the impact of ICTs is determined as much by the political and cultural contexts within which they are embedded, as it is by the nature of the technology itself.

It is equally misleading to view ICTs as politically "neutral" technologies. Walton gives us the perfect example to illustrate the dangers of

such an understanding when he describes how images recorded by
U.K.-manufactured cameras installed during the 1980s to monitor traffic in
Tiananmen Square were broadcast on Beijing television after the crushing
of the 1989 democracy movement in order to help the police trace and
punish participants in the events.[49] The installation of surveillance technology in Chinese ICTs is no more politically neutral than was the construction of low bridges on the roads to Long Island by Robert Moses was, for
the purpose of stopping immigrants and the poor reaching his beaches.

This is an important point to bear in mind when assessing the role of
investors and firms with their bases in North America and Europe. As
such actors are playing a decisive role in shaping the kind of architecture
that is being developed in China, they are already coming under scrutiny
from human rights organizations. This began to happen when the New
York-based Human Rights Watch started to call on foreign ICT firms to
stop turning a blind eye to repression after the arrest of Huang Qi and
his wife Zeng Li in June 2000. Their crime was to have allowed their
"www.6-4tianwang.com" website, used mainly to help find missing
people, to carry a demand for the political rehabilitation of the 1989
Democracy Movement by a former Beijing professor who had lost his
son in the Tiananmen Massacre.[50] Walton's report for the International
Centre for Human Rights and Democratic Development has taken the
criticism of the role of foreign firms in helping to construct a surveillance
state a significant step further.

Yet, if the globalization of ICTs is neither an automatic transmission
belt for liberal-democratic values, nor politically neutral, then the political dynamics that result from this process need to be properly addressed
by international institutions. Leaving the global governance of ICTs to
organizations concerned with trade and technical standards is far from
sufficient, and can even make the situation worse.

Managing the political impact of the Information Age demands that
our understanding of the relationship between security, communication,
and human rights is developed in ways that can keep up with the pace
of technological change. While maintaining international security will
remain of paramount concern, especially since September 11, 2001, if
appealing to the interests of states in their own preservation leads to the
building of a comprehensive and attributable global regulatory system,
this also needs to take into consideration human rights concerns. In a
world system that remains state-centric despite the globalization of
ICTs, taking concerns over security as the starting point from which to
address broader social issues may be a feasible project for those concerned
about the promotion of international human rights standards. It is

certainly a more effective way of addressing the real political problems that have to be faced in the Information Age than is starting out from assumptions that the social values of any particular society will inevitably be disseminated throughout the world.

Notes

1. This chapter was first published in French: "Pourquoi Internet ne démocratisera pas la Chine," *Critique internationale*, 15 (April 2002): 85–104.
2. J.A. Baker III, "America in Asia: Emerging Architecture for a Pacific Community," *Foreign Affairs*, 70, 5 (February 1991): 16.
3. W.J. Drake, "Dictatorships in the Digital Age: Some Considerations on the Internet in China and Cuba," *iMP: The Magazine for Information Impacts* (October 2000), URL (consulted November 2000): http:www.ceip.org.
4. WTO, "US–China WTO Agreement," URL (consulted November 2000): http://www.usChina.org/public/wto/ - bilat.
5. M. Bacchetta, P. Low, A. Mattoo, L. Schuknecht, H. Wagner, and M. Wehrens, *Electronic Commerce and the Role of the WTO* (Geneva: World Trade Organisation, 1998): 65.
6. State Council, "Hulianwang xinxi fuwu guanli banfa" (Methods for Managing Internet Information Service), URL (consulted November 2000): http://www.cnnic.net.cn/policy/18.shtml.
7. M. Kantor, "Foreign Direct Investment in Chinese Telecoms: Changes in the Regulatory Scheme," *Cambridge Review of International Affairs*, 13, 2 (2000): 147.
8. State Council, "Hulianwang xinxi fuwu guanli banfa."
9. S. Breslin, "The Virtual Market," *China Review* (Autumn/Winter 2000): 24.
10. Eastcom (2000), URL (consulted November 2000): www.eastcom.com.
11. D. Sutherland, "Policies to Build National Champions: China's 'National Team' of Enterprise Groups" in *China and the Global Business Revolution*, Peter Nolan (ed.) (Basingstoke and New York: Palgrave, 2001).
12. *IHT* (International Herald Tribune) (June 5, 2001): 13.
13. *The Guardian* (September 6, 2001).
14. *Financial Times* (September 5, 2001).
15. Y. Liu and W. Zhang, "High-Tech Development and State Security," *Jiefangjun bao* (Liberation Army Daily) (January 11, 2000): 6. (English version in BBC Summary of World Broadcasts, FE/3764 G/6.)
16. P. Nolan and M. Hasecic, "China, the WTO and the Third Industrial Revolution," *Cambridge Review of International Affairs*, 13, 2 (2000): 167–69.
17. G. Walton, *China's Golden Shield: Corporations and the Development of Surveillance Technology in the People's Republic of China* (Montreal: International Centre for Human Rights and Democratic Development, 2001), URL (consulted October 29, 2001): http://www.ichrdd.ca/frame.iphtml?langue=0.
18. L. Lessig, *Code and Other Laws of Cyberspace* (New York: Basic Books, 1999): 39–42.
19. J. Naughton, *A Brief History of the Future: The Origins of the Internet* (London: Weidenfeld and Nicolson, 1999).
20. C. Zhang and J. Ni, *Guojia Xinxi Anquan Baogao* (Report on National Information Security) (Beijing: Renmin Chubanshe, 2000): 35, 52.
21. P. Keller, "China's Impact on the Global Information Society," in *Regulating the Global Information Society*, Christopher T. Marsden (ed.) (London and New York: Routledge, 2000): 267.

22. B. Schneier, *Secrets and Lies: Digital Security in a Networked World* (New York: John Wiley and Sons Inc, 2000): 21.
23. H.H. Frederick, *Global Communication and International Relations* (California: Wadsworth, 1993): 245.
24. B. Schneier, *Secrets and Lies*: 67.
25. APEC, "APEC Leaders Statement on Counter-Terrorism" (October 21, 2001), URL (consulted October 2001): www.apecsec.org.sg.
26. C. Zhang and J. Ni, *Guojia Xinxi Anquan Baogao* (Report on National Information Security) (Beijing: Renmin Chubanshe, 2000): 271–92.
27. *The Guardian* (December 4, 2000).
28. T. Mathiesen, *On Globalisation of Control: Towards an Integrated Surveillance System in Europe* (London: Statewatch, 1999): 31.
29. House of Lords, Select Committee on the European Communities, *European Union Databases*, 23rd Report, Session 1998–99 (London: The Stationery Office, 1999): 17.
30. Ibid.: 12.
31. CSIS Taskforce, *Cybercrime . . . Cyberterrorism . . . Cyberwarfare . . . Averting an Electronic Waterloo* (Washington: CSIS Press, 1998).
32. Y. Liu and W. Zhang, "High-Tech Development and State Security."
33. G.D. Grove, S.E. Goodman, and S.J. Lukasik, "Cyber Attacks and International Law," *Survival*, 42, 3 (2000): 99–100.
34. H.H. Frederick, *Global Communication and International Relations*: 251.
35. Ibid.: 253.
36. "Hulianwang shang de jiaoliang" (Showdown on the Internet) *Beijing qingnian bao* (Beijing Youth Daily) (May 11, 1999): 2.
37. Liao, Minru, "Liang an haike zhan—bu fen wangyou fen tingzhi" (cross-straits Hacking War—Some Hackers Want to Call a Stop) *Lianhe Bao* (United Daily News, Taiwan—overseas edition) (August 14, 1999): 3.
38. Christopher R. Hughes, "Nationalist Chat," *The World Today*, 57, 6 (2001): 6–8.
39. Louis Althusser, "Ideology and Ideological State Apparatuses," in *Lenin and Philosophy and Other Essays* (Vol. 3) (New York: New Monthly Review Press, 1978): 244.
40. Christopher R. Hughes, "Nationalism in Chinese Cyberspace," *Cambridge Review of International Affairs*, 13, 2 (2000): 195–209.
41. L. Guo, "*Hulianwang shiyong zhuangkuan ji yingxiang de diaocha baogao*" (Report on a Survey into The Conditions and Influence of Internet Usage) (2001), URL (consulted July 1, 2001): www.Chinace.org.ce/itre.
42. "Zhunbei zao da" (Prepare to strike early, strike hard, strike with nuclear war), message posted on *People's Daily Strong State Forum* under pseudonym (2001), URL (consulted September 12, 2001): http://bbs.people.com.cn/.
43. P. Keller, "China's Impact on the Global Information Society": 265.
44. *IHT* (International Herald Tribune) (October 5, 2000).
45. D. Zinnbauer, "Whither the Panopticon?: Civil Society Activism and State Surveillance in the Age of the Internet, Some Evidence From Malaysia," research paper delivered to Development Studies Institute, L.S.E., November 2000: 38.
46. Lessig, *Code and Other Laws of Cyberspace*: 85–88.
47. Manuel Castells, *The Informational City* (Oxford: Blackwell, 1999): 21.
48. H. Bull, *The Anarchical Society* (London: Macmillan, 1977).
49. G. Walton, *China's Golden Shield*.
50. Human Rights Watch, "China: Foreign Companies Should Protest Internet Detention," URL (consulted June 27, 2000): www.hrwatchnyc.igc.org.

CHAPTER FIVE

Government Online and Cross-Straits Relations

PATRICIA BATTO

The election to the presidency of the Republic of China (ROC), on March 18, 2000, of Chen Shuibian, the candidate of the Democratic Progressive Party (DPP), started a new chapter in relations between the two sides of the Taiwan Strait. The DPP, formed in 1986, was born from the political opposition movement, which emerged in the 1970s and whose demands to the Nationalist government extended—becoming more radical—from the claim for democracy to the claim for the independence of Taiwan. After the DPP's victory over the Guomindang, the Nationalist Party (GMD), in March 2000, Beijing naturally has not cast off its irredentism, it reaffirmed more than ever its policy of national reunification, calling for Taiwan to return to the "motherland." As for Taipei, it is trying to fight against its international isolation, which has been increasing since October 25, 1971, when the United Nations Organization admitted the People's Republic of China (PRC) and expelled Taiwan. Parallel to this political evolution, since 1987, economic exchanges and trade links between the two Chinas have seen spectacular growth. The Internet, an essential means of communication and organization in all fields, has become for political actors "a privileged tool for acting, informing, recruiting, organizing, dominating and counter-dominating,"[1] and especially since 1995, when the World Wide Web first came to be used on a broad scale. In July 2001, Taiwan had 11.6 million Internet users, a penetration rate of 51.85 percent; the PRC at the same date had 26.5 million users, or 2.08 percent of the population.[2]

Taiwan is diplomatically isolated, and desperately needs international support in order to stand up to Beijing's irredentism. In the first part of this chapter, it will be seeked to establish, on the basis of a comparison between governmental sites run by Taipei and Beijing, whether Taiwan, taking advantage of its greater modernity, has been able to use the Internet to make itself better known internationally. In a second part, the content of various governmental sites will be examined, in order to compare the two Chinas' communication and information policies, in particular with respect to cross-straits relations. The third and final part will focus more closely at economics than at politics, to establish how economic and trade links between the two sides of the Taiwan Strait are perceptible on the Internet and what one can conclude from this.

Taipei Online: The ROC Shrunk Down to Taiwan

The Government Information Office, ROC, and Its Links

One of the main means of access to Taiwanese government news is the English-language site at www.gio.gov.tw. Its homepage is entitled *Republic of China on Taiwan, Government Information Office*. The mention "on Taiwan" is interesting: it comes across as indicating a focus by the ROC on the island of Taiwan. It is possible to consult the site in 12 languages: English, Chinese (both traditional and simplified characters: *zhongwen fanti, zhongwen jianti*), Spanish, French, German, Russian, Japanese, and also Korean, Dutch, Polish, Hungarian, and Czech.[3] The homepage contains a link to a "Periodicals" page, which gives online access to foreign-language publications by the Government Information Office (GIO), although only for the first seven languages listed earlier.[4] The "Publications" page gives access to *The Republic of China Yearbook—Taiwan 2002* and the *Who's Who in the Republic of China—Taiwan 2002*. These are online versions of books that are also available in print form. The name "Taiwan" was first used in the 2001 editions. Prior to that date, the first was entitled *The Republic of China Yearbook*, followed by the edition date, and the second, *Who's Who in the Republic of China,* also followed by the edition date. The change is a further indication of increased focus on Taiwan.[5] This change took place after 2000, when the Guomindang lost power to DPP's Chen Shuibian. This suggests that official information took note of the ROC's refocus on Taiwan, or even that it is leading the way in this matter.

Official Taiwanese information, on the Internet in particular, is mainly the responsibility of the Government Information Office (GIO). Until the end of martial law, on July 15, 1987, the GIO, which was set up in Nanjing on May 2, 1947, had complete control over the media under the authoritarian regime in power at that time in Nationalist China; the Guomindang's propaganda service was behind it.[6] But when the regime became more democratic, starting in the late 1980s, the GIO gradually lost its propaganda function.[7] The subheading "Goals" under the "Who We Are" heading on the homepage of the English-language site states: "The GIO has been offering information through the Internet since 1995. The GIO's Internet Team, part of the Department of International Information Services, was established in August 1999. This Internet Team is responsible for the GIO's foreign language websites".[8] The GIO operates numerous websites around the world "to enhance the international community's understanding of the ROC." "GIO departments and offices at home and abroad make active use of the Internet, grasping every opportunity possible to spread information about the ROC." There is no indication given as to the number of consultations on the site, which does not appear to be updated very often. Only the heading "Taiwan Headlines," which is accessed via a link, appears to be updated on a daily basis.

The www.gio.gov.tw site offers several links. Two of these lead to portals, "Interactive Government Directory" (http://portal.gio.gov.tw/gio/) and "Taiwan Related Links" (http://portal.gio.gov.tw/taiwan/). The first of these, "Interactive Government Directory," put online by the GIO on March 21, 2001, gives all ROC government sites in English, as well as a few others in Chinese. The second, "Taiwan Related Links," leads to nongovernment sites selected by the GIO.[9]

The "Interactive Government Directory" is divided into 15 headings, which are in turn divided into 49 subheadings.[10] The "External Affairs" heading contains three subheadings, "Foreign Relations," "Mainland Affairs" and "Overseas Chinese Affairs." This classification reflects the organization of the Central Government of the ROC: Mainland Affairs are distinct from Foreign Relations, suggesting that mainland China is not considered a foreign country for Taiwan; taking this logic to the full, Taiwan would not be a totally independent state relative to mainland China. Furthermore, the name Overseas Chinese Affairs indicates that Taiwan considers itself to be part of the Chinese world, which contradicts a number of Taiwanese declarations rejecting any "Chinese" identity for the island.

The Mainland Affairs Council, ROC: A Site Mainly Consulted Locally

The Mainland Affairs subheading leads to only one site, that of the Mainland Affairs Council (MAC), at www.mac.gov.tw/. The MAC was set up in October 1990. It is one of the three most important protagonists in mainland policy, alongside the President of the Republic and the Straits Exchange Foundation (SEF). The presidency is the key political institution in Taiwan; mainland policy, alongside foreign and security policy, is one of the President's preserves. The MAC, placed under the authority of the Executive Yuan, is responsible for implementing mainland policy set out by the President and the Executive Yuan. The SEF, set up in February 1991, is responsible for carrying out mainland policy; one of its particular responsibilities is sorting out technical problems caused by exchanges between Taiwan and mainland China; especially through dialogue with its counterpart in mainland China, the Association for Relations Across the Taiwan Straits (ARATS), set up by Beijing in December 1991.

The MAC site's homepage is entitled "Xingzhengyuan Dalu weiyuanhui" in Chinese, with an English subtitle, "Mainland Affairs Council." It is illustrated by the flag of the ROC, which is animated in order to make it look as though it is blowing in the breeze. This page gives the choice between three versions, one in traditional Chinese characters, a second in simplified characters and a third in English. The English-language site received 413,992 consultations between its creation on January 1, 1997 and November 15, 2002, compared with 810,851 for the version in traditional Chinese characters and 414,039 for the version in simplified characters; this suggests that the site is mainly consulted locally. I consulted each of its three versions regularly between October 15 and November 15, 2002, without noting any notable change, by which I mean a visible update.

The Office of the President, ROC, Focuses on Taiwan

The site of the presidency of the ROC, at www.president.gov.tw/, opens with a large map showing all of China in black and white, with only the minuscule island of Taiwan in color. This immediately gives way to an animation, a very quick zoom on Taiwan, the territory actually under the control of the ROC. In other words, the site features a very visual "focus" on Taiwan.

The homepage appears after that. It is illustrated with a color map of Taiwan, as well as the flag of the ROC, and is entitled "Zhonghua minguo zongtong fu," with an English subtitle, "The Office of the President of the Republic of China." The homepage offers three versions of the site: English, traditional, and simplified Chinese. A few pages are updated daily, but most of the site was not changed between October 15 and

November 15, 2002. Furthermore, the site carries no indication as to the number of consultations, in any of its three versions.

The SEF, ROC, Uses Traditional Chinese Characters Only

The SEF site (*Haixia jiaoliu jijinhui*), termed "a quasi-government agency" on the MAC site, at www.sef.org.tw, is not very rich, graphically speaking. It is entirely in Chinese, and in traditional characters only. It was not updated visibly between October 15 and November 15, 2002; as at November 20, 2002, the site had received 216,789 consultations since February 22, 1999.

Beijing Online: World Scale Ambition

The China Internet Information Center, PRC, in Ten Versions with Daily Change

The main point of access to government information concerning the PRC is the China Internet Information Center (*Zhongguo wang*), at www.china.org.cn or www.china.com.cn. The "About Us" heading at the bottom of the homepage indicates that this "authorized government portal site to China" is published under the auspices of the State Council Information Office and the China International Publishing Group. The site can be consulted in ten languages: Chinese, English, French, German, Japanese, Russian, Spanish, Arabic, Esperanto and . . . Big 5.

Comparing this choice of languages to that offered on the official Taiwanese site, at www.gio.gov.tw, shows that: (a) Two languages offered by Beijing do not appear on the Taipei site, Esperanto (the choice to include this is probably a hangover of the international Communist Utopia) and Arabic. Beijing however, differs from Taipei in its choice of not offering access in Korean, Dutch, Polish, Hungarian, or Czech. Beijing's choice looks to be better adapted to communication on a world scale than Taipei's;[11] and (b) On the government site of the PRC, "Chinese" (*zhongwen*) means simplified characters. Taiwanese sites generally offer versions in both traditional and simplified characters. On this site—and on others—Beijing does not refer to traditional characters as "Chinese," but rather as "Big 5," from the code name for these characters.

The "Chinese" and "Big 5" versions appear to be totally identical. There is no specific message to Taiwanese compatriots, who appear to be considered Chinese, just like mainland residents. But the site differs in each of its other languages.

The various versions of the China Internet center site, which make up as many distinct entities, do not come across as being any less modern than the Taiwanese government sites. Their homepages change daily for all versions, as a great deal of emphasis is placed on current events in these rather imposing sites. But none of the different versions gives consultation figures, and the "About Us" headings have much less detail than those of the Taiwanese sites.

We will look at the sites' contents later in this chapter. But it is worth pointing out at this stage that the Taiwan issue is not the object of any specific attention in either the "Chinese" or "Big 5" versions. However, a special heading is devoted to the issue in the English and French sites; a great deal of importance is also placed on Sino–American relations under these headings.

At the bottom of the china.org.cn homepage, there was, in early November 2002, a list of PRC government sites.[12] None of these directly touched on cross-straits relations; neither the presidency of the PRC nor the ARATS, the SEF's interlocutor, have their own sites. But Beijing carries out very strict control over the Internet, and the border between the "government" and "private" spheres is often very thin in the PRC.[13] Sites dealing with such a sensitive issue as Taiwan can only be "official," as it is the case for instance with the All China Taiwanese Association—ACTA (*Zhonghua quanguo Taiwan tongbao lianyihui*), at www.tailian.org.cn.[14]

Taiwanese government sites are more developed than their mainland equivalents, as they are more numerous; however, this does not mean that they are richer in content or that their design is more sophisticated. Mainland sites, which are most of the time updated daily, are often very imposing, and don't seem to be less advanced technically than their Taiwanese counterparts.

The PRC has adopted the stance of a great power with respect to the Internet. This is demonstrated by the choice of languages its sites offer for instance, but also—with respect to the issue of Taiwan—by its references to Sino–American relations, which illustrate a desire to present the country as being a partner, if not the equal, of the United States. In comparison, the ROC sends out a narrower image, which is largely attributable to its focus on the island of Taiwan. It would be tempting to use the adjective "provincial," if the word was not tainted by its use by supporters of reunification on both sides of the Taiwan Strait. On the Internet, Taiwan appears as a tiny island in the shadow of a powerful neighbor. Beijing is very visible on the Web, when it is Taiwan that has the greater need for international support.

Cross-Straits Relations Online: Taipei Stresses Public Opinion

The English-Language MAC Site Emphasizes Opinion Polls

The homepage of the MAC's English-language site is entitled "Mainland Affairs Council, Republic of China" and illustrated by the flag of the ROC.[15] It includes four main headings, set out in the four corners of the screen (Mainland Policy Documents; Organization and Function; Dialogue and Negotiation; Statistics). There are also three other headings, which are not given as much emphasis (Opinion Post; Briefing Room; For Foreign Guests), a heading for current events (What's New), and a link for people wanting to send an e-mail to the MAC's current President, Cai Yingwen (also transcribed as Tsai Ing-wen or Tsai Ying-wen).

The first of the four main headings, Mainland Policy Documents, brings together documents on Taipei's mainland policy, in five parts. Its first part, entitled "General Policy," consists mainly of official texts,[16] declarations by President Chen Shuibian[17] or Cai Yingwen. Documents on the Three Links and the Three Mini-Links are presented under the title "Social and Economic Policies," as well as conflicts concerning fishing and illegal immigration from the mainland.[18]

"Cross-Strait Exchanges" covers cultural exchanges between Taipei and Beijing, as well as cross-straits crime, particularly trafficking of drugs, arms, and other contraband; economic and trade links are not addressed. The fourth series of texts deals with Hong Kong and Macau, the fifth is made up of archives.

The second big heading, Organization and Function, goes back over the history of the MAC since its inception in 1990, after the liberalization of exchanges between the two sides of the Taiwan Strait on November 2, 1987. It sets out the MAC's structure and functions, and also presents the different entities, other than the MAC, in charge of mainland policy.

The site's third big heading, Dialogue and Negotiation, is divided into two parts. The first, "Major Events across the Taiwan Straits," lists major events in the Taiwan Strait between January 1912 and December 1999; it is accessible either by chronological order, starting with the founding of the ROC on January 1, 1912, or by theme (mainland Policy, cross-straits

Talks, mainland's Taiwan Policy, mainland's cross-straits Saber-rattling). This part gives the details of all talks between the SEF and the ARATS, as well as of the 1995–1996 missile crisis. The second part, "Cross-Strait Dialogue and Negotiation," includes official declarations, particularly those of Gu Zhenfu (1917), the President of the SEF.

The site's fourth big heading, Statistics, is also divided into two parts. The first, entitled "Statistics on Cross-Strait Exchanges," covers economic and trade flows between the two sides of the Taiwan Strait. This part gives access to the *cross-strait Economic Statistics Monthly* (*Liangan jingji tongji yuebao*), the most recent issues of which are available for online consultation. The second part of the Statistics heading, entitled "Public Opinion Surveys," is more of a surprise: it includes public-opinion polls carried out in Taiwan on the subject of cross-straits relations, filed under ten points.[19] The first point gives the results of a telephone poll, set out in nine charts. In the first chart, entitled "Unification or Independence?," six options are given: Status quo now/decision later, Status quo now/ unification later, Status quo now/independence later, Status quo indefi- nitely, Independence asap, Unification asap. The least popular option from September 1997 to August 2002 was "Unification asap," which fell from 3.1 to 1.9 over the period. The second least popular was "Independence asap," which fell from 9.0 to 5.5, despite peaking at 14.3 in August 1999. The most popular option is "Status quo now/decision later," which rose from 34.3 to 34.9, with peaks of around 42.[20]

The nine other points of "Public Opinion Surveys" include results for polls on the same theme, but sometimes give data dating back further than September 1997. Only the last of the ten points is different: enti- tled "Public Support for 'Special State-to-State Relationship', President Li Denghui's Remarks July 9 1999," it gives results of 14 public opinion surveys carried out between July 10–11 and September 14–15, 1999.[21]

These polls are given a good deal of emphasis in the MAC's English- language site. Not only are the results for the first point, set out on nine pages, made attractive by their presentation, but they also appear a number of times on the site. The first of the three smaller headings in the middle of the homepage, Opinion Post, also leads to these nine pages. Opinion Post has no content other than this, meaning that it is pure and simple overlap.

The second of the smaller headings, Briefing Room, gives MAC min- utes from 1999 to 2002. The third of the smaller headings, For Foreign Guests, offers a list of documents around five themes (On Policies, Public-Opinion Polls, cross-straits Economy and Trade, Culture Exchanges, Hong Kong Affairs). Public-Opinion Polls once again gives—and for the third time—the results of public-opinion polls!

These opinion polls suggest that a large majority of the Taiwanese population favors keeping the status quo, some simply by delaying any decision on the issue of independence or reunification, others by sticking to the status quo for an unlimited period; support for immediate independence or reunification is only marginal. The Taiwanese population also appears to leaning increasingly in favor of the development of cross-straits relations rather than foreign ties. Last, they make it clear that an aggressive attitude on the part of Beijing tends to exacerbate support for independence on the island.

These polls seem important for three reasons. First, their content is a response to Beijing's offer of reunification. And the response is very clear: the majority of the Taiwanese population is in favor of keeping the status quo and rejects Beijing's "one country, two systems" solution. Second, they emphasize the notion of public opinion. Being featured a number of times on the site, they help Taipei underline the democratic nature of the regime in place on the island. In a sense, they are a sort of referendum on the issue of reunification or independence. Third, the importance given to public opinion, as illustrated by the online presentation of opinion polling, is one aspect that sets Taiwanese government sites apart from those of the PRC.

The Chinese Versions of the MAC Site and the Practical Aspects of Cross-Straits Relations

The two Chinese-language versions of the MAC site are not structured in the same way as the English-language version, and there are even numerous small differences between the two Chinese versions, though the presentation of the homepage on both the Chinese-language sites is identical to that of the English-language site, with four main headings. The four big headings are entitled: (1) Mainland policy and situation (*Dalu zhengce yu qingshi*); (2) Structure and legislation (*zuzhi yu fagui*); (3) Exchanges and negotiations (*jiaoliu yu xieshang*); (4) Internet Resources (*wanglu ziyuan*). The headings in the middle of the page which receive less emphasis are: (1) News (*xinwen yuandi*); (2) Recent opinion polls (*zuixin minyi diaocha*); (3) Foundation for the development of China (*Zhonghua fazhan jijin*); (4) Recent information from the Executive Yuan (*Xingzheng Yuan jishi xinwen*); and (5) New, recent news (*New, zuixin xiaoxi*).

The Chinese site in traditional characters includes two more headings in the middle of the page than the site in simplified characters: (1) A link leading to the Mainland Affairs Information and Research Center, at

www.mac.gov.tw/rpir. This center has a library in Taipei that has—
among others things—a collection of all sorts of mainland publications,
including the *People's Daily*; one can also carry out online research, at
www.mac.gov.tw/rpir/macnet.htm (*Macnet Dalu zixun wang*); and (2) A
link leading to "The e-Government Entry Point of Taiwan," at
www.gov.tw/ (*wode e zhengfu*: "government Online"). This site is more
useful for people residing in Taiwan than for PRC citizens. At the bottom of the site in traditional Chinese, there is also an "ideas box" and six
small entries that mainly give access to regulatory texts, administrative
papers, etc. The site in simplified Chinese also has two entries at the bottom of the page: one leads to the Mainland Affairs Information and
Research Center, which is not given as much emphasis as on the site in
traditional characters.

There are differences between the two Chinese versions in the first of
the four main headings, "Mainland policy and situation." The heading
includes four subheadings in both versions; it is mainly the first,
"Mainland policy and public opinion" (*Dalu zhengce yu minyi*) that differs.
The site in traditional characters has two parts: (1) "Documents concerning mainland policy" (*Dalu zhengce xiangguan ziliao*), which includes
official texts: a number of declarations by President Chen Shuibian,
others by the MAC's Cai Yingwen, as well as texts concerning the entry
of the two Chinas into the World Trade Organization; and (2) "Opinion
polls" (*Minyi diaocha*), which gives the results of opinion polls in three
sections, in chronological order. The opinion-poll heading is a lot richer
than in the English-language site: it includes no less than 33 items,
compared with 10 for the English-language site.

In the site in simplified characters, the first subheading, also entitled
"Mainland policy and public opinion," has four parts, not two: (1) The first
part is identical to the site in traditional characters. It has the same official
texts, under the title "Documents concerning mainland policy"; (2) The
second gives access to the *Working Bulletin on mainland China* (*Dalu gongzuo
jianbao*), a monthly MAC publication of 20–30 pages. Issues dating back to
1998 can be consulted online; (3) The third, "Major Events across the
Taiwan Straits" (*Liangan guanxi dashiji*), includes first a detailed chronology
of the main events across the Taiwan Strait, month by month, from 1998 to
2002, and second the chronology from 1912 to 1999, accessible either by
date or by theme; and (4) The fourth part of the simplified-characters site
is identical to the traditional-characters site's second part: opinion-poll
results, with a lot more detail than on the English-language site.

The content of the second subheading is identical in both the
Chinese versions.[22] It starts with "Major Events across the Taiwan

Straits," which includes the detailed chronology from 1998 to 2002 and the chronology from 1912 to 1999. The second part of this subheading is the *Working Bulletin on Mainland China*. These two parts overlap on the site in simplified characters, as they also appear in the first subheading. The second subheading also contains statistical information about cultural, economic and trade links, as well as societal issues. These include data on illegal immigration from the mainland, fishing conflicts, but also a map of missile launches in 1995 and 1996 from mainland China in the direction of Taiwan, or statistics showing the extent to which Taiwanese businessmen are victims of growing lawlessness on the mainland. This leaves an impression of aggressiveness on the part of Beijing toward Taiwan.

The content of the third and fourth subheading, "Relations between Taiwan, Hong Kong and Macau" (*Tai Gang Ao guanxi*) and "Questions and Answers"(*Da ke wen*), are identical in both Chinese-language versions.

The content of the second heading, "Structure and legislation" (*Zuzhi yu fagui*), is more or less identical in the two Chinese-language versions. The same goes for the third, "Exchanges and negotiations" (*jiaoliu yu xieshang*). This third heading contains a page entitled, "Statistics concerning exchanges between the two sides of the Taiwan Strait" (*Liangan tongji*) in five parts: statistics concerning cultural issues (*wenjiao lei*), economics and trade (*jingmao lei*), society (*shehui lei*), Taiwan, Hong Kong, and Macau (*Tai Gang Ao lei*), as well as opinion polls (*minyi diaocha lei*), which once again gives the 33 items mentioned earlier.

The fourth heading, "Internet Resources" (*Wanglu ziyuan*), is made up mainly of links to other sites.

(1) A link to the site of the SEF (*caituan faren haixia jiaoliu jijinhui*), at www.sef.org.tw/.
(2) A link to the The Economic and Commercial Network of Taiwanese Businessmen on the mainland (*Dalu Taishang jingmao wang*), at www.chinabiz.org.tw/.
(3) Information about the MAC Foundation (*Zhonghua fazhan jijin*).
(4) and (5) Links enabling Internet users to carry out online searches for information on mainland China, at www.mac.gov.tw/rpir/macnet.htm and mac.gov.tw/rpir/sumain.htm (*Macnet Dalu zixun wang*).
(6) Lists of links to world media organs, from the *People's Daily* to the *Washington Post*, as well as the Hong Kong *Far Eastern Economic Review* and Taiwanese media.

(7) A link to the site of the ROC intended for members of the Chinese diaspora (*Zhonghua minguo haiwai Huaren fuwu wang*), at www.overseas.gov.tw/.

(8) A link to a government site dedicated to telephony (GSN) (*Zhengfu wanglu jichu fuwu wang*), at www.gsn.gov.tw.

The site in traditional Chinese characters has a further two points: the first is a link to the continuing professional education site in Taiwan (*gongwu renyuan zhongshen xuexi rukou wangzhan*), at http:/lifelonglearn.cpa.gov.tw/; the second gives information on the goals of the government of the ROC, ministry by ministry. Among the headings placed in the middle of the Chinese-language version's homepages, the one entitled "Recent opinion polls" (*zuixin minyi diaocha*) contains data from a single poll dating back to July 2002; this part of the site is not as rich as on the English-language version.

The two Chinese-language sites are not fundamentally different. The additional data contained on the site in traditional characters, as opposed to the one in simplified characters, mainly concerns administrative or practical information aimed at ROC citizens. The site in simplified characters emphasizes the chronology of cross-straits relations and the *Working Bulletin on Mainland China*, two headings that give the ROC's vision of cross-straits relations, presenting Taipei as rather full of goodwill and Beijing rather aggressive and acting in bad faith.

At the same time, the architecture of the two Chinese-language versions is not the same as that of the English-language version. The main difference is to be found in the fourth entry, "Internet Resources," which contains links, a lot of which lead to Taiwanese sites in Chinese, but also—under the heading media—to sites in the PRC or the United States for instance. Generally speaking, the Chinese sites contain a broader range of information and give a greater amount of practical information. The English-language version gives slightly greater emphasis to opinion polls, thereby underscoring the democratic nature of the regime in Taiwan. The Chinese-language versions stress the economic facet of exchanges across the Taiwan Strait, and the practical aspects of cross-straits relations, in particular the "government services" concerning exchanges.

The Site of the Taiwanese Presidency Shows Its Intention of Being Close to the People

The content of the site of the Taiwanese presidency is based around 15 sections in its English-language version.[23] The version in simplified

Chinese counts 12 sections,[24] compared with 22 for the site in traditional Chinese.[25] The elements given the greatest emphasis here are the same in all three versions: President Chen's Profile, Vice-President Lu's Profile, and the Presidential Building, all three illustrated by photos. The English-language version then emphasizes recent major broad policy declarations by the President and the Vice-President, under the titles "Hot News" and "Hot Topics."[26] This contrasts with the two Chinese-language sites, which stress Presidential internal policy declarations, and the President's day-to-day schedule.[27] The theme of cross-straits relations is not given any specific coverage on the site, even though the President is one of the main protagonists of mainland policy; no section is devoted to this single issue. The Presidential site gives greater focus to internal policy, relations between the governing class and the people, which once again would seem to suggest a focus on the island of Taiwan. The presidency tries to show itself as being close to the people, and not always without a dose of demagoguery, as illustrated for instance by the *Electronic Diary of President A-Bian* (*Abian zongtong dianzi bao*). The tone is set in the title: "A-Bian" is Chen Shuibian's diminutive, and as such denotes familiarity. The *Electronic Diary*, which comes out every week,[28] includes a cartoon strip, the two main characters of which are the President's two dogs. They suggest to Chen Shuibian that he call on the canine population in the fight against international terrorism, and give thanks that Chen Shuibian is not President of the United States, as that would mean he would have no time left to play with them . . .; this is a somewhat infantile vision of the presidency!

Naturally, cross-straits relations do appear at times on the site, whenever the President makes declarations on the topic, for instance, such as in the speech Chen Shuibian gave on the "Double Ten" National Day in 2002, which stressed Beijing's aggressiveness.[29] The cross-straits relations theme is also addressed on the Forum on National Concerns included in the traditional Chinese site, in which a very diverse range of views coexists.[30] The Presidential site gives the people a say, and tolerates all opinions.[31]

The site of the Taiwanese presidency also gives indications on Taipei's political communication. The section "About the Website" gives a run-down on the site's history. It was created on February 1, 1996, that is, under Li Denghui. Slight adjustments were made when Chen Shuibian took power on May 20, 2000, before broader changes in October 2000. The introductory text emphasizes democracy and public opinion. It stresses that in his inaugural speech on May 20, 2000, President Chen Shuibian stated: "The government exits for the people. The people are the masters and shareholders of the state. The government should rule on the basis of majority public opinion."

Taiwanese political culture took a major turn under Li Denghui. In February 1991, the magazine *Baoxue* published a file on spokespeople and public relations in which the main people in charge of Li Denghui's government communications gave their views.[32] Their declarations and their implications for institutional practice illustrated a transformation of the island's political culture, a new perception of relations between the government and the media. After the abolition of Martial Law on July 15, 1987 and the lifting of the press restrictions on January 1, 1988, and until the repealing of the Publication Law in 1999, the GIO had still the power to control the press, but claimed only a small degree of responsibility. The GIO's director, Shao Yuming, said: "The GIO contributed to national politics for some 40 years. But now that democracy is taking root in the country, the GIO's role should be simplified: previously responsible for government communications, political propaganda and press regulation, it should now only be in charge of government communications."[33]

As for the Office of the Presidential Spokesman (*zongtongfu fayanren shi*), established in 1990 and inspired by similar offices in Europe and the United States, its role is to "build a bridge between the President and the media," as "President Li Denghui considers that (. . .) in an open society, communications between the President and the people should be increased. The presidency should no longer remain a mysterious institution."[34]

Almost the same words are used, 11 years later, in 2002, at the start of the introductory text on the presidency's Internet site: "To many people, the 'Office of the President' seems like a remote and unreachable forbidden area under heavy guard. As a matter of fact, in a democratic Taiwan today, a visit to the Office of the President either by person or via its Website can be a matter of common practice. We hope that this worldwide information service will help change the image the Office of the President used to give to the public."[35]

Under the presidency of Li Denghui, in 1995, the Office of the President was opened to the public: nearly 60,000 people visited the Taiwanese presidency, "the symbol of highest power and once mysterious place in Taiwan," between January 1995 and September 2002. For those who cannot visit the presidency physically, the English-language and traditional-Chinese sites carry a Virtual Reality Tour and Web Video Tour within the presidency.[36] Once again, this shows the government's desire to bring itself closer to the people, a desire that is also perceptible in other headings on the site. Even though the process is not devoid of demagoguery, it does indicate that huge changes have taken place since the dictatorship of Chiang Kai-shek!

The Institutional SEF Site

The site of the SEF, at www.sef.org.tw, is very institutional in style. It presents the foundation and its members, and is mainly made up of official texts: government declarations, regulatory texts, statistical data, etc.

Six links are given at the bottom of the homepage. The first leads to the MAC site and the second to the government telephony site (www.gsn.gov.tw/). The third leads to a very rich page of links concerning relations between Taiwan and the mainland: sites,[37] search engines, as well as forums in which one can find the entire range of possible views on cross-straits relations.[38] The fourth link gives access to statistical data. The fifth lead to the Straits Exchange Foundation Taiwan Businessmen Information Web (*Liangan jingmao wang*), at www.seftb.org/. This site, which has a rather economic focus, is the equivalent of the SEF for practical questions, the SEF site itself being more political and institutional.[39] The sixth link leads to the Broadcasting Corporation of China (BCC) (*Zhongguo guangbo gongsi*).

Mainland Sites Constitute a "Closed Circuit"

The China Internet Information Center: No Links to Foreign Sites

As stated earlier, the "Chinese" and "Big 5" versions of the China Internet Information Center site, at www.china.org.cn and www.china.com.cn., look identical in all ways, and do not give the issue of Taiwan any special attention. It seems to consider the Taiwanese to be simply Chinese.

However, the site's English-language version devotes a special heading to Taiwan, "Taiwan Issues,"[40] made up of a presentation of the island,[41] and a choice of texts divided into two parts:

(1) "Speeches & Documents," which mainly contains official declarations emanating from the regime—by President Jiang Zemin above all—on the Taiwan Question and the Reunification of China. This part also includes the "Joint Communiqué on the Establishment of Diplomatic Relations between the People's Republic of China and the United States of America, January 1, 1979."[42]

(2) "News & Views," which gives information on relations between the two sides of the Taiwan Strait. Two types of text are stressed here: first, virulent criticism of Taiwanese described as "separatists" or accused of taking action in support of independence, and President Chen Shuibian in particular; second, information concerning various Taiwanese lobbies in favor of rapprochement with the mainland.[43]

Another heading on the English-language site, "Shanghai Communiqué 1972–2002," gives, for the 30th anniversary of this communiqué, a history of Sino–American relations ("China/US 30th Anniversary of the Shanghai Communiqué 1972–2002"). This includes the full text of the February 28, 1972 Communiqué, again that of the Joint Communiqué on the Establishment of Diplomatic Relations released at the end of 1978, and that of the China–US August 17, 1982 Communiqué.

The French-language site also features a special heading, "The Two Sides of the Taiwan Strait." It is not as rich as its English-language equivalent. It includes presentation of the island ("Taiwan, a Beautiful and Fertile Island"; "The Population"; "The History of Taiwan"),[44] opinions (messages from Mao Zedong to Taiwanese compatriots in 1958, from Deng Xiaoping in 1983, from Jiang Zemin in 1995, as well as from Li Peng, Zhu Rongji, and others), and two documents: the joint Sino–American Communiqué dating from 1981, and extracts from the joint Sino–American declaration at the time of Jiang Zemin's visit to the United States in 1997. Last, under the title "Information," one finds miscellaneous texts about opponents to independence for Taiwan and criticism of President Chen Shuibian. Articles include: "Chinese diaspora opposes 'independence for Taiwan' and supports 'reunification for the motherland'"; "Taiwan: protests after declarations in favour of independence by Chen Shuibian"; "Dangerous provocation by Chen Shuibian say Xinhua and *People's Daily* commentators"; "Chinese citizens living outside China criticise Chen Shuibian's secessionist language"; "Chen Shuibian's speech on 'independence' criticised by Taiwanese opinion"; "An organisation 'opposing independence and supporting reunification' proposed by Chinese citizens living in the US"; etc.[45]

There is no specific heading for Taiwan on the German-language site. But on the homepage, a small weather service gives the temperature for four Chinese cities: Beijing, Shanghai, Hong Kong, and Taipei. In other words, Taipei is presented as part of the country in exactly the same way as Beijing, Shanghai, and Hong Kong.

A number of links are included on the English-language homepage, leading mainly to media sites.

These sites include:

(1) The Xinhua News Agency, at www.xinhuanet.com. There are eight versions of this site: simplified and traditional Chinese, English, Spanish, French, Japanese, Russian, and Arabic.
(2) The *People's Daily*, at peopledaily.com.cn or www.people.com.cn, with the same eight versions.
(3) The *China Daily*, the PRC's official English-language daily, at www1.chinadaily.com.cn.[46]
(4) China Central Television—CCTV (*Zhongguo zhongyang dianshitai*), in simplified and traditional Chinese versions, as well as in English.
(5) China Radio International, at webcri.cri.com. This radio, founded on December 3, 1941, broadcasts programmes in 43 languages and Chinese dialects.[47]
(6) The weekly *Beijing Review*, at www.bjereview.com.cn. The Chinese edition is entitled *Beijing Zhoubao*, the English *Beijing Review*, and the French *Beijing Information*; there are also editions in German, Spanish, Japanese and other editions intended for English- and French-speaking Africa.
(7) The monthly *China Today*, at www.chinatoday.com.cn, in English, French, Spanish, German, Arabic, and Chinese versions.[48]

All the links lead exclusively to PRC sites; not a single foreign site is on offer, and—needless to say—none from Taiwan. In addition, information is sometimes used in loops: for instance, among the texts available under the heading "The Two Sides of the Taiwan Strait" in French-language version at www.china.org.cn, one can find: "Dangerous provocation by Chen Shuibian say Xinhua and *People's Daily* commentators." It is stated that this is an article published jointly by "informed commentators" of the *People's Daily* and Xinhua. But it so happens that the first two links on the French-language version of the site—and for the English-language version as well—lead to Xinhua and the *People's Daily*. This sort of "recycling" leaves one with an impression of stifling.

The All China Taiwanese Association—ACTA

The site of the All China Taiwanese Association—ACTA (*Zhonghua quanguo Taiwan tongbao lianyihui*), an organization set up by the PRC in Beijing on December 27, 1981, can be found at www.tailian.org.cn. There are two versions of this site, one in simplified characters and the

other in traditional characters, but the content is identical. Among other
things, the site offers all sorts of information about the association, but
also a rundown on Taiwanese investments in the mainland, information
for Taiwanese children attending school in the PRC, the most recent
legislation concerning Taiwanese people, etc. Most of this is practical
information. The site also includes a forum, which does not look to be
very popular, as it contains only 14 contributions, all very short, none of
which refers to the independence of Taiwan.

The homepage also offers links to 11 sites:

(1) The *People's Daily*.
(2) Xinhua News Agency.
(3) An information site on Beijing, at www.21dnn.com,
    www.qianlong.com, and www.beijingnews.com. The site was
    authorized by the State Council (*Guowuyuan*) and the
    Propaganda Department of the Communist Party of the City of
    Beijing (*Zhonggong Beijing shi wei xuanchuan bu*). Most Beijing
    media—press, radio, and television—participate.
(4) China News (*Zhong xinwen wang*), at www.chinanews.com.cn.
    This site was launched on January 1, 1999 and emanates from
    the official news agency Zhongxin (*Zhongguo xinwen she*).[49]
(5) China–Taiwan (*Zhongguo Taiwan wang*), at www.chinataiwan.org.
    This site has versions in simplified Chinese, in traditional
    Chinese, and in English. It falls under the responsibility of the
    China Taiwan Information Center (*Zhongguo Taiwan zixun
    zhongxin*), which is in charge of the Taiwan question and the
    development of cross-straits exchanges in order to achieve reuni-
    fication. The site is updated on a daily basis as it has a heading,
    "Daily Headline," which includes official texts concerning cross-
    straits relations, and "soundbites" such as "Despite difficulties
    over half a century, there's deep friendship across the straits," on
    the English-language site.

    Among the different headings, under "Highlights," one can
    find "The One-China Principle: the Key to Present Cross-strait
    Deadlock," with three points expanded upon underneath:
    "Origin of the One-China Principle," "KMT's Position on the
    One-China Principle," "DPP's Position on the One-China
    Principle." Under the title "News Features," one finds: "US Arms
    Sale to Taiwan," "One-China Principle," "Three Direct Links";
    just below that, one finds "One Country, Two Systems" and
    "Government White Paper on the Taiwan Issue."[50]

(6) China Jingwei Net (*Huaxia jingwei wang*), at www.viewcn.com and www.huaxia.com, launched on April 29, 2001, "with the support" of the State Council. This site, which has simplified and traditional Chinese versions as well as an English-language version, is also updated every day. It is less institutional and contains more practical information than the preceding one.

(7) China Bridge (*Zhongguo qiaolian*).[51]

(8) Taiwan Compatriots' House in Fujian (*Fujian sheng tailian*), at www.fjtl.org. This is a site for Taiwanese people in Fujian province, in simplified Chinese and Big 5 versions.

(9) Taiwan League (*Taimeng*), at www.taimeng.org.cn, simplified and traditional Chinese versions.

(10) Channel Online (*Haixia zaixian*), a site emanating from the Xiamen special economic zone in Fujian province, at www.twinland.com.

(11) Taiwan Merchants China (*Zhongguo taishang wang*), at www. china-taiwan.com.

The first two links offered are, once again, the *People's Daily* and the Xinhua News Agency, and all the other links lead also to PRC sites. PRC sites constitute a "closed circuit."

The main Taiwanese government site devoted to cross-straits relations—the MAC site—gives a lot of importance to public opinion in the island. Vis-à-vis the international community, Taipei has apparently decided to use the Internet to emphasize the democratic nature of the regime in power on the island, in contrast to an undemocratic PRC, the aggressiveness of which is highlighted. Vis-à-vis the Chinese community, and its own citizens in particular, Taipei is also interested in sorting out the practical problems that can arise from cross-straits exchanges. Generally speaking, the Taiwanese government comes across as trying to be close to its citizens, as not being immune to demagoguery on occasion, and by a desire for transparency, which is underscored by the huge amount of government information available online. Manuel Castells stresses that the Internet could be an ideal instrument for fostering democracy. The Internet facilitates the access to political information to such a degree that citizens could be almost as well informed as the governing class. Thanks to interactivity, the state would no longer keep citizens under surveillance, but rather the opposite. Unfortunately, he says, "governments at all levels, use the Internet, primarily, as an electronic billboard to post their information without much effort at real interaction."[52] Last, Taiwan government sites are characterized by their openness, which can be felt in the links they offer: a lot of these links lead to other Taiwan government sites, but others also lead to sites in the PRC and elsewhere.

Mainland sites differ in that they systematically send Internet users to other sites in the PRC, which, moreover, are often the same, such as the Xinhua News Agency or *People's Daily* sites. The fact that the Internet is not very well developed in the PRC and that there are not many sites available could explain why links tend to lead to the same sites. But this does not explain the lack of links to foreign sites.

In general, a lot of emphasis is put on news; but here again, information emanating from "authorised sources," that is, the Xinhua News Agency or the Zhongguo News Agency for instance. In other words, the severe control over information carried out by the state in the PRC is clearly perceptible on the Internet. The situation looks very similar to that prevailing in Taiwan before the end of the 1980s, when the Guomindang had control over all aspects of society, and information in particular (e.g. manuals for students of journalism, press organs and professional media organizations) thanks to martial law, which was in force until July 15, 1987, the Party's propaganda service, or the GIO.

Beijing's official line on cross-straits relations can be found intact on the Internet: Taiwan is presented as being part of China and—in order to support this affirmation—Beijing can point to the fact that the United States has acknowledged it.

Services Online to Taiwanese Businessmen on the Mainland: Taipei Turns to Beijing

Economic exchanges between Taiwan and the mainland took off spectacularly in the 1990s, leading to increasing interdependence between the two.[53] As early as 1989, Beijing, which has never sought to hide its intention to use economic arms in its battle for reunification, took the initiative of organizing and institutionalizing Taiwanese business people working on the mainland.[54] Taipei reacted by setting up its own network, the Taiwan Investors Associations.[55]

The Site Linked to SEF, ROC

The Straits Exchange Foundation Taiwan Businessmen Information Web, in Chinese (traditional and simplified characters), at www.seftb.org/, is the economic and practical side of the SEF's site [www.sef.org.tw], which is more political and institutional. It is made up mainly of practical information: laws concerning cross-straits economic and trade flows in Taiwan, the PRC, Hong Kong and Macau, how to invite PRC citizens to visit Taiwan, etc.

The site gives an enormous amount of importance to the Taiwan Investors Associations: it gives a list of 63 associations—updated on July 29, 2002—with all their contact details, the events they organize, their publications,[56] etc. It also gives particular emphasis to a SEF publication, the *Straits Business Monthly* (*Liangan jingmao*), which can be read online, and provides nine links to press sites. The first two lead to the Internet site of the Taiwanese press group United Daily News (*Lianhebao*), which lobbies for the reunification of the island and the mainland. The next two lead to the Taiwanese press group China Times (*Zhongguo shibao*), which has a more neutral editorial line. Another two links lead to media in the PRC[57] and another to a Hong Kong newspaper.[58] As at November 21, 2002, the site had been consulted 87,059 times.[59]

The Site Linked to the MAC, ROC

The Economic and Commercial Network of Taiwanese Businessmen on the Mainland (*Dalu Taishang jingmao wang*), at www.chinabiz.org.tw/, was born at the initiative of the MAC, which handed it over to the ROC's Council of Management Sciences (*Zhonghua minguo guanli kexuehui*) in 1997. It was set up by a university (*Zhongyuan daxue guanli xi*). As at November 21, 2002, this site, which is also made up mainly of practical information, had received 395,637 consultations since February 12, 2001.

This site is a good deal richer than that linked to the SEF. It includes directories, links to different ROC or PRC ministries, etc. It also gives contact details for the Taiwan Investors Association. The list is the same as that found on the site linked to the SEF, except that it has 65 items instead of 63. But this site also provides contact details for Taiwanese associations created at the initiative of Beijing: the Taiwan Merchant Association Shenzhen, for instance, the first of this type, founded on June 27, 1990, and whose Internet site can be consulted at www.tmas.org.

For current events, the site gives links to different media:

(1) The first leads to the Internet site of Taiwanese press group China Times, at news.chinatimes.com. This group is characterized by its relative neutrality on the subject of cross-straits relations; it is in favor of neither reunification, nor independence.

(2) The second leads to the site www.ettoday.com (Donglin), in
    traditional characters only.
(3) The third address given is www.sina.com.cn.
(4) The fourth leads to a site giving financial information in traditional
    characters only, at http://finance.cina.com.
(5) The fifth leads to the international edition of the *People's Daily*
    (*Renmin ribao haiwai ban*), at www.peopledaily.com.cn.
(6) The sixth leads to a table containing ten entries for Taiwan and
    eight for mainland China, one of which leads to the Xinhua
    News Agency site. One of the Taiwanese ten entries leads to the
    Central Daily News (*Zhongyang ribao*), the Guomindang daily, and
    another to the United Daily News site, the latter press group
    being in favor of reunification between Taiwan and the mainland.
    Another of the entries for Taiwan leads once more to the China
    Times, for which there is yet another link, in the top right-hand
    corner of the homepage. This site also offers online consultation
    of various publications, many of which emanate from the Taiwanese
    government.[60]

These ROC's two sites intended for Taiwanese business people
working on the mainland mainly contain practical information. The two
sites provide numerous links to PRC sites emanating from mainland
associations, institutions or media.

Taiwan Merchants—China, PRC: No Overt Political Message

The Taiwan Merchants—China site (*Zhongguo Taishang wang*), at
www.china-taiwan.com, exists in three versions: simplified Chinese, traditional Chinese, and English. The site's content is both technical and
practical. It is devoid of any overt political message. It is linked to the
Association of Taiwan Merchants, set up by Beijing in 1990 and based
in Shenzhen. The association has 20 or so branches outside Shenzhen,
particularly in the large Chinese cities.[61]

The site contains, among other features:

(1) A directory listing some 130,000 Taiwanese businesses operating
    in the PRC; as well as a ranking of these businesses by geographic
    presence and business.
(2) An online classified advertisement service: employment, office or
    factory space, supply or demand for raw materials, equipment and
    materials, etc.

(3) A list of investment opportunities on the mainland.
(4) Legislation concerning Taiwanese people living in the PRC.
(5) Stock-market information.
(6) Information on Taiwanese businesses (with links leading to Taiwanese sites, including that of the food corporation President (*Tongyi*), at www.pecos.com.tw or www.uni-president.com.tw).
(7) Information for everyday life, on transport, schools, accommodation . . . as well as the addresses of restaurants and bars.

This PRC site is very rich and comes across as being more complete than that linked to the MAC, in the ROC. But from mid-November to early December 2002 it was not possible to access it.

Taiwan Merchant Association Shenzhen, PRC: A Local Scope

There is another site that is also run by Zhongguo Taishang wang who owns the copyright to it, the site of the Taiwan Merchant Association Shenzhen (*Shenzhen Taishang xiehui*), at tmas.org. This site is a lot narrower in scope than the preceding one and has a local feel about it. This is highlighted by the six links it provides:

(1) Customs services in Shenzhen (*Shenzhen haiguan*: www. sz-customs. gov.cn).
(2) Quarantine services in Shenzhen (*Shenzhen jianyan jianyi*: www.szciq.gov.cn).
(3) Yahoo China (cn.yahoo.com).
(4) Sina (*Xinlang*: www.sina.com.cn).
(5) Sohu (*Souhu*: www.sohu.com).
(6) The China Shenzhen Machinery Association (*Zhongguo Shenzhen jixie wang*: www.chinaszma.com).

Sina, an Early Example of Tomorrow's Greater China Online?

The nongovernmental Sina site (*Xinlang*), looks to me to be of particular interest. It is accessible from a link on the MAC site, in the ROC [www.chinabiz.org.tw/], as well as from a link on the mainland Taiwan Merchant Association Shenzhen site. The address www.sina.com.cn corresponds to the Sina Beijing site, but Sina also has a site in the United States (www.sina.com), Hong Kong (www.sina.com.hk), and Taipei (www.sina.com.tw, in traditional characters, whereas all the other Sina sites use simplified characters).[62]

Sina was founded in March 1999, from the merger between the
Beijing based Stone Rich Sight Information Technology Company
(SRS) and U.S.-based sinanet.com. Online, Sina presents itself as follows:

> Sina.com (Nasdaq: Sina—News) is the leading online media and
> value-added infotainment service (VAS) provider for China and for
> global Chinese communities. With a branded network of 15 local-
> ized web sites targeting Greater China and overseas Chinese, Sina
> operates three major business lines including Sina.com (online
> media and entertainment service), Sina Online (consumer fee-based
> online and wireless VAS) and Sina.net (Small and medium-sized
> enterprises VAS) providing an array of services including online
> portals, premium email, wireless short messaging, search, classified
> information, online games, e-commerce, e-learning and enterprise
> e-solutions. With 60 million registered users worldwide and over
> 3 million active paid users for a variety of our fee-based services,
> Sina is the most recognized Internet brand name in China and
> among global Chinese. Our primary focus is in China where we
> generate 85% of our total revenues.

Sina also presents its management team, made up of nine people. Most
of them have degrees from prestigious universities in both China and
abroad—American for the most part.[63] Their nationality is not given,
but their academic background and other indications given suggest that
four of them come from the PRC, two or three from Taiwan, the
remainder possibly being members of the Chinese diaspora.[64] In a press
release, issued October 1, 2002, both in Beijing, China, and San Mateo,
California, Sina announced it relocated its worldwide headquarters from
Beijing to Shanghai, in order to focus on opportunities in China and on
cross-straits business.[65]

The example of Sina is interesting in that it appears to be an online
illustration that Taiwan and mainland China are in fact a lot closer than
the political stance of the respective governments, particularly on their
Internet sites, would suggest.[66] ROC sites aimed at Taiwanese business
people include a lot of links to PRC sites. This fact is corroborated by
one of the GIO's two portals, "Taiwan Related Links" [http://portal.gio.
gov.tw/taiwan/]. Under the portal's second heading, "Business and
Economy," there is a subheading, "Mainland Business Information,"
which provides four pages of links, most of which lead to Chinese-
language sites in the PRC, some of which clearly present themselves
as being government emanations.[67] In order to keep the Taiwanese

population informed about the PRC, the ROC in a certain sense looks obliged to turn to Beijing. The ROC can do no better than give "second hand" information, as the PRC has the upper hand. Take for instance legislation concerning Taiwanese citizens living in the PRC. As Beijing has the initiative concerning domestic legislation, mainland sites can immediately react to decisions taken, while Taipei can only report the decisions with a delay—however short it may be.

Mainland sites aimed at Taiwanese business people are characterized by an absence of any overt political message: they are solely practical and appear to suit to their mission, which is to provide a service for Taiwanese people. In addition, these sites look to be better adapted, for some services, than ROC sites: it seems not very logical for two Taiwanese business people both working in mainland China to hop over to Taiwan to buy or sell to each other equipment owned in the mainland. Mainland sites are no doubt also better in helping Taiwanese business people find staff in mainland China.

Conclusion

The control exercised by the Chinese state over information in general and over the Internet in particular, means that PRC government sites reproduce faithfully the official line on cross-straits relations. The Internet looks like being a means of getting its message across, alongside other media such as the *People's Daily* and the Xinhua New Agency. Beijing's irredentism nevertheless comes across more clearly in foreign-language versions; in Chinese-language sites, the Taiwanese are not given separate treatment, they look to be already considered as PRC citizens just like any others.

Mainland sites aimed more specifically at Taiwanese business people are not described as "government" sites by Beijing, but as "private" sites. They emphasize business over politics and do not convey any overt political message, preferring to offer practical information, services, etc. Politically speaking, on the Internet, the PRC comes across as an important power; economically, Beijing looks to be more in control than Taipei.

On Taiwanese government sites, Taipei's official line is also very clear: the sea change in the government's information policy at the end of the 1980s is manifest. It was at this time that Taipei started to move away from pure and simple propaganda. Today, Taiwanese government sites give a very broad range of views on cross-straits relations. The ROC which turned its focus to the island of Taiwan, is seeking to emphasize public opinion, the democratic nature of the regime, as opposed to the aggressive nationalism that Taipei claims characterizes the PRC.

The Internet is less developed in the PRC than in the ROC, and this means that the inhabitants of mainland China are less exposed to Taipei's views than the other way round. However, it is no doubt true that Taiwanese people are less sensitive to political propaganda since democratization. The Internet is nevertheless spreading fast in the PRC. According to a ROC Defence White Paper published in July 2001, the mainland will have become a real threat for Taiwan by 2010 as it becomes more skilled in computer and electronic warfare, as some mainland hackers' actions already show it nowadays.[68] PRC authorities are confronted with a dilemma: the Internet can be beneficial to economic growth in the country, but it can also pose a threat to state control over information. It is not sure that Beijing will still be able to exert such severe control over the Internet in 2010.

Notes

1. Manuel Castells, *The Internet Galaxy: Reflections on the Internet, Business, and Society* (Oxford and New York : Oxford University Press, 2001): 137.
2. These figures are those of the NUA, a privately run online information company specializing in the demography and change of the Internet, at www.nua.com/surveys/. The estimate for Taiwan was established by Nielsen NetRatings, the one for China is that of the CNNIC (*Zhongguo hulian wangluo xinxi zhongxin*), at www.cnnic.net.cn. Internet is developing at a very fast pace in China: in July 2002, the CNNIC estimated that 45.8 million Chinese people used the Internet, a penetration rate of 3.58%. According to Castells, *The Internet Galaxy*, 212, "in China, the three largest cities, Beijing, Shanghai, and Guangzhou, in September 2000, according to NUA surveys, accounted for about 60 percent of Internet users. In contrast, the penetration rate for the country as a whole remained at less than 2 percent of the population."
3. On the Chinese-language GIO site, at www.gio.gov.tw/info/index_c.html, only the first seven languages are available: Chinese (traditional and simplified characters), English, French, Spanish, German, Japanese, and Russian. These seven languages seem to be considered the most important.
4. There are nine online periodicals: *Taipei Journal* and *Taipei Review* in English, *Sinorama* in English, Chinese (simplified and traditional characters) and Japanese, *Noticias* and *Taipei Hoy* in Spanish, *Taipei aujourd'hui* and *Les Echos-Taiwan Info* in French, *Taipei Heute* in German, and *Taibeiskaya Panorama* in Russian.
5. The history of the Yearbook is a lot longer and even more significant. Editions published in 1972–1973, 1974, and 1979, i.e. before diplomatic relations were established between Beijing and Washington, were entitled *China Yearbook*, followed by the edition date. In 1986, 1987, and 1988, the book was called *Republic of China*, followed by the edition date. In 1989, 1990–1991, and 1991–1992, it took on the title of *Republic of China Yearbook*, followed by the edition date. From 1993 to 2000, it became *The Republic of China Yearbook*, followed by the edition date. But its last two editions have been called *The Republic of China Yearbook, Taiwan 2001* and *2002*. The key word is "Yearbook," and in second position "Taiwan," which is in a bigger typeface than "The Republic of China." Similarly, up to the 2000 edition, the book opened on a double-page map including mainland China and Taiwan, with the legend "The Republic of China"; a detailed

map of Taiwan was given overleaf. But the 2001 and 2002 editions open on a double page including a color map of Taiwan on the left, above which there is a part of what is designated as the "Chinese Mainland"; on the right, there is a more detailed map of Taiwan, with "Taiwan" in large typeface and "Republic of China" underneath, in smaller typeface.

6. The GIO lost power over the press only on January 25, 1999, with the repealing of the Publication Law.

7. Under the heading "Who We Are" on the English-language site's homepage, the subheading "Organizations" includes the following text: "The GIO is responsible for clarifying national policy, publicizing governement ordinances and administrative achievements, releasing important information at home and abroad, actively developing overseas information and cultural projects, and strengthening cultural communication to the Chinese Mainland."

8. Under the subheading "Functions," one can read the following text: "GIO's Department of Planning and Evaluation is responsible for the overall planning of information affairs at home and abroad; handling Mainland, Hong Kong and Macau affairs; collecting, assessing, and making use of information on Mainland affairs; computerizing GIO operations; and maintaining the GIO's chinese language website."

9. The "Taiwan Related Links" portal includes 12 headings: (1) Arts and Humanities; (2) Business and Economy, including the subheading "Mainland Business Information"; (3) Computer and Networks; (4) Education and Learning; (5) Entertainment; (6) Health; (7) Investment and Financing; (8) Libraries and References; (8) Natural Sciences; (9) News and Media; (10) Recreation; (11) Social Sciences; and (12) Society and Culture.

10. The heading, (1) Agriculture & Food includes two subheadings; (2) Arts & Culture has five; (3) Central Government Organs has seven (Presidential Office, National Assembly and the five Yuans); (4) Defense only has one subheading; (5) Economy has three; (6) Education has four (Departments, Museums, Universities, Research Bodies; the Universities subheading gives access to the Internet sites of 29 Taiwanese universities, eight of these sites are in Chinese only); (7) External Affairs has three subheadings: Foreign Relations, Mainland Affairs, and Overseas Chinese Affairs; (8) Health Environment has three; (9) Local Governments has four; (10) Public Safety has three; (11) Recreation has three; (12) Reference has three: Libraries, Research Bodies for the second time, and Statistics; (13) Science & Technology has three; (14) Society has three; (15) Transportation & Communications has two.

11. The importance Taipei attaches to languages like Dutch, Hungarian, etc., surely illustrates its efforts to break out of the isolation the ROC is victim to internationally. It can also be related to trading links: the Netherlands, for instance, are a very significant trading partner of Taiwan, the second in Europe after Germany, far before France. In 2001, Taiwanese exports to Germany amounted to 4,480 thousands of U.S.$, to the Netherlands to 4,229 thousands, to France to 1,166 thousands; the imports from Germany amounted to 4,246 thousands of U.S.$, from the Netherlands to 1,524 thousands, from France to 2,131 thousands.

12. All these government sites are supposed to have Chinese and English-language versions, but the English version seems not always available. Three of them have other versions, in addition to Chinese and English. These are the National Tourism Association, the State Council Information Office and the Xinhua News Agency: (1) Ministries and Commissions under the State Council: Ministry of Foreign Affairs (www.fmprc.gov.cn); State Economic and Trade Commission (www.setc.gov.cn); Ministry of Science and Technology (www.most.gov.cn); Commission of Science, Technology and Industry for National Defense (www.costind.gov.cn); Ministry of Finance (www.mof.gov.cn); Ministry of Land and Resources (www.mlr.gov.cn); MII (www.mii.gov.cn); China Electronic Industry Information Net (www.ceic.gov.cn); Ministry of Foreign Trade and Economic Cooperation (www.moftec.gov.cn); and State Family Planning (www.sfpc.gov.cn). (2) Organizations Directly Under the State Council: General Administration of Customs (www.customs.gov.cn); State Intellectual Property Office (www.cpo.gov.cn); and National Tourism Administration (www.cnta.com, versions in Chinese, "Big 5," English and Japanese). (3) Others: Special Economic Zone Office of the State Coucil (www.sezo.gov.cn);

State Coucil Information Office (www.china.org.cn presented earlier, in ten different languages); and China Council for the Promotion of International Trade (www.ccpit.org). (4) State Bureaus under the Jurisdiction of Ministries and Commissions: State Administration of Light Industry (www.clii.com.cn); State Tobacco Monopoly Administration (www.tobacco.gov.cn); State Post Bureau (www.chinapost.gov.cn); State Administration of Textile (www.ctei.gov.cn); State Administration of Non Ferrous Metal Industry (www.atk.com.cn); State Administration for Entry-Exit Inspection and Quarantine (www.ciq.gov.cn); and State Administration of Traditional Chinese Medicine (www.satcm.gov.cn). (5) Institutions directly under the State Coucil: Xinhua News Agency (www.xinhua.org, in simplified and traditional Chinese, English, Spanish, French, Japanese, Russian, and Arabic); Chinese Academy of Science (www. cahq.ac.cn); Chinese Academy of Social Sciences (www.cass.net.cn); Chinese Academy of Engineering (www.cae.ac.cn); and China Securities Regulatory Commission (www.csrc.gov.cn).

13. Françoise Mengin and Jean-Louis Rocca, "Introduction: Analyzing Changes Through Overlapping Spheres," in *Politics in China, Moving Frontiers*, Françoise Mengin and Jean-Louis Rocca (eds.) (New York: Palgrave, 2002): x–xxviii.

14. Among the mainland sites devoted to Taiwan, one can also find "Hello Taiwan" (*Ni hao Taiwan*), at www.nihaotw.com, in simplified Chinese only, which was first put online on May 18, 2001, and which is run by the China National Radio (*Zhongyang renmin guangbo diantai*), as well as the Reunification Front site (*Zhonggong zhongyang tongyi zhanxian gongzuo bu*), at www.zytzb.org.cn, in simplified Chinese as well; this site's presentation and content are as outdated as its name.

15. Its address is www.mac.gov.tw/english/Welcome.html. The homepages of the two Chinese versions (www.mac.gov.tw/Chinese.htm for traditional characters, www.mac.gov.tw/gb/Welcome.htm for simplified characters) have titles in Chinese "Xingzhengyuan Dalu weiyuanhui" and sub-titles in English "Mainland Affairs Council"; neither contains mention of the "Republic of China."

16. For example, "Guidelines for National Unification" adopted by the National Unification Council (NUC) on February 23, 1991 and the Executive Yuan on March 14, 1991.

17. Extracts from speeches on January 1, 2002, December 31, 2000, his inaugural speech on May 20, 2000, etc.

18. Between 1987 and November 30, 1999, Taipei arrested an average of 250 illegal mainland immigrants per month, costing it NT$ 600 millions. The Kinmen Agreement obliges the mainland to take back its citizens within 20 days. But in reality, it takes an average of 150 days; Taipei underlines Beijing's lack of cooperation in this respect. Between 1987 and 1999, 37,000 people (out of about 38,000) were repatriated.

19. They come under the following titles: (1) Public Opinion on Cross-Straits Relations in the ROC, August 2002; (2) Unification or Independence ?, July 2002;. (3) Public Opinion on Cross-Straits Relations in the ROC, May 2002; (4) 2001 General Analysis of People's Views on the Governement's mainland Policy and Cross-Straits Relations, February 2002; (5, 6, 7, 8) Public Opinion on Cross-Straits Relations in the ROC, February 2002, July 2001, March 2001, June 2000); (9) How Taiwan People view Cross-Straits Relations, February 2000; and (10) Public Support for "Special State-to-State Relationship," September 1999.

20. The sample of the telephone poll, carried out between September 1997 and August 2002 in conjunction—among other intervening parties—with the National Chengchi University Taipei's Election Study Center, is made of 1,000 Taiwanese people aged between 20 and 69. The second chart gives the same results as that of the first chart, in a different graphic presentation. The third chart gives the question: "If developing foreign ties would lead to rising tension on cross-straits relations, would you agree with such an effort ?," which gets a majority of affirmative responses. But the majority is declining: from 71% in September 1997 to 54.5% in July 2002. The fourth shows the response to the question: "Whether to develop foreign or cross-straits relations as a priority"; the answer "developing cross-straits relations is more important"

rose from 17.9 in 1997 to 35.0 in 2002. The fifth deals with "The Pace of Cross-Straits Exchanges." Fewer Taiwanese people are finding the pace "Just right," and increasing numbers are saying "Don't know." The sixth, "Beijing's Hostility toward ROC," shows that the Taiwanese are more sensitive to "Hostility toward ROC Government" (around 60%, with a peak of 88.5% in August 1999 corresponding to the peak of 14.3% in desire for independence), than to "Hostility toward ROC people." The seventh shows that a large majority of 70–85% of the Taiwanese population does not subscribe to the "One Country, Two Systems" formula as a solution to solve the problems across the straits. The eighth shows that the question "How should our governement handle Taiwanese investment on Mainland China?," receives a majority reply of "Increase Restrictions Regulations." The ninth, "Should we open up direct transportation links with mainland China?," shows that most people think the country "should conditionally open up direct transportation links" rather than go ahead with unconditional liberalization.

21. All the results are favorable to Li Denghui, despite the fact that they emanate from institutes as diverse as the United Daily News Poll Center, of the *United Daily News*, in favor of reunification, and Shan Shui Poll Survey Co., trusted by Global Television and *The Journalist*, which rather support independence.

22. The second point on the site in traditional characters is entitled "Situation in the Taiwan Strait and in Mainland China" (*Liangan ji Dalu qingshi*). Despite the content being identical, the same page on the site in simplified characters is called "Economic Situation in the Taiwan Strait and in Mainland China"(*Liangan ji Dalu jingji qingshi*); the title includes the word "jingji," and thus emphasizes the economic aspect.

23. The 15 sections of the Taiwanese presidency's site in english, at www.president.gov.tw/, are: (1) News Releases: providing the latest news on the Office of the President and other government websites; (2) Introduction of ROC; (3) Presidential Office Organization; (4) President Chen's profile; (5) Vice-President Lu's profile; (6) Forum on National Concerns: offering the public a channel to voice opinion on national affairs; (7) Tour Guide and Art Gallery: introducing the Presidential Building through different perspectives; (8) Open-House Tours; (9) Special Subjects; (10) For Kids: vividly introducing the Office from children's perspective; (11) For Youth; (12) About this Website: introducing the construction history of the website; (13) Related Websites; (14) English Version; and (15) Simplified Chinese Character Version.

24. The three sections removed from the English-language version are: Forum on National Concerns, Open-House Tours, and For Youth.

25. The seven sections added to the English-language version are: (1) A detailed agenda, day by day, of the President and the Vice-President (*meiri huodong xingcheng*); (2) Opinion polls carried out by the presidency (*zongtongfu mindiao*), mainly concerning the Internet site itself or internal Taiwanese issues such as the revision of the Constitution. Out of 21 items, only one concerns Beijing: it was a poll carried out before Beijing won the 2008 Olympics, asking Taiwanese people whether they were for or against a win by Beijing and, in the event of Beijing winning, what they thought the impact would be on cross-straits relations; (3) The *Electronic Diary of President A-Bian* (*Abian zongtong dianzi bao*); (4) Official statements by the presidency (*Zongtongfu gongbao*); (5) Public services (*bianmin fuwu*); (6) Official publications (*gongbu lan*); (7) Audiovisual materials (*yingyin yuandi*).

26. This is a digest of the most important recent texts given in the "News Releases" section.

27. The first heading,"Hot News and Hot Topics" (*zuixin xiaoxi yu remen huati*) is a digest of "News Releases." The second, entitled "Important Agenda Activities" (*meiri zhongyao huodong*), is a digest of the President's main meetings during the day. The simplified Chinese version does not include the Presidential agenda but does include the daily digest.

28. The issue dated November 14, 2002, is number 57.

29. "With regard to cross-strait relations, the government will continue to advocate 'goodwill, active cooperation and permanent peace' and promote the normalization of cross-strait

relations. However, in the face of the PRC's ever increasing threats and intimidation, and its aggressive campaign to suffocate Taiwan on all international fronts, we harbor no illusions. We do know that Taiwan's sovereignty is inalienable and cannot be infringed upon. The will of the Taiwanese people to pursue freedom, democracy and peace can never be compromised. On behalf of all citizens of the Republic of China (Taiwan), I solemnly call upon the leaders of the People's Republic of China (PRC) to immediately remove the 400 missiles that are deployed along the Taiwan Strait, and to openly renounce the use of force against Taiwan. For, only by engaging in rational discussions and allowing the 'doors of dialogue' to be reopened can the antagonistic deadlock in cross-strait relations be resolved."

30. Contributions assembled on October 29, 2002 in a subject on the Forum entitled "The Three Links" (*liang an san tong*): Taiwan is not a state, it's the ROC that is a sovereign state (*Taiwan bu shi yi ge guojia, Zhonghua minguo cai shi yi ge zhuquan guojia*); Taiwan is not a nation, Taiwan is a special state of the United States of America (*Taiwan bu shi yi ge guojia, Taiwan shi Meiguo de yi teshu zhou*); Taiwan, the equivalent of the ROC, is a state, but is not a Chinese province (*Taiwan dengyu Zhonghua minguo shi yi ge guojia, bu dengyu Zhongguo de yi ge sheng*), etc.

31. There is no forum on the site in simplified characters. Perhaps it is feared that a forum for PRC citizens would open the door to Beijing propaganda . . . But PRC citizens can perhaps participate in discussions on the English or traditional characters sites.

32. See "Fayanren yu gonggong guanxi zhuanji" (File on spokespeople and public relations") *Baoxue* (*Journalism*) VIII, 4 (February 1991): 6–71. *Baoxue*, launched on July 20, 1951, folded after 1996. Bi-annual but irregular, it was published by the ROC Editor's Association (*Zhonghua minguo xinwen bianjiren xiehui*), a professional organization controlled by the Guomindang. *Baoxue*'s lay out was severe and outdated, its content was very academic and relatively conservative.

33. Shao, Yuming, "Tan zhengfu fayanren de yunzuo" (On functioning of government spokespeople) *Baoxue*, VIII, 4 (February 1991): 20–23.

34. Qiu, Jinyi, "Wei zongtong yu xinwenjie da yi zuo qiao—Zongtong fayanren de jiaose yu gong-neng" (Building a bridge between the presidency and the media: the role and function of the presidency spokesperson) *Baoxue*, VIII, 4 (February 1991): 8–18.

35. The text concludes as follows: "The Internet has become an indispensable part of our daily life. In a democratized Taiwan, Presidential Building now belongs to all citizens. Therefore, the success or failure of this Website depends on the concern and participation of all the citizens, while we try to make it a 'Window on the Republic of China'."

36. The theme of visits to the Presidential palace is not given as much emphasis on the site in simplified characters, certainly because it is difficult for PRC citizens to go to Taiwan.

37. For example, Straits Exchange Foundation Taiwan Businessmen Information Web (*Liangan jingmao wang*), at www.seftb.org/ (traditional and simplified characters); The Economic and Commercial Network of Taiwanese Businessmen on the mainland (*Dalu Taishang jingmao wang*), at www.chinabiz.org.tw (traditional characters only); Services Online for Economy and Commerce across the Taiwan Straits (*Liangan jingmao fuwu wang*), emanating from the Association of Mainland-investing Taiwanese businessmen (*Dalu touzi Taishang lianyihui*), at www.ssn.com.tw (traditional characters only), etc.

38. Eight forums are proposed: (1) The Peace Forum (*heping tanqu*) at www.dsis.org.tw/peace.htm, on the DSIS site, "Division of Strategic and International Studies, Taiwan Research Institute," in three versions (simplified and traditional characters, English); (2) Peace for Future China (*weilai Zhongguo*), at www.future-china.org.taiwan; (3) Cross-Straits Forum (*liangan luntan*), at tc.pauo.com/forum.pl; (4) Forum on Cross-straits Relations (*liangan guanxi luntan*), an emanation of the Singapore press, at www.zaobao.com/special/china/taiwan/forum.html; (5) Forum on Asia-Pacific Public Affairs (*Yatai gonggong shiwu luntan*), at www.appaf.nysu.edu.tw; (6) National Forum on Sustainable Development (*guojia yongxu fazhan luntan*), at sd.erl.itri.org. tw/forum/sd_index.html; (7) Discussion Space on Taiwan–China Relations (*Tai, Zhong guanxi taolun qu*), at newcongress.yam.org.tw/taiwan_sino; and (8) World Forum on Military Affairs

(*Shijie junshi luntan*), at www.wforum.com/wmf, which is probably linked to Beijing as it exists only in simplified characters and in English.

39. There are two links to this site on the SEF site. It is also placed third in the list of links on relations between Taiwan and the mainland.
40. Tibet also receives special treatment in the English site.
41. Various aspects are discussed: History, Agriculture, Climate, Culture and Institution, Economy, Forests and Fishery, Geography, Landscape, Language, Mining and Quarrying, Population, Resources, Transportation, Vegetation and Animal Life. The first point, History, starts as follows: "Lying off the southeastern coast of the Chinese mainland, Taiwan is China's largest island and forms an integral whole with the mainland. Taiwan has belonged to China since ancient times."
42. The Communiqué was released on December 15, 1978, in Washington and Beijing. This Communiqué states: "The United States of America recognizes the Government of the People's Republic of China as the sole legal Governement of China." (. . .) "The Governement of the United States of America acknowledges the Chinese position that there is but one China and Taiwan is part of China."
43. Articles include: "Taiwan Independence Intolerable," "Taiwan Lawmakers Propose Charter Flight to Mainland," "Most Taiwanese Favor Direct Transport Links with Mainland: Poll," "Businessmen Urge Direct Cross-Straits Links," etc.
44. In French: "Les deux rives du détroit de Taiwan," "Taiwan, une île belle et fertile," "La population," "L'histoire de Taiwan."
45. In French: "Les Chinois d'outre-mer s'opposent à 'l'indépendance de Taiwan' et soutiennent la 'réunification de la patrie' "; "Taiwan: Protestations contre les propos indépendantistes de Chen Shui-bian"; "Provocation dangereuse lancée par Chen Shui-bian, selon des commentateurs de Xinhua [Chine nouvelle] et du *Quotidien du peuple*"; "Des ressortissants chinois résidant dans certains pays critiquent les propos sécessionnistes de Chen Shuibian"; "Le discours de Chen Shuibian sur 'l'indépendance de Taiwan' a été critiqué par l'opinion taiwanaise"; "Une organi- sation 'contre l'indépendance et pour la promotion de la réunification' proposée par les Chinois résidant aux Etats-Unis," etc.
46. The *China Daily* site not only gives access to the daily, but also to affiliated English-language publications: *Hongkong Edition, Business Weekly, Shanghai Star, 21st Century* and *Beijing Weekend*.
47. Seventeen versions are available on the homepage.
48. Then follow *China Pictorial* (*Renmin huabao*), at www.china-pictorial.com; *Renmin Zhongguo* in Japanese, at www.peoplechina.com.cn; *El popola Cinio* in Esperanto at www.chinareport.com. cn; *Chinese Literature*; Beijing Portal at www.beijingportal.com.cn; and a list of other links.
49. The Zhongxin Agency launched an Internet site in Hong Kong as early as 1995, at www. chinanews.com.
50. Among the five links offered by the Chinese-language versions of the China-Taiwan site, one leads back to *People's Daily* and another to Xinhua News Agency.
51. This site should be at www.qiaolian.org, but I have not managed to consult it as the ACTA link leads to a pornographic site, perhaps the result of hacking.
52. Castells, *The Internet Galaxy*, 155.
53. Cross-straits trade amounted to $78 millions in 1979, $1.5 billion by 1987 and more than $30 billions in 2000, according to the MAC. As for direct Taiwanese investment on the mainland, Taipei has identified some 24,000 projects worth nearly $20 billions. Beijing has identified nearly 51,000 projects, the contracted being nearly of $55 billions and the realized amount around $30 billions.
54. Françoise Mengin, "Taiwanese Politics and the Chinese Market: Business's Part in the Formation of a State, or the Border as a Stake of Negotiations," in *Politics in China, Moving Frontiers*, Françoise Mengin and Jean-Louis Rocca (eds): 232–257: "(T)he Chinese authorities have anticipated the formation of [Taiwan Merchants] pressure groups, probably because they were fearing it, and have taken the initiative in institutionalizing this community in order to better

surpervise it. In March 1989, an Association of Taiwan Invested Businesses (*Taizi qiye xiehui*) was established in Beijing, and in June of the same year, an Association of Taiwan Merchants (*Taishang xiehui*) in Shenzhen. During the following years, about 20 of such bodies came into being in the major cities where Taiwan firms had invested. Although this network is highly decentralized, (. . .) (it) is closely controlled: its administration is staffed by members of the United Front as well as by members of the various local Taiwan Affairs Offices, while members of the party are appointed on an honorary basis."

55. Ibid.: the Taiwan Investors Associations (*Dalu Taishang xiehui*), established by the Chinese National Federation of Industry and Commerce (the Taiwanese employer's organization that was closely supervised by the Guomindang), "have been, in a large measure, boycotted by the small- and medium-sized firms, which have considered the move of their governement, both too late and too dominated by the large-sized firms."

56. Seven journals are presented on the site: those of associations in Dongguan, Fuzhou, Shenzhen, Guangzhou, Hangzhou, Foshan, and Shanghai.

57. The *People's Daily* and the *International Business Daily* (*Guoji shang bao*), at www.ibdaily.com.cn.

58. *Mingbao*, at www.mingpaonews.com.

59. It is not made clear when they started counting.

60. The four publications emphasized are: the monthly *Professor Zhang, Taiwanese Businessman* (*Taishang Zhang laoshi*), *Fortune China Monthly* (*Touzi Zhongguo*), the bi-monthly *Information on Hong Kong's Economic and Trade*(*Xianggang jingmao baodao*) and the MAC's *Cross-straits Economic Statistic Monthly* (*Liangan jingji tongji yuebao*). Seven other journals are listed; they also emanate from ROC government bodies. They are not given as much emphasis. Then follows a choice of magazines, including lots of business and finance titles from Taiwan (18) and the PRC (28).

61. According to the site, there are branches in Beijing, Shanghai, Hangzhou, Changsha, Guangzhou, Shantou, Shenyang, Mudanjiang, Wuhan, Quanzhou, Dongguan, Nanjing, Yuezhong, Suzhou, Guilin, Fuzhou, Baoji, Hongkong, Taipei, Taizhong, and in Japan. The Beijing and Shanghai branches both have small single-page sites that give the contact details of the local association.

62. Sina also has local sites in the PRC: in Shanghai, sh.sina.com.cn; Guangdong, gd.sina.com.cn; Chongqing, cq.sina.com.cn; Fujian, fj.sina.com.cn; Sichuan, sc.sina.com.cn; Hunan, hn.sina. com.cn; Yunnan, yn.sina.com.cn; Guangxi, gx.sina.com.cn; Yangzhou, yz.sina.com.cn. There is also a site in English, at englishcenter.sina.com, as well as sites for Japan, Korea, Australia, and Europe.

63. (1) Daniel Mao, Chief Executive Officer, holds degrees from Stanford University and Jiaotong University in Shanghai. (2) Wang Yan, President: University of Paris. (3) Charles Chao, Executive Vice-President (EVP), Chief Financial Officer: University of Texas in Austin, University of Oklahoma, Fudan University in Shanghai. (4) Hurst Lin, EVP of Global Business Development, US General Manager: Stanford University and Dartmouth College. (5) Yuan Chao-yan, Senior Vice-President, Chief Technology Officer: Huazhong Institute of Technology. (6) L.C. Chang, Senior Vice-President, Sales and Marketing, and Brand Management Center: Taiwan Fu Jen Catholic University and Taiwan University. (7) Chen Tong, Vice-President of China Web Operations and Coordinator of Chief Editing Center: Beijing Institute of Technology and Beijing Polytechnic University. (8) Benjamin Tsiang : Vice-President of Sina Global Products, General Manager of Sina Taiwan and East China, Executive Deputy General Manager of Sina Online: National Taiwan University and Stanford University. (9) Albert Yen, General Manager of Sina Hong Kong and South China: no information.

64. Three of the four top managers have worked for major American firms. Daniel Mao served as Vice-President of Walden International Investment Group, overseeing investments in technology-based companies in the United States, China, and Hong Kong. Charles Chao served as an experienced audit manager with Pricewaterhouse Coopers LLP, providing auditing and consulting services for high-tech companies in Silicon Valley. Hurst Lin served as consultant with Ernst & Young Management Consulting Group, focusing on marketing and operations in telecommunications and technology companies.

65. "Since the integration of our Taiwan operations into our East China Operations, we have seen a rise in our cross-strait business where we are better able to serve our Taiwan clients on both sides of the Taiwan Strait," says Benjamin Tsiang, General Manager of Greater East China Region. "As more and more Taiwan and Hong Kong firms increase their investments in the Shanghai-East China region, our worldwide operations center in Shanghai will further enhance our ability to follow these companies' business from Hong Kong and Taiwan to China."

66. Sina is also an excellent illustration of an article by Leng, Tse-Kang, "Economic Globalization and IT Talent Flows across the Taiwan Straits: the Taipei-Shanghai-Silicon Valley Triangle," *Asian Survey* XLII, 2 (March/April 2002): 230–250, or Ngai-Ling Sum's chapter in this volume.

67. These sites include directories: Changxun's Yellowpage (www.csgcc.com), China Big Yellowpage (www.chinabig.com) . . .; sites of large sectors including the China Leather Industry Association (www.china-leather.com) or the Eastern Textile (www.ecf.com.cn); local sites such as China Quanzhou Enterprise Information Website (www.qze.gov.cn), Datong Industry Web (www.dtjww.gov.cn), Ningbo Economic & Technical Development Zone—NETD (www.netd.com.cn et www.netd.gov.cn), etc. The NETD site (*Ningbo jingji jishu kaifa qu*) looks very high-tech, and offers consultation in Chinese (both traditional and simplified characters), English, French, Japanese, and Korean. Consultation figures are given for three versions: as at November 15, 2002, the simplified-characters site had received 57,068 visits, the traditional-characters site 15,384 and the English site 972,687. This means the site is consulted a lot from abroad. According to the site, the NETD, set up by the Chinese government in October 1984, had at the end of 2000 approved 533 foreign-capital companies for an investment totalling $4.6 billions, of which $1.4 billion had actually been realized. Companies include Exxon, BP, Messer, Itochu as well as Taiwanese companies such as Tianyin Computer, Panyin Computer, Jianlong Chemicals, etc. The modern aspect of the site and its heavy traffic in English is worth looking at in the light of observations made by Leng, Tse-Kang, "Economic Globalization and IT Talent Flows across the Taiwan Straits": "Regardless of political differences, overseas Taiwanese entrepreneurs are helping to introduce the Silicon Valley model to China. Mutual economic benefit, rather than political interest, motivates this move. Numerous ethnic Chinese technology asociations in the Silicon Valley region serve as a bridge to link technology and talent between US and Greater China area. The alliance of National Business Information (NBI) and Ningbo City governement is a typical case. In 2000, NBI, an association of Chinese–American computer companies of which Taiwanese firms constitute the majority, helped establish a cooperative relationship with industrial-park developers in Ningbo. Member firms of NBI set up software-development base and other joint ventures in Ningbo. NBI leaders stress that the strength of NBI is its dense network of people in the three largest growth markets in the world—namely China, Taiwan and Silicon Valley."

68. The ROC's French-language online information site, at http://taiwaninfor.nat.gov.tw, signaled on September 11, 2002, that the Taiwanese authorities had just issued a call for hackers to try to get into the various government sites in order to test security measures and that those who succeed would receive a reward. Between November 2001 and July 2002, it went on, hackers based in Wuhan had successfully entered 216 sites spread across 42 state bodies. According to other sources, in the same way that mainland Chinese hackers would have successfully put the Chinese flag on U.S. military sites, they have reportedly replaced the ROC flag with that of the PRC on Taiwanese official sites.

Main Websites Studied (October 15–November 15, 2002)

ROC

www.gio.gov.tw Republic of China, Government Information Office
www.mac.gov.tw/ Mainland Affairs Council
www.President.gov.tw/ The Office of the President

www.sef.org.tw Straits Exchange Foundation
www.seftb.org/ The Straits Exchange Foundation Taiwan Businessmen Information Web
www.chinabiz.org.tw/ The Economic and Commercial Network of Taiwanese Businessmen on the Mainland

PRC

www.china.org.cn, www.china.com.cn China Internet Information Center
www.tailian.org.cn All China Taiwanese Association
www.china-taiwan.com Taiwan Merchants—China
www.tmas.org Taiwan Merchant Association Shenzhen

Useful links

www.cnnic.net.cn China Internet Network Information Center
www.sina.com Sina

CHAPTER SIX

The Internet and the Changing Beijing–Taipei Relations: Toward Unification or Fragmentation?

CHIN-FU HUNG

Introduction

Information and its technologies facilitate the exercise of what has been called "soft power," a concept that differentiates information from the conventional dimensions of "hard power," which is mainly associated with military force and economic influence. Soft power, according to Nye, a former Assistant Secretary of Defense of the United States, means that "A country may obtain the outcomes it wants in world politics because other countries want to follow it, admiring its values, emulating its example, aspiring to its level of prosperity and openness. In this sense it is just as important to set the agenda in world politics and attract others as it is to force them to change through the threat or use of military or economic weapons."[1]

It is becoming a shared belief that the new communications, symbolized by the Internet, demonstrate the most far-reaching force in the changing role of nation-state, in the shaping of new players on the international stage, and hence transforming a novel paradigm in world politics.[2] Internet-based globalization will certainly contribute to the future development of power relations across the Taiwan Strait as a Singaporean minister argues, "the modern nation is like a cell in a larger organism: porous in some respects, walled off in others, part of larger structures, containing substructures, ultimately in control of its own actions."[3] It may be of great significance to examine how and to what extent the cross-straits relations will evolve under the Internet-based globalization.

According to conventional wisdom, cross-straits relations have been a thorny issue that involves much in the historical legacy of the sovereignty dispute arising from the civil war between 1945 and 1949, with each side proclaiming absolute sovereignty over the whole of China. It was not until early 1990s that cross-straits relations moved forward as the first round of the "Koo-Wang Talks" was held in Singapore in 1993, in which "four agreements"[4] were signed to inaugurate at least a more constructive mechanism of official dialogues. Nevertheless the standoff between Republic of China (ROC)—People's Republic of China (PRC) as well as mutual mistrust remain and from time to time severely deteriorate when a critical event springs up, for example, the missile crisis during 1995–1996,[5] following former Taiwan President Li Denghui's visit to the United States as well as the historical first election of state president on the basis of direct universal suffrage. All in all, it is generally perceived that the fundamental cross-straits political deadlock remains unchanged since 1979, even in the wake of the rise of the Chinese third generation of Jiang Zeming's era from 1997 onward and Chen Shuibian's accession to the presidency of Taiwan from May 2000.[6]

While military and political tensions are deadlocked in current Beijing–Taipei relations, trade and investment relation are soaring across the Taiwan Strait and this marks a potentially pivotal area of interaction between the two Chinese societies. This trend is even more prominent now that Taiwan is suffering from an economic recession and ineluctable adjustments of its industry to the intensified new global production network, primarily resulting from China's accession to the World Trade Organization (WTO). Exponentially increasing amounts of overseas investment were pouring from Taiwan into mainland China, with personnel in previous years who were unwilling to work there ironically now wishing to go. It has long been contended that the cross-straits relations would aptly be characterized as "political alienation cum economic integration."[7] It appears even evident from the 1990s onward when Taiwanese electronic/computer industry is being incrementally integrated into an international production network, distribution, and management of goods and services within the globalization context, that transborder investment in mainland China could further reinforce the economic integration within "Greater China,"[8] coupled with the accession of both sides of the Taiwan Straits to the WTO in late 2001. The Internet, an essential component and medium to the globalized network production, is to assume to be part of the driving force that may reshape not only the changing economic and sociocultural conjunction, but also the new epoch of power relations into the twenty-first century linking both sides of the Taiwan Straits.

My main research questions pose: (a) how and to what extent this new Information Technology (IT) of the Internet might reshape cross-straits relations; and (b) to which trajectory would it lead: to unification or fragmentation? These are two primary research questions that this chapter endeavors to answer. It takes as a premise in this research chapter that, in order to elucidate contemporary global political and economic phenomena with particular reference to cross-straits relations, a deeper understanding of the new media—Internet as well as exploration of the Internet's impacts are critical, if not necessary. By employing the International Political Economy (IPE) approach into this chapter, it aims to show that although the Internet will strength Greater China in terms of increasingly integrated economics and socioculture, it seems unlikely to facilitate the political integration process while eroding the sovereignty claims from both sides of the Taiwan Straits, as some Internet pundits claim.

The scheme of the chapter begins with a literature review of general studies of the Internet and power relations, and then moves on to specifically practical Greater China's context. By way of examining relevant literature can we reinforce the belief that the IPE approach may more adequately provide an analytical framework in this chapter. After conceptually elaborating on the interactions between globalization and the NIT, it moves on to consider the Internet development and diffusion in China and Taiwan, intending to investigate whether this globalized phenomenon has had any impact on the new Beijing–Taipei relations. It then shifts to the second question by separately investigating the economic, sociocultural and political dimensions, in turn, within this new context, hoping to probe whether the new direction of relations mediated by the new IT is moving along unification or fragmentation, and in so doing, should shed some light on the study of IT and Beijing–Taipei relations.

International Political Economy Approach

As contended, the relationship between Taiwan and mainland China has been so rigid and Taipei's and Beijing's policies toward each other have been so predictable that for decades they have attracted little attention. Only did it emerge as a contentious policy issue-area and a field of

serious academic study in the late 1980s when the people (not yet
governments) at first began to interchange in various way.[9] More specifically, it turns to be one of the international focus in Asia-Pacific region
since the "missile crisis" held between 1995 and 1996.[10] It attracted
more academic attention in the aftermath of Taiwan's 2000 presidential
election in particular. There are indeed plenty of papers debating the
recent cross-straits relations and the *Cambridge Review of International
Affairs*, is one of them highlighting the *Convergence, Collision or the Status
Quo* for the new era of China–Taiwan relations on its April 2001 issue
and further reviews in 2002. Papers in both issues present a comprehensive review of cross-straits relations from different perspectives: diplomacy, historical background, domestic politics, socioeconomic
developments, national identity, "one country, two systems" formula,
geographic strategic concerns, third-party (particularly the United
States) factors, concerns and interests for the power balance in the Asia-
Pacific, . . . and so forth. Nevertheless it seems rather little work has
been done with regard to the dynamics of information and communication technologies (ICTs). In other words, insufficient literature has
been considering the emerging importance on whether the new global
media—symbolized by the Internet—may be playing a vital part in the
reshaping of power relations across the Taiwan Strait. In addressing the
Internet's impact upon the changing Beijing–Taipei relations, this preliminary study wishes to add to the multifaceted literature that deals
with cross-straits relations studies. Given the inherent constraints upon
ongoing Internet development and complex power structure of both
polities as well as historical legacy of the civil war, it is argued in this
chapter that while the increasing economic and sociocultural interaction
and integration under the globalized Internet context is dramatically
evolving, the political stalemate over the sovereignty dispute still exists
and is likely to remain, at least in the short to medium term.

Ngaire Woods characterizes IPE in the age of globalization as having
three major aspects: internationalization, technological revolution and
liberalization. Internationalization refers to the increase in transactions
among states reflected in flows of trade, investment, and capital. Its
process has been facilitated and is shaped by interstate agreements on
trade, investment, and capital, as well as by domestic policies permitting
the private sectors to transact abroad. The technological revolution effect
of new electronic communication permits firms and other actors to
operate globally with much less regard for location, distance, and borders.
Liberalization is the policy undertaken by states that have made a new
global economy possible.[11] In another article, she reminds us that in

order to understand what is new about globalization, we need carefully to distinguish two aspects of change: a quantitative dimension and a qualitative one. Globalization quantitatively refers to an increase in trade, capital movements, investments, and people across borders, but this assumption could be somehow misleading.[12] Instead, she argues that the answer to the new globalization lies in qualitative changes in international politics—changes in the way people and groups think and identify themselves, and changes in the way states, firms, and other actors perceive and pursue their interests.[13] Woods' insights indeed shed light on the further investigation of the Internet and cross-straits relations, that albeit cross-straits relations are quantitatively and rapidly evolving in terms of economic and sociocultural integration, where the core of relations may likely hinge upon qualitative factors, such as the political constraints in which it still deserves to be weighed highly in the new epoch of relations.

Internet Diffusion and Its Governance

The ICT pervades the whole realm of human activities and is reshaping at accelerated pace the material basis of society. Manuel Castells contends that a technological revolution, centered around information, is fundamentally altering the way we are born, we live, we learn, we work, we produce, we consume, we dream, we fight, or we die.[14] It seems we live in a world that in the expression of Nicholas Negroponte, has become digital.[15] Castells later describes in another work the specific role of the Internet as "the fabric of our lives," adding that "If information technology is the present-day equivalent of electricity in the industrial era, in our age the Internet could be likened to both the electrical grid and the electric engine because of its ability to distribute the power of information throughout the entire realm of human activity."[16] However, this chapter does not suggest that technology absolutely determines society, nor does the realm of society and politics condition the entire course of technological change. Instead, it is likely to be a dialectical interaction that captures the development of both technology and society.

In the Chinese context, as mainland China is gearing up to transform its economy from a central planning into one of the world's key IT-driven economies (dubbed the "New Economy" or "e-commerce"), it provides a crucial test case for other like-minded regimes in the Asian region—Vietnam and North Korea, for example—as to how governments might handle the threat or grasp the opportunities of cyberspace.

A Chinese scholar, Hu Angang, aggressively holds that China, under economic globalization, ought to adopt the knowledge-driven strategy as its most significant national development strategy in the twenty-first century. It is primarily because it can not only narrow the divide between China and developed countries in terms of knowledge development, but also shrink the digital gap between western and eastern China.[17] To date, Internet access is expanding rapidly and extensively chiefly due to direct support by the Chinese government, and the government goes on to promote the use of IT. As we may observe in the recent semiannual survey report on the development of China's Internet, released by the quasi-official China Network Information Centre (CNNIC), the estimated total number of Internet users by mid-2002 is about 45.8 million as Table 6.1 illustrates. If the figure is credible, it has outstripped Japan as the world's second largest Internet user.[18] Anyhow, such an amazing achievement within a rather short period of time coincides with the argument that, although China is a latecomer to the Internet world, once the Chinese leaders become convinced of its significance toward enhancing China's economic prosperity and growth, they begin to play critical roles in unleashing its potential.[19]

Undeniably the Chinese government has acted as a vital driving force for boosting Internet and e-commerce diffusion. In retrospect, it was in 1993 that the authority began to take swift action in embarking upon a series of so-called "Golden Projects"[20] to give it information on and control over the rapid decentralization of decision-making that was taking place as a result of the move toward a market economy.[21] On one hand,

Table 6.1 Internet growth in China

	Computer Hosts	Internet users domain	Names (.cn)	Web sites	International Bandwidth (Mbps)
November 1997	299,000	620,000	4,066	1,500	18.64
July 1998	542,000	11,750,000	9,415	3,700	84.64
January 1999	747,000	2,100,000	18,396	5,300	143
July 1999	1,460,000	4,000,000	29,045	9,906	241
January 2000	3,500,000	8,900,000	48,695	15,153	351
July 2000	6,500,000	16,900,000	99,734	27,289	1,234
January 2001	8,920,000	22,500,000	122,099	265,405	2,799
July 2001	10,020,000	26,500,000	128,362	242,739	3,257
January 2002	12,540,000	33,700,000	127,319	277,100	7,597.5
July 2002	16,130,000	45,800,000	126,146	293,213	10,576.5

Source: CNNIC, *Semiannual Survey Report on the Development of China's Internet* (several years), available online via: http://www.cnnic.net.cn/ develst/repindex-e.shtml.

this was aimed at laying the infrastructure for the digitization of China's telecommunications network, on the other, the central government began using the Internet's infrastructure to improve its own administrative control over provincial and local offices.[22] In November 1998 the authorities further announced the "Government Online Project" that by the end of 1999 and 2000, at least 60 and 80 percent, respectively of China's government offices and ministries were going online: all ministries and provincial authorities would establish their own websites for citizens to consult.[23] China even christened 1999 "The Government Online Year"[24] and 2000 "Enterprise Online Year." As the official *People's Daily* boasted, "While drafting the outlines for China's 10th Five-Year Plan, the State Development Planning Commission received more than 10,000 submissions—of which over 300 were adopted—from ordinary people through special websites."[25] In short, it should be stated that the "Government Online Project" is in fact sponsored by China Telecom and the Information Centre of State Economic and Trade Commission, while funds often come out of the existing budgets of various governmental agencies. The objective is obvious that it may propel government agencies to adopt the Internet and e-commerce.

On the other side of the Taiwan Strait, Internet use in Taiwan began with the Taiwan Academic Network (known as TANet), an academic network built by the Ministry of Education in 1990. Hinet, affiliated to Taiwan's dominant telecommunications operator Chung-Hua Telecom, established their inaugurating commercial Internet service some time later in March 1994. Strengthening its own comparative advantages as well as enhancing global information infrastructures, Taiwan's government has during the previous years advanced the liberalization process of telecommunications sector. The governmental boost of physical resources into the ICTs has also promoted greater Internet use not only in schools, but vigorously throughout various sectors, primarily in the commercial and industrial arenas. Based on a recent survey conducted by Taiwan's Transportation and Communications Ministry in March 2002, Taiwan had an Internet penetration of 37.5 percent, or 8.34 million users out of total population of 23 million.[26]

The Taiwan President Chen Shuibian has also emphasized that in order to rapidly develop a knowledge-based economy and to build Taiwan into a "green silicon island," it will be necessary to develop a "Greater Internet Taiwan." As a result, Taiwan is actively engaged in the work of Internet construction, including an Internet backbone network, an Internet access network, and international Internet links, in order to provide the country's people with rapid, convenient, and inexpensive

Internet services.[27] In line of the grand vision of "Greater Internet Taiwan," the Taiwanese government formulated the *Challenge 2008* comprehensive six-year national development plan in May 2002. Within the plan, it acknowledges that the global economic recession and the transfer of its manufacturing industries into the Chinese mainland have seriously affected Taiwan. It is hoped that Taiwan will take advantage of IT to strengthen research, apply and renovate relevant technologies, upgrade industrial development, and ultimately promote a digital Taiwan in the years ahead.[28]

Electronic Commerce Across the Taiwan Strait

Nicolas Negroponte argues the power of the IT in *Being Digital*: "Like a force of nature, the digital age cannot be denied or stopped. It has four very powerful qualities that will result in its ultimate triumph: decentralising, globalising, harmonising, and empowering."[29] Theorists Alvin and Heidi Toffler in *Creating A New Civilization—The Politics of the Third Wave* foresee that globalization of business and finance required by the advancing "Third Wave" (Information) economies will compel nations to "surrender part of their sovereignty and to accept increasing economic and cultural intrusions from one another."[30] In other words, IT has the ability not merely to make small and medium enterprises as well as large business more competitive in domestic and global markets,[31] but also to reduce time and distance barriers, thereby making commercial transactions from distant and remote areas more economical and efficient. It may be comprehensively depicted in the Foreward of *Report on E-commerce and Development (2002)* within the United Nations Conference on Trade and Development:

> E-commerce is one of the most visible examples of the way in which information and communication technologies (ICT) can contribute to economic growth. It helps countries improve trade efficiency and facilitates the integration of developing countries into the global economy. It allows businesses and entrepreneurs to become more competitive. And it provides jobs, thereby creating wealth.[32]

In developing countries like China,[33] the government there has initiated the so-called "twin-track strategy" that ambitiously try to integrate industrialization into the grand process of informatization.[34] In an official presentation, the Fifth Plenary Session of the 15th Central

Committee of the Chinese Communist Party (CCP) unambiguously pointed out that "Informatisation is the key in promoting industrial advancement, industrialisation and modernisation. Therefore, promoting national economic and social informatisation is a strategic action in the fulfilment of the whole modernisation construction plan."[35] It can be summarized that fostering IT manufacturing industry, telecommunications industry, software industry, and promoting the progress of the national economies as well as social informatization in China become the top priority mission of the Ministry of Information Industry (MII). Based on the *Outline of the Tenth Five-Year Plan for National Economy and Social Development (2001–2005)* proposed by the MII, the importance and the role of the IT in the national economy will principally serve as the basic, pioneering, supporting and strategic industry of the national economy, and increasingly play an important role in promoting the domestic economy, national safety, the welfare of citizens and social development.[36] Premier Zhu Rongji made this clear when delivering the *Tenth Five-Year Plan* at the Fourth Session of the Ninth National People's Congress (NPC) on March 5, 2001. He stated:

> Developing new and high-tech industries, and using information technology to stimulate industrialization. . . . We also need to develop the software industry, strengthen the development of the information infrastructure, and apply digital and network technologies extensively in the technical development, production and marketing activities of enterprises, and in public services and government administration, so that industrialization and the information revolution go hand in hand.[37]

Here informatization is projected as the "engine" of development in the next five years or so. It was no coincidence that, when delivering the keynote *Report* to the 16th Party Congress of the CCP on November 8, 2002, President Jiang Zemin again outlined the main tasks for China's economic development and reform in the first two decades of the twenty-first century. Jiang said that to fulfill the tasks, China must take a new road to industrialization—namely, determinedly to persist in using IT to propel industrialization, which would, in turn, stimulate IT application, blazing a new trail to industrialization.[38] On the other hand, the IT industry in Taiwan has been progressing rapidly for the past decades. It has effectively laid the foundation to become one of the most important high-tech industries in Asia-Pacific. As mentioned earlier, Taiwan has had an Internet penetration of 37.5 percent so far. Competition has intensified in the broadband services market, with the entry of private fixed networking companies. Asymmetric Digital Subscriber Line (ADSL) and cable modem subscribers totaled 920,000 and 210,000, which reflected respective growth rates of 700 percent and 89 percent from 2000.[39] Stimulated chiefly by the wide spectra of opportunities, IT has been pushing the transformation of Taiwan's economy traditionally labor-intensive to knowledge-based industries. However, faced with a massive relocation of production activities to mainland China, the Taiwan government is trying to prevent the domestic industries from hollowing out by encouraging local firms to embrace new ITs to strength their ties to multinational companies.[40] Taiwan is one of the world's largest manufacturers of electronics components and products. As such it is a major consumer and producer of electronics manufacturing equipment, wafer production equipment, IC chips, specialized IT components, and so forth. Nonetheless it should be noted that Taiwan's e-commerce strength, different from that of their counterparts in China, largely owes more to private sector efforts to make their companies locally and globally competitive, and the bulk of the e-commerce development is taking place in the high-tech sector among companies linked to Japanese, European, and American technology firms.[41]

In the late 1990s, the world economy is undergoing a fundamental structural change driven by both globalization and the revolution in ICTs.[42] In line with the global trend of the "digital economy" in industrialized countries and most major developing ones, China and Taiwan are both participating in economic globalization, where the Internet economy is heavily dependent upon infinite expansion of knowledge, high-speed networks, Internet applications, digital marketing and tools, and electronic intermediaries to increase the efficiency of Internet-driven business. It is fairly distinct from the old economy that was primarily based on raw materials and finite resources. It takes as its premise that the diffusion of information is essential to the generation of knowledge, and this in turn is dependent on ICTs, of which the most dynamic is, in turn, the Internet. Compared to overall Internet development in mainland China, Taiwan has the edge in engaging more e-commerce activities. Since Internet diffusion is one of the dominant components of digital economy, it is argued that the rapid growth of IT in China should enhance: the availability of qualified personnel, the diffusion of personal computers, the development of telecom infrastructure, the deployment of digital networks, and active foreign direct investment.[43] Meanwhile, Internet development cannot take off without the fundamental support of related industries such as the ongoing liberalization and reform of the telecommunications sector.

In China, the telecommunications sector is arguably the jewel in the crown of the socialist market economy in terms of growth and revenue. It is accordingly the case that China was consistently frugal in its infrastructure expansion of the basic network, and in so doing managed to resist pressures to enlist significant amounts of foreign capital. However, the China's reform-minded leadership also appreciate the significance of the magnitude of a prosperous telecommunications infrastructure for the success of sustained economic growth, and as a consequence, the government has been struggling to move forward with requisite changes necessary for the accession into the WTO chiefly in the aspects of laws and regulations to assure compliance with its commitments.[44] In a word, given the specific economic, infrastructure and policy environments, e-commerce in China could be characterized as being in a start-up stage with uneven diffusion among different geographic areas and different sectors with their own unique implementation strategies.[45]

There is broad agreement that science, technology, and innovation increasingly determine the performance of modern economies and the competitiveness of industries. Fostering the production and diffusion of scientific and technical knowledge has thus become crucial to ensuring the sustainable growth of national economies in a context of increased competition and globalization as well as the transition to a more knowledge-based economy.[46] In sum, it appears evident that the e-commerce is also driving the two sides of the Taiwan Strait closer, further interconnected and interrelated, partly because of the burgeoning economic ties across the region. Though it is also acknowledged that different rules about foreign exchange, business investment, and freedom on economic activities may hinder freer market growth of the Internet economy, the business dynamics from entrepreneurs from both sides may still manage to overcome by following a carefully crafted path in between government directives and business profits.

The Impact of the Internet upon
Sociocultural Interaction

Technological systems are socially produced. Social production is culturally informed. The Internet is no exception.[47] As such, the Internet as a communication tool provides conduits for different groups of people, who previously would not interact, to connect with one another. In this regard, it imposes cultural exposure and exchange as information is made available regardless of social and cultural boundaries and the policies of nation-states. Therefore ICTs can be argued to be a cultural tool to enable each individual to create, share, and experience a multitude of cultural products.[48] When dealing with the cultural impact of the Internet, it is contended that its impact hinges upon several assumptions and a tight chain of logic: IT brings increased exposure to cultural content; artifacts produced by nonindigenous foreign cultures will lead to rejection of, and decline in, adherence to local values and their substitution by either anomic or foreign values. Change in values and attitudes will, over time, lead to changes in behavior inappropriate to and injurious to the health of indigenous society as a whole.[49] In parallel, Pippa Norris provides an analytical cultural approach, aiming to understand the impact of the Internet by examining whether the predominant values, attitudes, and beliefs found within the online world are distinct from the broader political culture. Specifically, she argues that if the culture (society) on the Internet affects both new groups and new values, then this has the potential for the greatest transformation of public opinion.[50] Both arguments about the impact of the Internet upon culture/society have contributed to a better understanding of the ongoing changes in the two Chinese societies. Nonetheless, retrospectively one should also take notice of the phenomenon of dramatic change presented in modern China: China formerly shares common roots of Confucianism but later displays a unique communist culture characterized as collectivism in general and its own political culture in particular. During the Cold War, culture and media were capitalized by both Taiwan and China to play an opposing role in the propaganda battles for respective legitimacy consolidation. Nonetheless, the most recent change in the cultural relations has symbolized the beginning of a new direction toward the normalization of their cultural relations.[51] With the continuing deep-rooted economic reform and especially Internet diffusion in recent years, the convergence of two distinct cultures is now emerging in many respects. Pop culture is no doubt one of them.

A Singaporean scholar wrote about the phenomenon of present-day pop culture in Greater China, depicting it as follows: "In contrast to the absence of a common grand philosophical discourse on Chinese culture and identity, in this age of globalized consumption, there is no doubting of the fact that there are floods of popular cultural products in various Chinese languages crossing borders everyday among the overseas Chinese communities globally."[52] David Shambaugh further stresses that the Chinese popular culture now being shared among all three societies—China, Taiwan, and Hong Kong—has become a vital component linking Greater China together.[53] It is virtually true but it presents a slightly different picture nowadays because the Internet and new media technologies have been enriched by the cultural development. For instance, recently the much-adored Taiwanese TV shows, Meteor Garden and F4 (Flowers Four), made a swift hit among Chinese communities, despite China's ban on them as a threat to young minds. The episodes are overwhelmingly popular, facilitated significantly by the new technology—the Internet, and a Chinese youth culture that spans Taiwan and Hong Kong as well as overseas Chinese communities, shows, commercial interests and popular demands are competing directly with the CCP's orthodoxy—and increasingly bending the Party to their will. As argued, although popular culture around the world often has taken on the established order, here the battles rage within the CCP itself as well. Some parts of the ruling machinery try to harness the market to produce booming profits—government policy for the last two decades—while other parts attempt vainly to maintain ideological and cultural control, fearing power could slip from their hands.[54]

When the China State Administration of Radio, Film, and Television banned the Taiwanese series "Meteor Garden" in March 2002 because it "misleads teenagers,"[55] Chinese youth were forced to switch to watching it on the Web or bought pirated video compact discs. Despite the government's regular heavy-handed crackdowns, Internet cafés in their thousands are flourishing all over China and they provide many outlets for cultural and even political opposition to government policies.[56] In this case, more evidence has shown that censorship is not as easy as the authorities envisaged in the age of the Internet.[57] As the technology has substantially improved and more and more Netizens can afford to get wired, the sociocultural integration across the Taiwan Strait appears apparent.[58] And we may even proclaim that a digital revolution is forging new bridges between youth from each side of Chinese societies, regardless of the prevalent political skirmishes. In this sense, culture in modern societies is "extensively" and increasingly mediated by the institutions and mechanisms of mass communication.[59] To put it bluntly, contemporary culture is manifestly more heavily information-laden than any of its predecessors.

With the introduction of many-to-many communications capabilities like the Internet, the modern societies like Taiwan and China are increasingly reminded of the complex global networks that participate in the mediation of culture.[60] Networked communications provides a means through which both sides of the Taiwan Straits can insure connections with the latest news, entertainments and information. Take the recent tragedy occurred in mainland China for example, a mass food poisoning case occurred on September 14, 2002 in Nanjing, capital of east China's Jiangsu Province. The victims were mostly students from four schools and transient workers from a construction site in Tangshan, a small town to the east of Nanjing. An early report put the death toll at more than 40, but the official Chinese news agency would only say, "a number have died." In fact, the Chinese government tried to clamp down on reports of a mass fatal poisoning like this, but provoked a wave of criticism, for instances, on the "Qiangguo Luntan" (Strong Country Forum) run by the *People's Daily* or chat room in sina.com. Angry comments were posted asking why it was taking so long for casualty figures to be released, while others compared the Chinese media unfavorably with the western press.[61]

Indeed, reports in China's state-controlled media on the exact numbers of casualties have been mixed and confused. The official *Xinhua News Agency* reported that 41 people had died and up to 400 had been made ill by the poisoning. Nevertheless, that report was quickly deleted and replaced by an earlier story saying only that "a number of victims" had died and more than 200 were poisoned. Such confusion is not unusual in the reporting of disasters in China where the state media often face strict controls in their coverage of incidents deemed sensitive by the central government.[62] In the meantime, this mass poisoning incident was without delay disseminated to Taiwan's audiences either through traditional media of TV or the Internet. In fact, people from both sides of the Taiwan Straits are showing much concern about things directly and indirectly affecting them, since increasing tourists and business people are both touring and making business trips to and within the Greater China. As a matter of fact, tourism has recently also contributed to heightened economic and cultural activities across the Taiwan Strait. Apart from the commercial and business concerns, the impact of tourism as part of a global flow of information can be seen at least on two interrelated layers: societal and individual.[63] Based on the latest figures released by the Taiwan Mainland Affairs Council, the exchange of visits from 1988 to June 2002 across the Taiwan Strait has risen exponentially, totaling more than 25,257,000 numbers of person trips across China, within which 777,479 have crossed to Taiwan, from the year of lifting visit exchange ban in 1988, beginning with 437,700 and 381, respectively.[64] This stepping up of contacts is now spawning a pan-Chinese culture that is spreading and gaining speed as the digital global village links the two sides of the Taiwan Straits into an arguably "virtual" union.[65]

This social dimension of the Internet across the Taiwan Strait seems to propel or favor the development of new and virtual communities, rather than inducing citizen isolation, severing people's ties with society, and eventually, with their "real" world.[66] However, the profound impact of the new knowledge revolution on intersociety as well as interculture can not only be a force of globalization as both sides of economies integrate more closely into each other—albeit not necessarily on equal terms—but also a force of fragmentation as it subverts, to some extent, the capacity of national government to manage its effects. As a result, while cultural affinities, societal connections, and economic interaction mediated by IT may lay the foundation for future political integration,[67] a formal unification framework that would eventually resolve the sovereignty issue seems unlikely in the short or medium run as discussed in the ensuing section.

Internet, Sovereignty, and Its Fragmentation Relations

The growth of Internet diffusion has also been one of the most crucial aspects when considering future bilateral relations across the Taiwan Strait. It is mainly because some works have convincingly held the belief that the IT is able to erode the sovereignty of the state in all societies, in particular developing ones.[68] In other words, such commentators proclaim that the traditional concept of sovereignty is being challenged and may even decline with the diffusion of IT associated with globalization. Proponents have seen in the Internet a threat to sovereignty because the Internet challenges the three historic functions of the state: providing national security, regulating economic activities, and protecting and promoting civic and moral values. In short, the Internet threatens the government's ability to control power, wealth, and morals within specified territory.[69] Most discussions of the fact that state sovereignty is being eroded by the Internet in the globalized context are concerned fundamentally with questions of "control" not authority.[70] In fact, there are two ways in which they may assault the sovereignty of nation-state: "top-down" and "bottom-up" trajectories, both driven and empowered by the IT and new communication technologies. On one hand, the "top-down" trajectory results from the many cross-border flows that intrude onto the traditional areas of rights and responsibilities of central governments. On the other, the "bottom-up" trajectory, refers to the use of IT by grassroots nongovernmental actors, such as nongovernmental organizations (NGOs), small businesses, and individuals.[71] What I have argued earlier about the economic, societal and cultural aspects can also come convergence within the question of state sovereignty on both sides of the Taiwan Straits in the Information Age. Consequently, the discussion later intends to disprove the contending hypothesis that the Internet will eventually create a borderless state since the sovereignty is stifled, and answer the second research question that to what trajectory would it lead to unification or fragmentation?

To begin with, I will examine the "bottom-up" force in considering the practical development of both sides of the Taiwan Straits. In Taiwan, as it has democratized and more importantly "Taiwanized" (*bentuhua* or localized) over the last two decades, the political clout of the "One China" stance has been diminishing and blurring. Kenneth Lieberthal potently argues that there are at least three reasons associated with this phenomenon: first, Taiwan's population is overwhelmingly Taiwanese, with mainlanders (those who crossed over the mainland at the conclusion of the civil war) a small minority of less than 10 percent; second, Taiwanese lived under the rule of Japan from 1895 to 1945, but under the aegis of the mainland for only a few years in the late 1940s before the seat of the ROC government moved to Taipei; third, by the late 1990s, Taiwan had developed a (political) culture quite different from that on the mainland—highly educated, heavily middle class, Western orientated, and democratic.[72]

So far, however, Beijing seems either unable to appreciate or to deal effectively with Taiwan's changing political climate. The rise of Chen Shuibian's Democratic Progressive Party (DPP) has challenged and questioned mainland China by denying the "1992 consensus" (dubbed as *Jiuer gongshi*) of the "one China principle" and by rejecting Beijing's requirement that Taipei accepts the "principle" as a prerequisite for dialogue, preferring instead to put the "principle" itself up for one of the issues for future political dialogue. Without offering enough and effective incentives for Taipei to consider political reconciliation, Beijing continues to practice intimidation tactics, including the rapid and huge deployment of missiles across the Strait, no matter how repeatedly it indicates its preference to reach a peaceful settlement over the "Taiwan Question." This coercive policy has proven counterproductive, reducing rather than enhancing the confidence and trust necessary for any constructive dialogue to be resumed.[73]

Regardless of Beijing's efforts to increase its economic clout over Taiwan, the stout hold on the sovereignty persistently remains uncompromising,[74] but the Internet itself provides a crucial and approachable means to verify whether the sovereignty concern is being challenged or even eroded as some pundits predict. The core concept employed here is "public opinion" that is mediated by the Internet—which is nicknamed the *Dianzi dazibao* (electronic version of the big-character posters, which is believed to be the most efficient and effective means of mobilizing public opinion during the Cultural Revolution). One of the Internet's impact upon public opinion is that it provides opportunities for individuals to air their political views in chat forums, on bulletin boards, and so on, where previously they only talked among themselves.

We may observe the rapidly growing popular nationalist reaction partook by the Internet chat rooms, when, for example, atrocities committed against ethnic Chinese in Indonesia during a riot in May 1998 took place. The Internet became a conduit to disseminate and publicize information of outrage first arising from neighboring Southeast Asian countries, and then Taiwan, Hong Kong and the rest of world, particular in the United States, and finally reached Netizens in mainland China. It is of great significance as Christopher R. Hughes argues that the Internet in that event became a site for expressing dissent by calling into question the nationalist credentials of the CCP after the Beijing authorities refused to grant permission for the demonstration.[75] The Chinese "hackers"[76] (*Hongke*), claimed as their first patriotic nationalist defense on the Chinese Internet history, vandalized or defaced lots of Indonesian websites, including Government and Business webpages, with obscene or racist anti-Indonesian rhetoric. For instance, a certain Indonesian website (http://tokobudi.co.id) was hacked, leaving the message that follows:

YOUR WEB SITE HACKED BY A GROUP OF HACKERS FROM CHINA!!
STOP KILLING CHINESE!!!!
MOB STOPPING ATROCITY!!!
SHIT!!! (Friday, August 07, 1998; 11:59:48 +0900)[77]

Widespread public debates on politically sensitive issues like the cross-straits relations are usually unseen by the traditional media, but may be revived in Internet chat rooms. For example, when the "Special State-to-State" (*teshu de guo-yu-guo de guanxi*) relations, commonly referred to as the "Two-States Theory," was proposed by former President Li Denghui in July 1999 to characterize cross-straits contacts, it extremely angered both CCP leaders and lots of Chinese mainlanders. This sort of over-reaction, in particular from the mainland side was spiritedly debated on the Internet in the real time across the Taiwan Strait, with later hactivism being rampant across both sides of the Taiwan Straits, leading to defacement of public as well as business Web servers with populist sentiment expressions.[78] It was further fueled when George W. Bush stated that the United States would do whatever it takes to help Taiwan defend itself from Chinese attack, and the sale to Taiwan of a robust package of defensive arms, after the Sino–U.S. relations deteriorated following the Spy Plane collision on April 1, 2001. Alan R. Kluver argues: "In a time of international crisis, the Internet did little to alleviate tensions," after examining another fervently online issue of the U.S. Spy Plane incident.[79] Shanthi Kalathil similarly contends that the Beijing leadership is aware that it must deftly manage nationalist sentiment on the Internet in order to maintain their legitimacy. If properly massaged, such sentiment can significantly bolster the popularity of the CCP.[80] Indeed, PRC textbooks and the official press socialize people into a highly suspicious attitude toward governments in Japan, the United States and Taiwan, as they are the "hot-button" issues of Chinese nationalism, and the rapidly growing popular press and Internet chat rooms often take an even harder line.[81] Yet, it should also be acknowledged that hackers' interests are not necessarily molded by nationalism; they hack governmental institutions and multinational corporations as well.

Second, I will consider the "bottom-up" force to the challenge of sovereignty from domestic civil societal organization. The best-known Internet-based challenge arises from the Falun Gong group.[82] It was a large Falun Gong-led demonstration, mostly silent and composed, involving 10,000 of the group's followers outside the government leadership compound at Zhongnanhai in April 1999, that first drew the Beijing authorities' attention to the severe threat. As Vivienne Shue contends, because the Falun Gong precisely does represent such a deep-going challenge—a challenge to the very foundations of the state's authority and legitimacy—government officials insist on extermination of the threat.[83] By labeling the group *xie jiao* (heterodox organization or evil cult) and cracking down relentlessly on its practitioners, the Falun Gong, within and outside physical territory, has been forced to rely heavily upon the Internet to wage campaigns or conduct online and offline dialogues despite official hostility.[84] The Falun Gong story appears to be as much about technology as it is about religion; it offers a fascinating glimpse of an ancient religious tradition that is mutating rapidly as it makes the leap into cyberspace.[85] Virtually there are also supporters all over the world, including Taiwan and Hong Kong. The most recent incident that arose uneasy tension between authorities in Beijing and Taipei was that supporters of the outlawed Falun Gong movement had staged a "TV hijacking" on September 9, 2002 by interrupting transmissions on a satellite system that broadcasted to every corner of China.[86] Beijing then charged that Falun Gong followers had used Taiwan as a base to hack into China's satellite television stations. But Taiwan downplayed an allegation and government spokesman instead alleged Chinese hackers had targeted Taiwan, and had broken into 42 government computer systems and 216 Taiwanese websites from November 2001 to July 2002.[87] China's Taiwan Affairs Office held a press conference to demand that Taiwan takes immediate steps to halt the illegal broadcasts because the Falun Gong had been sabotaging cross-straits relations over the years, and Taiwan's conniving with them had compounded the problem.[88]

No matter which version is true, what mostly has drawn attention here is whether dissident groups within or outside China like the Falun Gong have effectively challenged the authorities' capability to defend sovereignty in the Information Age. Regrettably, there is relatively little evidence to date that the group has had any significant political impact on the heavy-handed initiatives from Chinese government. Rather, an increasing number of works, such as recent one by Shanthi Kalathil, has argued, "Albeit some mainland Chinese followers possess the technical prowess necessary to access overseas Falun Gong sites and evade capture, the government's campaign to eradicate the bulk of the domestic movement—partly through arrests and brainwashing—appears to be succeeding."[89] A timely report conducted by RAND has similarly suggested that Beijing's countermeasures have been relatively successful to date in tackling the political use of the Internet by Chinese dissidents, no matter whether they are from the Falun Gong group, Tibetan exiles, or others who use the Internet for purposes considered subversive by Beijing, no matter where they are at home or overseas.[90] It seems unlikely in the political arena that the new technology could in the short term effectively erode the sovereignty of the Party state like Communist China primarily due to government's relentlessly repressive initiatives, let alone facilitate the easing of cross-straits tensions in terms of political as well as military threats.

In summary, authorities across the Taiwan Strait have so far maneuvred adequately to both alleviate cyber-nationalism and transform the cyber popular sentiments into individual legitimacy consolidation, particular on the part of Beijing. There is to date insufficient evidence to suggest that "top-down" as well as "bottom-up" force have effectively deprived much rights or responsibility associated with the State's sovereignty. Given the prevalent and frequent references to sovereignty, one would anticipate officials in both sides of the Taiwan Straits to be wary of the corrosive effects of globalization on sovereignty. Simply put, it seems that the Internet's impact on the erosion of sovereignty can be exaggerated whether to establish constructive political integration or even to carve out a timetable for future unification. Instead, it may present a trajectory neither toward unification nor fragmentation, but a dialectical relationship, depending upon internal as well as external forces mediated by the Internet for either future convergence or divergence to happen.

Conclusion

As Peter Ferdinand argues, "So far the assessment of the Internet impact upon politics has been cautious. But over a longer period of time it still seems reasonable to assume that the Internet will transform politics, both domestically and internationally. This is because it will be reinforced by another major factor—generational change."[91] Since the widely held agreement about the striking effects of the Internet is to demonstrate its ability to spread ideas and products across national boundaries chiefly attributed to the potency of globalization,[92] we may, by the same token, have reasons to extrapolate the long-term impact of the Internet upon cross-straits relations to be greater integrated and unified, since the youths from both sides are becoming more familiar with computers and the World Wide Web as they have grown up. But in the short to medium term, the political relations seems uncertain and may thereby exhibit a dialectical relationship, depending upon internal as well as external forces for convergence or divergence. In addition, it ought to be reminded that we are still in the early stage of technological innovation, with probably the first glimmers of Internet implications/impacts ahead. It is in fact too soon to make a final judgment at this phase. Nevertheless, one thing seems certain: China's and Taiwan's modernization is being inextricably linked with the global phenomenon of the Internet.

To sum up, one of the objectives of this chapter has been to dissect cross-straits relations in the light of the Internet. Though there are great deal of articles tackling cross-straits relations, there have been relatively few works concentrating on the impact of the Internet on this theme. Being a preliminary research, it hopes to shed some light on NITs and power relations in the Greater China's political economy studies. In this chapter, the striking characteristics of economic integration, the triangle economies (China, Taiwan, and Hong Kong), e-commerce vibrancy and sociocultural interaction across the Taiwan Strait are basically driven by private initiatives or market forces; intergovernmental coordination has been relatively weak, and cross-straits relations have also been political unstable and unsettled. The Internet has at least contributed to a mediating role in improving cross-straits relations. We may anticipate that it may play an even more important part as both sides of the Taiwan Straits are increasingly drawn into the magnet of globalization.

Notes

1. Joseph S. Nye Jr, *The Paradox of American Power: Why the World's Only Superpower Can't Go it Alone* (Oxford: Oxford University Press, 2002): 8–9.

2. There are increasingly a great deal of articles and books dealing with ITs and global politics. See, for example, James N. Rosenau and J.P. Singh (eds.), *Information Technologies and Global Politics: The Changing Scope of Power and Governance* (Albany, NY: State University of New York Press, 2002); W. Lance Bennett and Robert M. Entman, *Mediated Politics: Communication in the Future of Democracy* (Cambridge: Cambridge University Press, 2001).

3. G. Yeo, "The Soul of Cyberspace," *New Perspectives Quarterly*, 12, 4 (1995): 23.

4. This first round of Koo-Wang talks resulted in several agreements dealing with document authentication, mail, and future meetings. Provisions were made for regular and non-periodic meetings between the Straits Exchange Foundation (SEF) and the Association for Relations across the Taiwan Strait (ARATS) officials.

5. There are lots of works tackling this theme, see, for example, Zhao, Suisheng (ed.), *Across the Taiwan Strait: Mainland China, Taiwan, and the 1995–1996 Crisis* (New York and London: Routledge, 1999).

6. T.Y. Wang, "Lifting the 'No Haste, Be Patient' Policy: Implications for Cross-Strait Relations," *Cambridge Review of International Affairs*, 15, 1 (April 2002): 131–139; Linda Chao, Ramon H. Myers, and Jialin Zhang, "A China Divided since the Turnover of Political Power in Taiwan," *Cambridge Review of International Affairs*, 15, 1 (April 2002): 115–122; Steven M. Goldstein, "The Taiwan Strait: A Continuing Status Quo or Deadlock?" *Cambridge Review of International Affairs*, 15, 1 (April 2002): 85–94; Jean-Pierre Cabestan, "Integration without Reunification," *Cambridge Review of International Affairs*, 15, 1 (April 2002): 95–103; John Fuh-sheng Hsieh, "How Far Can Taiwan Go?," *Cambridge Review of International Affairs*, 15, 1 (April 2002): 105–113; Dennis Van Vranken Hickey and Li, Yitan, "Cross-Strait Relations in the Aftermath of the Election of Chen Shui-bian," *Asian Affairs*, 28, 4 (Winter 2002): 201–216; T.Y. Wang, "Cross-Strait Relations in the Aftermath of Taiwan's 2000 Presidential Election," paper presented at the 2001 Annual Meeting of the American Political Science Association; Zheng, Shiping, "Changing Dynamics and Future Scenarios of Cross-Strait Relations," *Cambridge Review of International Affairs*, 14, 2 (July 2001): 175–186; Zhang, Wei, "Economic Integration and Its Impacts on Cross-Strait Relations," *Cambridge Review of International Affairs*, 14, 2 (July 2001): 201–211; Cheng, Tun-jen and Vincent W.C. Wang, "Between Convergence and Collision: Whither Cross-Strait Relations?," *Cambridge Review of International Affairs*, 14, 2 (July 2001): 239–256.

7. Wu, Yu-Shan, "Liangan guanxi de bianhua yu qianjing: jingji hezuo, zhengzhi shuli" (The Change and Prospects of cross-straits Relations: Economic Cooperation and Political Alienation) in *Maixiang ershiyi shiji de Taiwan* (Taiwan: Moving Towards the 21st Century), Hsu, Ch'ing-Fu (ed.) (Taipei: Cheng-chung, 1994).

8. Economically speaking, Greater China involves the expanding commercial interactions among mainland China, Taiwan, and Hong Kong. For more about the concept of "Greater China": its origins, usages, variations, difficulties, and realities, see Harry Harding, "The Concept of 'Greater China': Themes, Variations and Reservation," in *Greater China: The Next Superpower?*, David Shambaugh (ed.) (Oxford: Oxford University Press, 1995): 8–34.

9. Su, Chi, "Domestic Determinants of Taiwan's Mainland Policy," paper presented at the Peace Across the Taiwan Strait Conference, 23–25 May 2002, Asian Studies Centre, Oxford University.

10. Wu, Yu-shan, "Theorizing on Relations across the Taiwan Strait: Nine Contending Approaches," *Journal of Contemporary China*, 9, 25 (November 2000): 407–428.

11. Ngaire Woods, "International Political Economy in an Age of Globalization," in *The Globalization of World Politics: An Introduction to International Relations*, John Baylis and Steve Smith (ed.) (Oxford: Oxford University Press, 2001): 290.

12. She illustrates the misleading phenomenon with an example on the basis of an empirical survey of data, transfer in goods, movement of capital or people in 17 countries from 1913–1993. It manifests there is no necessary causality between globalization of IPE and interdependence or transnationalism because the measured items do not increase dramatically. See Ngaire Woods, "The Political Economy of Globalization," in *The Political Economy of Globalization*, Ngaire Woods (ed.) (London: Macmillan Press, 2000): 1–2.

13. Ibid.

14. Manuel Castells, *The Rise of the Network Society* (Oxford: Blackwell, 2000).

15. Nicholas Negroponte, *Being Digital* (London: Coronet Book/ Hodder & Stoughton, 1995).

16. Manuel Castells, *The Internet Galaxy* (Oxford: Oxford University Press, 2001): 1.

17. Hu, Angang, *Zhongguo zhanlue gouxiang* (Strategy of China) (Hangzhou: Zhejiang renmin chubanshe, 2002): 15.

18. "China Surpasses Japan in Internet Population, Rating Service Says," *People's Daily Online* (April 23, 2002), available online via: http://english.peopledaily.com.cn/200204/23/print20020423_94532.html (accessed: October 19, 2002).

19. Dali L. Yang, "The Great Net of China," *Harvard International Review*, 22, 4 (Winter 2001): 64–69.

20. The "Golden Projects" consists of several sub-projects, including primarily, Golden Bridge—a national public economic information communication network aiming to connect ministries and state-owned enterprises and to build the infrastructure backbone over which other information services will run; Golden Card—an electronic money project which aims at setting up a credit-card verification scheme and an inter-bank, inter-region clearing system; Golden Customs—a national foreign economic trade information network project; Golden Marco—a national economic macro policy technology system; Golden Tax—a computerized tax return and invoice system project; Golden Gate—a foreign trade information network aimed at improving export–import trade management; Golden Enterprise—an industrial production and information distribution system; Golden Intelligence—the China education and research Network (CERnet); Golden Agriculture—an overall agricultural administration and information service system; Golden Info—a state statistical information project, and Golden Cellular—a mobile communications production and marketing project.

21. This concept is claimed somewhat akin to the idea prevalent in the USSR in the 1980s that IT could be used to make central planning more effective and to better manage the Soviet economy. See Marcus Franda, *Launching into Cyberspace: Internet Development and Politics in Five World Regions* (Boulder, Colorado: Lynne Rienner Publishers, 2002): 188; Frank Ellis, *From Glasnost to the Internet* (London: Macmillan Press, 1999).

22. See, for example, Zhang, Junhua, "China's 'Government Online' and Attempts to Gain Technical Legitimacy," *ASIEN*, 80 (July 2001), available online via: http://web.syr.edu/~ztan/Gov2.pdf (accessed: October 20, 2001). Meanwhile, China is also hoping to introduce more computer and IT into its taxation system in a bid to improve efficiency and revenue. See, "China to Increase Use of IT in Tax-collection," *Xinhua News Agency* (July 31, 2002), available online via: http://202.84.17.73:7777/Detail.wct?RecID=26&SelectID=1&ChannelID=6034&Page=2 (accessed: September 25, 2002).

23. *Zhengfu shangwang gongcheng: Huigu yu zhanwang* (Government Online Project: Review and Goals and Aspirations), available online via: http://www.gov.cn/govonlinereview/6future/01.htm (accessed: March 6, 2001). Besides, more detailed accounts of Internet development and diffusion in China can be found in William Foster and Seymour E. Goodman, *The Diffusion of the Internet in China*, available online via: http://cisac.stanford.edu/docs/chinainternet.pdf

(accessed: December 20, 2000); Milton Mueller and Tan, Zixiang, *China in the Information Age: Telecommunications and the Dilemmas of Reform* (Westport: Praeger, 1997); Lin, Jintong, Liang, Xiongjian, and Wan, Yan (eds.), *Telecommunications in China: Development and Prospects* (Huntington, NY: Nova Science Publishers, 2001); Fan, Xing, *Communications and Information in China: Regulatory Issues, Strategic Implications* (Lanham, MD: University Press of America, 2001); Tan, Zixiang, William Foster, and Seymour Goodman, "China's State-Coordinated Internet Infrastructure," *Communications of the ACM*, 42, 6 (June 1999): 44–52.

24. "1999: The Government Online Year," *People's Daily* (January 3, 1999): 4.
25. "Internet Brings Sweeping Changes to China," *People's Daily* (October 20, 2002), available online via: http://english.peopledaily.com.cn/200210/20/eng20021020_105367.shtml (accessed: October 25, 2002).
26. ROC, Government Information Office (June 2, 2002). available online via: http://www.gio.gov.tw/ (accessed: September 18, 2002).
27. ROC Ministry of Transportation and Communications, *Annual Report 2000—Internet Development—Bringing the Internet into Everyday Life Roaming the Virtual E-world*, available online via: http://www.dgt.gov.tw/English/About-dgt/publication/89/development-89.htm (accessed: March 12, 2002).
28. ROC Government Information Office, *Challenge 2008—The Six-year National Development Plan* (May 21, 2002), available online via: http://www.gio.gov.tw/taiwan-website/4-oa/20020521/2002052101.html (accessed: August 7, 2002).
29. Nicholas Negroponte, *Being Digital*, 229.
30. The Third Wave is being argued as what the world is entering now. The previous waves were the agricultural wave—the first wave, and the industrial wave—the second wave. The third wave that the Tofflers speaks of basically involves the advent of computers, and their involvement into our daily lives. See Alvin and Heidi Toffler, *Creating A New Civilization—The Politics of the Third Wave* (Atlanta: Turner Publishing Inc., 1995).
31. Hernan Riquelme, "Commercial Internet Adoption in China: Comparing the Experience of Small, Medium and Large Businesses," *Internet Research: Electronic Networking Applications and Policy*, 12, 3 (2002): 276–286.
32. United Nations Conference on Trade and Development (UNCTAD), *E-commerce and Development Report, 2002* (Ref. No: UNCTAD/SDTE/ECB/2) (November 18, 2002), available online via: http://www. unctad.org/en/docs//ecdr2002_en.pdf (accessed: November 30, 2002).
33. Other developing countries such as Vietnam have pursued a similar strategy to China. For example, in the Directive No. 58-CT/TW of October 17, 2000, which was promulgated by the Central Executive Committee of Communist Party of Vietnam, it amplified on the possibilities to leapfrog in successfully realizing the cause of industrialization and modernization by the use and development of IT. See The Central Executive Committee of Communist Party of Vietnam, *Directive No. 58-CT/TW of October 17, 2000* (unofficial translation), available online via: http://www.gaia.ca/appendixd.pdf (accessed: November 30, 2002).
34. For more about China's "twin-tract strategy," see, for example, Dai, Xiudian, "Towards a Digital Economy with Chinese Characteristics?," *New Media and Society*, 4, 2 (June 2002): 144.
35. Ministry of Information Industry (MII), *Tenth Five-Year Plan (2001–2005)—Information Industry*. The English translation is provided by the Telecommunications Research Project of Asian Studies at the University of Hong Kong, available online via: http://www.trp.hku.hk/infofile/china/2002/10-5-yr-plan.pdf (accessed: September 14, 2002).
36. Ibid.
37. *Outline of the Tenth Five-Year Plan for National Economy and Social Development (2001–2005)* Part II, available online via: http://www.chinatranslate.net/en1/era/era02.htm (accessed: August 16, 2002).
38. "Jiang Zemin Outlines Main Economic Tasks for China," *China Daily* (November 8, 2002), available online via: http://english.peopledaily.com.cn/200211/08/eng20021108_106484.shtml (accessed: November 8, 2002).

39. Government Information Office, *The Republic of China Yearbook 2002—Taiwan 2002 (Science and Technology)*, available online via: http://www.gio.gov.tw/taiwan-website/5-gp/yearbook/chpt18-3.htm#box18-6 (accessed: July 17, 2002).

40. Chen, Tain-Jy, *Globalization and E-Commerce: Growth and Impacts in Taiwan* (November 2001). Publication of the Center for Research on Information Technology and Organization, University of California, Irvine, available online via: http://www.crito.uci.edu/git/publications/pdf/taiwanGEC.pdf (accessed: September 20, 2002).

41. Charles V. Trappey and Amy J.C. Trappey, "Electronic Commerce in Greater China," *Industrial Management & Data Systems*, 101, 5 (2001): 201–209.

42. Matti Pohjola, "The New Economy: Facts, Impacts and Polices," *Information Economics and Policy*, 14, 2 (June 2002): 133–144.

43. Zhao, Hongxin, "Rapid Internet Development in China: A Discussion of Opportunities and Constraints on Future Growth," *Thunderbird International Business Review*, 44, 1 (January/February 2002): 124–127.

44. Kenneth J. DeWoskin, "The WTO and the Telecommunications Sector in China," *The China Quarterly*, 167 (September 2001): 630–654.

45. For more about recent discussions, see, for example, Tan, Zixiang (Alex), and Wu, Ouyang, *Global and National Factors Affecting E-Commerce in China* (August 2002). Publication of the Center for Research on Information Technology and Organization, University of California, Irvine, available online via: http://crito.uci.edu/publications/pdf/GEC2_China.pdf (accessed: September 20, 2002). In addition, a special survey conducted in 2001 by China's State Economic and Trade Commission specified nine factors that hindered China's e-commerce development: network safety, internet infrastructure construction, social business credit problem, e-commerce related laws and regulations, standardization problem, network payment, canonization degree of enterprises on e-commerce, network market scale, IT and management talents. See, "Nine Factors Hampering China's E-commerce Development: Survey," *People's Daily* (December 21, 2001), available online via: http://english.peopledaily.com.cn/200112/20/eng20011220_ 87144.shtml# (accessed: October 13, 2002).

46. OECD, *OECD Science, Technology and Industry Outlook 2002* (Paris: OECD, 2002): 23.

47. Manuel Castells, *The Internet Galaxy*, 36.

48. Brian Carolan, "Technology, Schools and the Decentralisation of Culture," *First Monday*, 6, 8 (August 2001), available online via: http://www.firstmonday.dk/issues/issue6_8/carolan/index.html (accessed: December 17, 2001).

49. Ernest J. Wilson III, *Globalization, Information Technology, and Conflict in the Second and Third Worlds: A Critical Review of the Literature* (New York: Rockefeller Brothers Fund, 1998): 24. available online via: http://www.rbf.org/Wilson_Info_Tech.pdf (accessed: September 26, 2001).

50. Pippa Norris, *Digital Divide?: Civic Engagement, Information Poverty, and the Internet Worldwide* (Cambridge: Cambridge University Press, 2001): 195–216.

51. Hong, Junhao and Sun, Jungkuang, "Taiwan's Film Importation from China: A Political Economy Analysis of Changes and Implication," *Media, Culture & Society*, 21, 4 (1999): 543.

52. Chua, Beng-huat, "Pop Culture China," *Singapore Journal of Tropical Geography*, 22, 2 (2001): 115.

53. David Shambaugh, "Introduction: The Emergence of Greater China," *The China Quarterly*, 136 (December 1993): 653–659.

54. John Pomfret, "Band Hits Sour Note in China: Group's Appeal Shows Rift between Culture, Party," *Washington Post* (June 10, 2002): A01.

55. "Beijing Bans Taiwanese Drama," *BBC News* (March 12, 2002), available online via: http://news.bbc.co.uk/ 1/hi/entertainment/tv_and_radio/1868693.stm (accessed: July 28, 2002).

56. Leslie Sklair, *Globalization: Capitalism and Its Alternatives* (Oxford: Oxford University Press, 2002): 270.

57. There are some more evidence that support this argument. For example, "We sold over 50 sets within a week of the ban," Li Xia, a saleswoman who runs a small video shop just next door to the district court in Beijing's Chaoyang district. One of the mainland's top Internet

providers, NetEase, said that within 24 hours of the ban, more than 70,000 users logged on to discuss and complain about the ban on the soap opera. Even *Southern Weekend*, a state-run weekly newspaper, commissioned a poll and found that 78 percent of those surveyed in Beijing, Shanghai, and Guangzhou opposed the state's judgement that the series promoted "a decadent luxurious life" and the "worship of money." See Jasper Becker, "A Soap Opera, China's Teens, and a Cyber-revolt," *The Christian Science Monitor* (May 24, 2002), available online via: http://www.csmonitor.com/2002/0524/p01s04-woap.html (accessed: September 23, 2002).

58. I found an interesting phenomenon when I was doing my field research in China in the summer of 2002. I stayed at the school hostel in Beijing College of Information Technology, where I visited their students very often. I noticed that lots of students downloaded several Taiwanese and HK's TV shows from the Internet websites, which are set up either inside or outside China. They could also exchange downloaded files of TV programmes with their classmates and friends studying at other institutions across China through the Internet.

59. John B. Thompson, *Ideology and Modern Culture: Critical Social Theory in the Era of Mass Communication* (Cambridge: Polity, 1990).

60. The theorist of global cultural approach to globalization, Marshall McLuhan, famously addressed the idea of "global village," in which he pointed out that the spread of the mass media, especially television and now the Internet, would expose everyone in the world to the same imagines, almost instantaneously. See Marshall McLuhan and Bruce R. Powers, *The Global Village: Transformations in World Life and Media in the 21st Century* (Oxford: Oxford University Press, 1989).

61. John Gittings, "China Masks a Mass Poisoning: Reporting Ban on Deaths from Foodstall Breakfasts," *The Guardian* (September 16, 2002), available online via: http://www.guardian. co.uk/china/story/0,7369,792886,00.html (accessed: September 22, 2002).

62. "China Deaths Blamed on Rat Poison," *CNN* (September 16, 2002), available online via: http://www.cnn.com/2002/WORLD/asiapcf/east/09/15/china.poisoning/ (accessed: September 18, 2002).

63. Hamid Mowlana, *Global Information and World Communication: New Frontiers in International Relations* (London: SAGE, 1997): 131–145.

64. ROC Mainland Affairs Council, *Preliminary Statistics of cross-straits Economic Relations (June 2002)*, September 11, 2002.

65. Kevin Platt, "Pop Culture Bridges Political Gap," *The Christian Science Monitor* (January 7, 1999).

66. A recent empirical research centered upon Internet use and sociability in mainland China and Hong Kong suggests that the Internet users live in both the online and offline world, and can shift back and forth between the two worlds simultaneously. See Betty K.M. Lee and Jonathan J.H. Zhu, "Internet Use and Sociability in Mainland China and Hong Kong," *IT & Society*, 1, 1 (Summer 2002): 219–237.

67. Some political scientists who subscribe to the functionalist approach suggest that economic and sociocultural interaction would create a basis for a thickening web of structures and procedures in the form of institutions. And that successful cooperation in one functional setting will eventually enhance the incentive for collaboration in other field, such as political realm. See, for example, James E. Dougherty and Robert L. Pfaltzgraff Jr, *Contending Theories of International Relations: A Comprehensive Survey* (London: Longman, 1997): 422.

68. Walter Wriston, for example, states about the revolution of the Information Age as "Sovereignty, the power of a nation to stop others from interfering in its internal affairs, is rapidly eroding." See Walter B. Wriston, "Bits, Bytes, and Diplomacy," *Foreign Affairs* (September/October 1997): 172–174. James Rosenau suggests that the basic nature of the international system is changing. The scope of activities over which states can effectively exercise control is declining. See James Rosenau, *Turbulence in World Politics: A Theory of Change and Continuity* (Princeton, NJ: Princeton University Press, 1990): 13.

69. Henry H. Perritt, "The Internet as a Threat to Sovereignty?: Thought on the Internet's Role in Strengthening National and Global Governance," *Indiana Journal of Global Legal Studies*, 5, 2

(Spring 1998), available online via: http://ijgls.indiana.edu/archive/05/02/perritt.shtml (accessed: November 18, 2001).

70. As a matter of fact, those analysts who are concerned about state sovereignty within globalization mainly focus upon the concept of the "control" capability, other than the "authority." See, e.g., Janice E. Thomson, "State Sovereignty in International Relations: Bridging the Gap between Theory and Empirical Research," *International Studies Quarterly*, 39 (1995): 213–233.

71. Ernest J. Wilson III, *Globalization, Information Technology, and Conflict in the Second and Third Worlds*, 28.

72. Kenneth Lieberthal, "Cross-Strait Relations," in *China under Jiang Zemin*, Tien, Hung-mao and Chu, Yun-han (eds.) (Boulder, Colorado and London: Lynne Rienner, 2000): 184.

73. The Guomidang government first initiated the "National Unification Council" and then promulgated the "Guotong gangling" (Guidelines for National Unification) in 1991, craftily setting a "three-phase" process to achieve eventual (re)unification, i.e., exchanges and reciprocity in the short term, followed by mutual trust and cooperation in the medium, and eventually consultation and unification in the end.

74. Jiang Zemin reaffirmed the determined sovereignty claim in delivering the keynote Report to the 16th National Congress of the CCP, stating "We Chinese people will safeguard our state sovereignty and territorial integrity with firm resolve, and will never allow anyone to separate Taiwan from China in any way." See "16th CPC Party Congress Opens in Beijing," *People's Daily* (November 8, 2002), available online via: http://english.peopledaily.com.cn/ 200211/08/ eng20021108_106479.shtml (accessed: November 8, 2002).

75. Christopher R. Hughes, "Nationalism in Chinese Cyberspace," *Cambridge Review of International Affairs*, 13, 2 (Spring/Summer 2000): 196.

76. There are two distinctive expressions concerning the term "hacker" in China: "Red Guest" (*Hongke*) and "Black Guest" (*Heike*). While "Black Guest" is a Chinese slang term for any computer intrusions by hackers, the "Red Guest" mainly refers to Chinese hackers because they normally do not act out of malice but of patriotism.

77. Wang, Yunbin (ed.), *Hongke chuji: Hulianwang shang meiyou xiaoyan de zhanzheng* (Hackers' Raid: A War without Smoke of Gunpowder on the Internet) (Beijing: Jingji Guanli, 2001): 22.

78. Ken Grant, "Weekly Press Review," *Virtual China* (August 13, 1999), available online via: http://www.virtualchina.com/archive/infotech/reviews/review-081399.html (accessed: September 17, 2002); Vincent Wei-cheng Wang, *Winning The War Without Fighting? Overcoming The Superior With The Inferior? China's Information Warfare Strategies and Implications for Asymmetric Conflict in the Taiwan Strait*. Paper presented at the 2002 Annual Meeting of the American Political Science Association, Boston, available online via: http://www.la.utexas.edu/research/ cgots/Papers/53.pdf (accessed: October 12, 2002). In fact, similar heated online debates were provoked when Taiwan President Chen Shuibian remarked on the cross-straits relations as "One Country on Each Side," on August 3, 2002.

79. Alan R. Kluver, "New Media and the End of Nationalism: China and the US in a War of Words," *Mots pluriels*, 18 (August 2001). Available online via: http://www.arts.uwa.edu.au/ MotsPluriels/MP1801ak. html (accessed: January 12, 2002).

80. Shanthi Kalathil, *Nationalism on the Net* (Carnegie Endowment for International Peace, February 22, 2002). Available online via: http://www.ceip.org/files/news/ kalathil_Bushtrip.asp?p=5 (accessed: February 27, 2002).

81. Susan L. Shirk, *Chinese Nationalism and Policies Toward the United States, Japan and Taiwan* (The ASPEN Institute Policy Programs—US–China Relations, March 29–April 7, 2002): 9–47. Available online via: http://www.aspeninst.org/congressional/pdfs/shirk.pdf (accessed: October 26, 2002); Pei, Minxin, "Hearing the Voice of the People at Last: Chinese Gain an Indirect Role in Shaping Policy," *Newsweek* (May 7, 2001): 21.

82. For an organizational analysis of the Falun Gong, see James Tong, "An Organizational Analysis of the Falun Gong: Structure, Communications, Financing," *The China Quarterly*, 171 (September 2002): 636–660.

83. Vivienne Shue, *State Legitimation in China: The Challenge of Popular Religion*. Paper presented at the 2001 Annual Meeting of the American Political Science Association, San Francisco.

84. Fang, Hanqi, "Falun Gong yu Hulianwang" (Falun Gong and the Internet) in *Zhongguo chuanboxue: Fansi yu qianzhan* (China Mass Communications Studies: Introspection and Prospect) (Shanghai: Fudan University Press, 2002): 173–191; Stephen D. O'Leary, "Falun Gong and the Internet," *Online Journalism Review*, 15 (June 2000). Available online via: http://ojr.usc.edu/content/story.cfm?id=390 (accessed: May 22, 2001); "Falun Gong Used Internet to Mobilize Demonstrations," *Hong Kong Voice of Democracy* (May 1999). Available online via: http://www.democracy.org.hk/EN/may1999/mainland_09.htm (accessed: June 28, 2001); Arnold Zeitlin, "Falun Gong Sect Show Power of Web, Hong Kong Press," *Freedom Forum* (July 27, 1999). Available online via: http://www.freedomforum.org/templates/document.asp? document ID=5961 (accessed: June 28, 2001).

85. Stephen D. O'Leary, "Falun Gong and the Internet," in *Falun Gong's Challenge to China: Spiritual Practice or "Evil Cult"?*, Danny Schechter (eds.) (New York: Akashic Books, 2000): 208.

86. "Falun Gong Hijacks Chinese TV," *Associated Press* (September 24, 2002). Available online via: http://www.wired.com/news/politics/0,1283,55350,00.html (accessed: September 29, 2002).

87. "Taiwan Downplays China's TV Hacking," *CNN* (September 26, 2002). Available online via: http://asia.cnn. com/2002/WORLD/asiapcf/east/09/25/taiwan.falungong/index.html (accessed: September 29, 2002).

88. Ko, Shu-ling, "China's Falun Gong Claims Denied," *Taipei Times* (September 26, 2002). Available online via: http://www.taipeitimes.com/News/archives/2002/09/26/0000169475 (accessed: September 29, 2002).

89. Shanthi Kalathil and Taylor C. Boas *Open Networks, Closed Regimes: The Impact of the Internet on Authoritarian Rule* (Washington DC: Carnegie Endowment for International Peace, 2003).

90. James Mulvenon, Stuart Johnson, and Nina Hachigian, *You've Got Dissent! Chinese Dissident Use of the Internet and Beijing's Counter-Strategies* (Santa Monica, CA: RAND, 2002). Available online via: http://www. rand.org/publications/MR/MR1543/ (accessed: September 5, 2002).

91. Peter Ferdinand (ed.), *The Internet, Democracy and Democratization* (London: Frank Cass, 2000): 180.

92. Ibid., 11.

PART 3

Global Networking and Economic Interactions

CHAPTER SEVEN

The Information Technology Industry and Economic Interactions Between China and Taiwan

BARRY NAUGHTON

The information technology (IT) hardware industry in China has grown rapidly over the past 20 years, and recent evidence indicates that the foundation has been laid of a world-class electronics industry. The industry's recent growth in China began with the movement of labor-intensive stages of electronics assembly to the mainland from Taiwan and other Asian locations during the 1990s. Since about 2000, though, this development has reached a new level of sophistication. On one hand, the existing electronics assembly industry is out-competing other Asian locales and gaining global market share. On the other hand, production within China is moving rapidly into the more technology and capital-intensive upstream stages of the electronics industry. Particularly impressive is the rapid movement into sophisticated integrated-circuit (IC) production, a development that is evident only in the post-2000 period. The first section of this chapter documents these developments.

What are the most important sources of the dynamism of China's IT hardware industry? In particular, how should we assess the interrelationship between market forces and government policy? To what extent are recent developments under the control of Chinese domestic actors, and to what extent do they reflect the impact on China of international market forces? These questions motivate the description of China's IT hardware industry that follows. The chapter attempts to shed light on these questions by describing some of the main economic and political forces at work on the industry. Among economic factors, the chapter examines the role of Taiwan investors in the Chinese industry, and then the broader context of IT industry development. Turning to policy factors, the chapter examines technology policy in China and then in Taiwan. The chapter concludes that the Chinese electronics industry is currently in a position where market forces and government policy have come together to reinforce the dynamism of the industry. Taiwan companies have played a key role in that dynamism, and the interaction between the Taiwan and China IT industries will continue to develop over the foreseeable future.

The Emergent Electronics Industry

The development of a modern, export-oriented electronics industry in China began with the restructuring of the electronics industries in neighboring economies, and especially Taiwan. In the late 1980s, Taiwan firms began moving the most labor-intensive stages of electronics production to the China mainland, starting with assembly of keyboards, mice, and monitors. Initially, only the simplest assembly processes were transferred, but the movement gradually expanded to include nearly all assembly operations.[1]

Since 2000, this assembly industry has continued to grow rapidly, and China is establishing itself as the most competitive location for electronics assembly in the Asia region. During the first half of 2002, while the global electronics industry overall stagnated, and electronics exports from most East-Asian economies declined, Chinese exports of computers and computer components increased by 50 percent, exports of telecommunications equipment increased 28 percent, and exports of electrical machinery increased 21 percent.[2] The Japanese *Nihon Keizai Shimbun* recently surveyed 16 major electronics product categories (projecting output for all of 2002), and found that China had garnered the largest share of eight, including most of the assembled final product categories. Rapid increases in share—shown in figure 7.1—are particularly striking for DVD players, of which China now accounts for more than half of world output, for desktop and notebook computers, and for cell phones.[3]

The recent growth phase follows the pattern of comparative advantage established in the earlier phases of electronics industry restructuring in East Asia. The activities in which China has established a predominant position are all relatively labor-intensive, final assembly stages of light

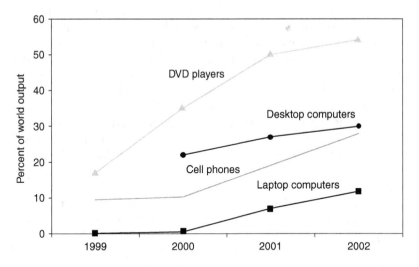

Figure 7.1 China's share of world production.

electronics goods. However, the recent improvement in the competitive position of these Chinese industries reflects the burgeoning Chinese supply base. Increasingly, suppliers of components and subassemblies are locating production close to the final assemblers who are their customers, creating agglomerations of producers with more comprehensive capabilities and lower costs. These productive regions support firms with superior competitive ability. Complex networks of contracting and subcontracting develop in these regions. "Flagship" multinationals with well-known brands, often headquartered in the United States, Japan, or Europe, contract with a first tier of suppliers, who are often headquartered in Taiwan. First-tier suppliers manage their own networks of second-tier suppliers, producing predominantly in China.[4]

Two significant agglomerations are emerging in China. The first is the area of Guangdong province centered on the cities of Dongguan and Shenzhen, primarily engaged in the production of desktop computers. Of the components of a desktop computer (by quantity, not by value) 95 percent are produced within a 50-mile radius of Dongguan. Most of the producers are foreign-invested firms, and 80 percent of those are from Taiwan.[5] The second agglomeration is the greater Shanghai region, which is rapidly developing capabilities in virtually all types of electronics production. Greater Shanghai—with its satellite production centers including Suzhou, Wuxi, and Kunshan—has superior human resources to Guangdong and a larger market in its immediate hinterland. The development of supply bases has corresponded with a steady movement from the labor-intensive production activities that were the first to cluster, into progressively more capital and technology-intensive production stages. In recent years, the movement of more sophisticated, higher-technology suppliers has begun to reach critical mass.

The most important recent milestone has been the rise of the China IC industry. IC production is very technically demanding, and the world IC industry has been characterized by sustained rapid technological progress. The pattern of technological progress was characterized early on in "Moore's law," an observation that the number of transistors put onto a single silicon IC—or "chip"—could double every 18 months.[6] Remarkably, Moore's law has turned out to be an accurate prediction, such that the number of transistors on a personal computer central processing unit (CPU) has increased from 2,250 in 1971 to 42 million in a Pentium 4, first produced in 2000. Such progress implies that the cost of computational power is being cut in half approximately every 18 months, and that new types of functionality and smaller, lighter weight products are being enabled.

The remarkably steady, linear progress of technology in the IC industry makes it possible to measure the technological progress of follower nations such as China. Although many difficult technical problems must be resolved to move to denser and more complex ICs, there is a simple metric that captures much of this progress: ICs can carry more transistors when the circuits etched onto silicon wafers are narrower. Smaller line widths (narrower circuits) enable more circuits to be compressed into a given area of silicon. In practice, "generations" of standardized line widths succeed each other every 2–3 years. We can measure the technological progress of China's IC industry by tracking the number of generations Chinese IC producers lag behind the world leaders. In addition, chips are cut out of larger silicon wafers, and wafer size is also an index of technological progress. Larger wafers increase the number of "chips" that can be produced in a given production run, increasing "yield," and lowering costs.

New generations of chips are designed and small numbers of samples produced well before the IC factory (or "fab") is ready for mass production. Since our focus is the economics of IC production, we are most interested in the technologies actually employed in mass production. As of late 2002, the world technological frontier (or "leading edge") in mass production was defined by the manufacture of chips with a line width of 0.13 micron (130 nanometers (nm)). The dominant leading edge

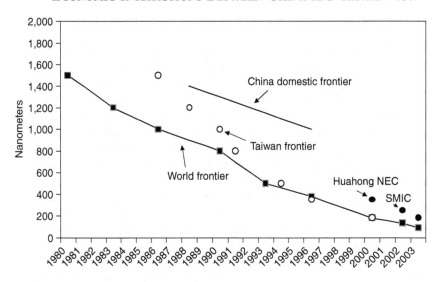

Figure 7.2 Width of Integrated Circuit lines.

manufacturer, Intel, began large volume shipments of Pentium 4 processors with a line-width of 130 nm, etched on 300 millimeter (mm) wafers, in the first quarter of 2002. Many of the world's premier chip makers have now begun to produce 130 nm chips on 300 mm wafers.[7] Thus, line-width, and the switch over from 200 mm (8-inch) to 300 mm (12-inch) wafers are the key indices of technology that is "advanced" in the context of the world IC industry as of the second half of 2002.[8] While leading edge manufacturers command premium prices for their product, the bulk of IC output actually comes from "trailing edge" producers. In late 2002, three-quarters of world IC wafer fabrication took place at the "trailing edge," at 250 nm or thicker. The trailing edge is everything two generations or more behind the leading edge dimension of 130 nm.

Figure 7.2 displays the worldwide decline in line-widths since 1980, showing that progress has been steady and continuous. Because of the steady and continuous decline in line-widths, the difference in technological capacity between different economies can be converted into a time-lag, simply by plotting the line-width of a producer at a given time, and tracing horizontally back to the global frontier. The horizontal distance equals the technological lag. Figure 7.2 shows Taiwan production in circles. It shows that Taiwan IC producers were 6 years behind the global frontier in 1986, but then began a rapid catch-up process that brought them to the frontier by 1995–96.

China's technological position can be located in a similar fashion. First, as of the mid-1990s, China had still not succeeded in implementing submicron technology (i.e. less than 1,000 nm) in its IC production. That implies that China was 9–10 years behind the technological frontier. More striking is that China, following a technology strategy based on domestic producers purchasing equipment and technological services that embodied key technology, had been unable to shrink the technological gap since the mid-1980s when it first entered world technology markets.[9] The clear failure of China's indigenous firm-based technology policy of this period is not really surprising. IC production is extremely technologically demanding, and China lagged not only in production technology as such, but also in many areas of basic science, and, perhaps most importantly, in managerial expertise. Moreover, the world frontier itself was moving extremely rapidly. It would be much more likely that China would shrink the technological gap by attracting foreign-invested fabs, which were willing to transfer close-to-best-practice technologies to China to take advantage of lower labor and land costs, and access the growing Chinese market. This has indeed been the case.

The pace of investment in China's IC industry has accelerated dramatically since about 1999, and the pace of technology transfer has shown dramatic results since 2001. China now has ten main IC fabrication companies in operation or under construction, and the chip sector is said to have attracted about $10 billion in foreign investment since 1999.[10] Six out of ten of these firms are located in the Shanghai area, with three of the most important within sight of each other in Pudong: Semiconductor Manufacturing International Corporation (SMIC), Grace, and Belling. These firms represent a clear acceleration of the pace of IC industry development. As of 1998, China had succeeded in attracting commitments from Japan's NEC and U.S. Motorola to build large and relatively sophisticated chip fabs, which were expected to begin production at 500 nm, and migrate to 350 nm by about 2000. Predictions were that 350 nm technology would be widespread by 2005.[11] Progress has in fact been more rapid than this, and a key role has been played by Taiwan-linked companies that have leap-frogged the developed country multinationals.

The clear technology leader in China is SMIC, which opened its first fab in late 2001, using 250 nm design rules on 200 cm wafers, both of which were firsts for China's IC industry: volume production was reached during 2002. SMIC is already transitioning to 180 nm at a second Shanghai fab (during the second half of 2002), and is also beginning trial runs of 130 nm processes. If things continue to go well, SMIC can expect to begin production at 130 nm by the end of 2003.[12] Following close behind, Grace Semiconductor Manufacturing Corporation, currently under construction, will start pilot runs at 250 nm in January 2003. Grace has aggressive plans to move to mass production of 180 nm chips before the end of 2003. The 2003 movement to line-widths thinner than 250 nm is significant for two reasons: first, it provides clear evidence of a shrinking of the technology gap with the world cutting-edge firms to less than 4 years (see figure 7.2). It is roughly consistent with an independent analysis by the U.S. General Accounting Office that argues that some Chinese firms are only 2 years behind the world industry. While SMIC has clearly not narrowed the lag behind the most advanced cutting-edge firms (such as Intel) to 2 years, it has moved rapidly to a position where it is about 2 years behind standard mass production technology in countries with technologically advanced IC industries. As of 2001, 250 nm had become the most widely operated line width in the world industry: China's advanced producers are about 2 years behind that standard. Finally, as we will discuss later, the 250 nm "line" has recently been defended by both the United States and the Taiwan governments as a dividing line for sensitive or critical technologies which they are unwilling to see transferred to China.[13] The rapid breaching of this line thus indicates a technological, managerial, and political breakthrough.

Despite its bland name, SMIC is an interesting company. Its CEO, Richard Chang (Zhang Rujing), worked for Texas Instruments for a decade, setting up state-of-the-art manufacturing operations around the world. He returned to his native Taiwan and established a successful semiconductor company there—Worldwide Semiconductor Manufacturing—which was sold out from underneath him to his arch-rival Taiwan Semiconductor Manufacturing Corporation (TSMC). Although the sale made Chang a rich man, it also left him frustrated and inclined to seek new challenges, motivated by a combination of rivalry and idealism. Chang has brought more than one hundred Taiwan engineers to Shanghai, including many who worked with him previously at Texas Instruments or Worldwide.[14]

The largest shareholder of SMIC is Shanghai Industrial, the holding company arm of the Shanghai city government, listed on the Hong Kong stock exchange. However, Shanghai Industrial holds only 17 percent of the company, and other shareholders include U.S. investment bank Goldman Sachs, fund manager H&Q Asia-Pacific, and venture capitalists

Walden International and Vertex Management.[15] Chang has maintained an aggressive growth strategy, and in addition to the two Shanghai fabs, now has two fabs under construction in Beijing. He has arranged technology sources for the new fabs, and has hinted that one of the Beijing plants might install a 300-mm production facility.[16] It is by no means clear that the enormous expense of a cutting-edge 300-mm fab—well over U.S.$2 billion—makes practical or economic sense. Both SMIC and Grace are involved in a symbolic game of announcing technological achievements that they *might* attempt in the future. Much of this is for public relations purposes, to which Grace is especially susceptible. From the outset a high-profile undertaking, Grace has been spearheaded by Jiang Mianheng—son of Jiang Zemin, first secretary of the CCP until 2002—and Winston Wong—son of Wang Yung-ching, Taiwan plastics tycoon and one of the most prominent businessmen in Taiwan. In fact, Grace has experienced significant problems in building its first facility, and is now about a year behind its initial (extremely ambitious) schedule. SMIC, by contrast, has managed to keep production ramp-up generally on schedule, and has developed a reputation for reliability.

With all this activity, China's IC industry has moved onto the world stage. It is still well behind the technological frontier, but it has moved to a position where it plays a significant role and must be taken seriously. The IC story is being repeated with liquid crystal displays (LCDs). For now, China does not produce large (17" or larger) LCDs, which are currently produced in about equal parts by Japan, South Korea, and Taiwan. But Taiwan has dramatically increased its production of both small and large LCDs in the past three years, and now accounts for 60 percent of the number (not value) of LCDs produced. The production of small LCDs, largely destined for notebook computers, has begun to move from Taiwan into China, following the transference of much notebook assembly to the mainland.[17] During 2003, both Taiwan and Japan companies will construct facilities to make large LCDs in China, and shift in production location, already underway, should accelerate.

The Role of Taiwan

Taiwan's economic interactions with mainland China are important in virtually every sector, but nowhere more than in electronics. The Taiwan government-sponsored research agency, the Institute for Information Industry's Market Intelligence Center (III MIC) collects data on the output of Taiwan-owned IT companies that is produced in Taiwan, in mainland China, and elsewhere. By the first quarter of 2002, the share of Taiwan's IT industry's total production (by this definition) that was actually produced in Taiwan was only 38 percent (down from 47 percent in full-year 2001). The share produced on the mainland, by contrast, was 49 percent (up from 37 percent for 2001).[18] Other regions—primarily Southeast Asia—dropped from 16 percent to 12 percent of the total, demonstrating that movement to the mainland is accelerating, and that China's competitiveness vis-à-vis Southeast Asia is improving. Right now, a majority of the output value of Taiwan's IT hardware industry is produced in mainland China.[19]

Indeed, it appears that the relative importance of Taiwan in the mainland China economy is increasing. This proposition, at first glance, seems to be contradicted by official data from both China and Taiwan that show Taiwan direct investment declining as a share of China's inbound foreign direct investment (FDI).[20] Figure 7.3 shows Taiwan investment and other data that may offer an explanation. The official Chinese data show Taiwan investment reaching its peak as a share of total incoming FDI in 1993, at about 12 percent of the total, and then declining to a low of less than 7 percent in 2000, before rebounding slightly in 2002. Some of this is real. When China really began to open its markets to foreign-invested firms in 1992–93, Hong Kong and Taiwan firms, given their proximity, were the first to take advantage of the new opportunities, and their share of incoming FDI reached historic highs.

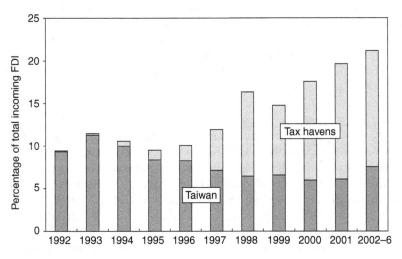

Figure 7.3 China incoming FDI: share from Taiwan and tax havens.

Subsequently, as slower moving US, European, and Japanese multinational firms moved in, incoming FDI soared to over $45 billion in 1997, and the relative share of Taiwan (and Hong Kong) declined. But as figure 7.3 shows, since 1998 the share of FDI coming into China from tax havens—the Cayman Islands, Virgin Islands, Samoa, Bermuda, and Panama—has soared. A great deal of this "laundered" FDI is coming from Taiwan, which tightened restrictions on investment in the mainland in 1996, and which shows significant outflows to the main tax havens in its official data.[21] Some tax haven investment may come from Hong Kong as well, but Taiwan investors face by far the strongest incentives to re-route their investments, since they face the largest barriers against investment, especially in high-tech industry. If we estimate (conservatively) that half of the tax haven investment is from Taiwan, then Taiwan accounted for 14–15 percent of incoming FDI in China. This places Taiwan's share of the total well above its previous peak, and second only to Hong Kong. It also implies that Taiwan invests substantially more in the mainland than does Japan, the United States, or the European Union.

The Chinese IT Industry

The development of China's IT industry can be understood by putting it in the context of downstream final markets. There are three main final markets for IT hardware: computers, telecommunications, and consumer electronics. China's current movement upstream into technologically more sophisticated sectors is being driven by the fact that each of these three downstream markets has reached a critical mass, and yet each seems poised for continued growth. Earlier, we described the evolution of China's electronics industry primarily through the development of export industries in the personal computer sector (where the connection to Taiwan is especially strong). Final demand for China's IT hardware is created not only by the export markets, but also by China's large domestic market for consumer durables and electronics and, especially, by China's large market for telecommunications services. Moreover, export markets have now expanded to include consumer appliances and consumer electronics, goods which are also sold in China. Thus, China has been the world's largest producer of color televisions for a decade, and it has recently also become the world's largest producer of DVD players. The broad base and rapid growth of downstream demand strongly encourages investment in the technically demanding upstream sectors.

The Chinese market for telecommunications equipment is now one of the largest in the world. The increase in subscriber numbers clearly demonstrates this. Fixed line subscribers increased by 34 million in 2002 to reach 214 million. Even more impressive is the growth of mobile phone subscribers, which increased a whopping 61 million in 2002 to reach 206.6 million.[22] While prices and profit margins are lower in China than in other markets, the differences are not large enough to challenge the conclusion that China's telecom market is the second largest in the world, and not far behind that of the United States. It is worth underlining how remarkable this is. It is commonplace to refer to the potential of the vast China market, but in nearly all other sectors, the China market is still very much a medium-sized market, much smaller than markets available in the larger developed countries. Enthusiasm for the China market in these sectors is based on China's population and rapid growth, and essentially represents hopes for the future. But in the telecommunications sector, the large market is a reality today.

Telecommunications generates demand for a variety of hardware products. At one end of the spectrum is the market for mobile phones. Here China is far and away from the world's largest volume market and producer, with an estimated 106 million mobile phones to be shipped during 2002. Moreover, domestic Chinese companies have made significant inroads into this market, muscling in alongside established foreign firms like Nokia and Motorola. By the end of 2002, it is projected that Chinese companies will account for 21 percent of phones shipped, and Taiwan companies 6 percent.[23] Many electronics assembler and home appliance manufacturers in China have entered this market, making it extremely competitive. At the other end of the spectrum are new telecommunications technologies generated by continuing demands on the telecom system. Demand pressure is intense to continue to hook up large numbers of households to the network, and to provide broadband connections to those who need them. The rapid growth of the Chinese phone market, combined with the still huge submerged demand among under-served households, is generating a search for new, more efficient, technologies to provide peak-load service in China's crowded cities, and new approaches to connecting up vast rural areas. China has already developed a tier of domestic telecommunications manufacturers—such as Huawei and Zhongxing Telecom (ZTE)—that carved out a position for themselves in the market for digital switching systems for fixed line telecommunications. As low cost producers, they entered the market in the traditional way, from below, competing on price, with adequate quality. These producers are now graduating to a range of more sophisticated technological solutions tailored to China's unique challenges and opportunities. For example, there is a lively rivalry underway concerning the best technology for improving the speed of data transmission through urban fiber-optic rings, with different suppliers offering competing solutions.[24]

The demand for broadband connections to the network has created an environment in which different technological solutions are in competition, and in which newly emerging technologies are constantly disrupting existing solutions. The recent completion of a national optical-network backbone enabled much faster connection rates and lower costs of bandwidth. Currently, four different broadband solutions are competing in China. Ethernet connections to new high-rise building complexes were the first widespread providers of broadband access. Subsequently, asymmetric digital subscriber lines (ADSLs) grew rapidly, and China became a significant market for digital subscriber lines. More recently, though, China's cable television industry—a highly dispersed industry under the general supervision of the State Administration of Radio, Film and Television (SARFT)—began a drive to supply cable modems to the roughly 90 million cable subscribers in China. Finally, a new entrant is local multipoint distribution service (LMDS), which enables wireless broadband connections of various types. Thus, fierce competition among four different broadband access technologies characterizes the Chinese market.[25]

The downstream markets that incorporate telecom, computers, and consumer electronics are large, diverse, and growing rapidly, and they guarantee a large market for upstream products like ICs. Moreover, the dynamism of the downstream markets implies a demand for professional engineering and design services that can create hardware products appropriate to those markets. In this respect, China is in a rather unusual situation. The large downstream market creates a market for ICs, which fosters the growth of a domestic IC industry. However, currently most of the downstream demand is satisfied by imported ICs. China produced 2.6 billion ICs in the first half of 2002, but this only satisfied 20 percent of domestic demand, with the remainder coming from imports.[26] At the same time, China's top foundries, such as Huahong-NEC, mainly produce for foreign clients, since these clients are more capable of providing the completed designs for IC production. Worldwide, the standardization of design tools and the improvement of communications networks allow IC design to be physically separate—and geographically distant—from the actual fabrication of ICs.[27] This is what has permitted the development of "pure play" IC foundries, on the one hand, and "fabless" firms, on the other hand, in the global IC industry. Thus, China's chip fabs are not dependent on the existence of a domestic design industry, nor does the demand they create automatically call such an industry into existence. Indeed, China's IC design capabilities have typically been seen as weak, by some estimates, about ten years behind world standards. IC design should be seen as another "upstream" activity—in this case upstream of the IC fabs—which requires a great deal of sophistication and technological expertise. China needs additional time to develop this sector, and to build a well-rounded IT industry.

In this sense the movement upstream from electronics assembly to IC fabrication, and from IC fabrication to IC design, replicates familiar stages of economic development in all economies. Most successful developing countries moved from early industries (garments, food products) upstream to more capital and technology-intensive middle and late industries (heavy and chemical industries, etc.) But the progress from IC fabrication to IC design occurs under different economic principles than did the progression from assembly to fab. The progression to IC design is the progression to a *more* labor-intensive activity, albeit one which relies on highly skilled professional labor. But there is no reason why an economy can't proceed directly to transforming its low-cost labor advantage into a low-cost *skilled* labor advantage, such as India has done in the software industry. China can develop IC design in tandem with IC fabs, or as a separate initiative.

In fact, China has recently begun to make progress in IC design. Part of this is due to substantial government help, and part due to the growth of downstream demand.[28] But once again, a crucial factor has been substantial involvement with Taiwan companies and engineers. Taiwan companies that set up design services in China need only a good lab, which can be modest sized. Taiwan engineers have been migrating to China to start, or work in, Chinese IC design companies. A survey of IC design companies carried out by *EETimes-China* in July 2002 revealed just how intertwined Chinese and Taiwan companies are. The Chinese firms employed an average of 264 people, and 58 IC design engineers. The government provided only 18 percent of start-up capital. Of these companies, 52 percent designed for foundries (fabs) located in China, and 33 percent designed for foundries located in Taiwan.[29] A third of the companies surveyed, in other words, are linked to Taiwan production systems. Prospects are for this sector to continue to develop, with a high degree of integration with Taiwan.

The evidence is thus compelling. China's IT industry is developing rapidly into a world-class IT hardware industry. Powerful development processes are at work in downstream and upstream stages of the industry. Taiwan companies are deeply involved in virtually all stages, from the downstream (computers, more than telecom or consumer electronics), to the upstream (IC design and fabrication). We will see later that this increased collaboration is spilling over into the all-important definition of technical standards as well. There is evidence that, with the confluence of these developments, China has landed at the "sweet spot" of technology industry development, in which low costs and accelerating capabilities lead to explosive growth, improved profitability, and increased competitiveness.

Technology Policy

Technology promotion has been a constant objective of China's economic policy since the founding days of the People's Republic. But technology policy has undergone numerous twists and turns as policymakers sought a successful model. However, since the end of the 1990s, China's technology policy seems to have settled into a more stable and promising configuration. The year 1999 has emerged as a turning point. Government proclamations in that year emphasized the increased priority the Chinese government was giving to technological development.[30] In fact, the resources committed to research and development (R&D) and technological development in general have increased substantially beginning in 1999. A census of R&D activity was carried out in 2000, and that survey showed that R&D outlays amounted to 1 percent of GDP in 2000, and 1.1 percent in 2001 and 2002. The data from this census are far better than earlier China data on R&D, but unfortunately lack comparability with earlier data. Nevertheless, figure 7.4 shows the new data in juxtaposition to the earlier data and reveals some consistent aggregate trends.[31] According to official figures, total R&D spending as a share of GDP reached a low point of 0.56 percent of GDP in 1994, before beginning a slow, steady increase. The data slightly undercounted R&D outlays at the low point, since it excluded some portion of enterprise—especially non-state enterprise—expenditures on R&D, which were captured after 2000. Nonetheless, the pattern of change is likely to be robust, and the upward trend reliable. The years 1994–95 were also the low point of budgetary revenues and outlays as a share of GDP, and R&D expenditures to some extent follow this larger pattern. The jump in R&D is thus not as abrupt as the figures seem to show, but still accurately reflects a real increase in R&D outlays since 1995, boosted by the impact of more comprehensive statistical collection.

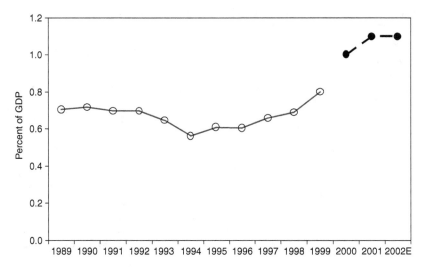

Figure 7.4 R&D as a share of GDP.

The impact of an increased government commitment of resources to technology development is also evident in the increasing supply of engineering talent (this is separate from, and not captured by, the R&D figures). In recent years, foreign-invested firms in China have increasingly reported that they are able to hire engineers with decent skills at reasonable wages. China's educational institutions are turning out significant numbers of engineers and technologists. In 2000, China graduated 350,000 engineers (including 140,000 from 3-year technical colleges) and 100,000 scientists.[32] China's universities have become more aggressive in their curriculums, and more practical in the subject content. This has provided abundant middle-tier talent, but for now still leaves China dependent on the inflow of top-tier manufacturing talent from other locations, especially Taiwan and the United States.

Table 7.1 shows that 60 percent of China's R&D outlays were made by enterprises, according to the 2000 survey. This is considerably higher than previous estimates (1997 data are given for comparison), and once again the jump reflects both real underlying trends and the effect of better collection of statistics. The 2000 survey made an effort to include non-state and especially small start-up firms, which are particularly prominent in high-tech sectors. The survey gives data by "ownership" as well as institution, so if we assume that all research institute and university in R&D is "state-owned," then it emerges that enterprise R&D is

Table 7.1   R&D expenditures: by type and agent, 1997 and 2000 (Billion yuan)

	Research Institutes	Universities	Enterprises and other	Other	Total
1997 expenditures, R&D					
Basic research	1.5	1.0	0.3		2.7
Applied research	7.0	3.2	2.9		13.1
Development & applications	12.2	1.6	18.5		32.3
Total	20.7	5.8	21.7		48.1
	43%	12%	45%		100%
2000 Expenditure, R&D					
Basic research	2.5	1.8	0.2	0.1	4.7
Applied research	6.7	4.0	3.8	0.7	15.2
Development & applications	16.6	1.9	49.7	1.5	69.7
Total	25.8	7.7	53.7	2.4	89.6
	29%	9%	60%	3%	100%

Source: China Statistical Yearbook on Science & Technology, 1998: 6–7, 14–17, 23, 77, 123. China Statistical Abstract 2002: 169.

done 35 percent by traditional state-owned enterprises (SOEs), 43 percent by various hybrid ownership forms (joint stock, limited liability, cooperatives, etc.), 20 percent by foreign-invested firms, and 4 percent by registered private firms. Although the private share may seem small, the beginning of a shift away from SOE dominance reflects a sea change in Chinese technology policy.

Through the 1980s and 1990s, policy moved from a unitary state-dominated "technology push" model, to one that combined elements of state leadership with market demand pull in an environment in which many diverse actors participate in technology development. Nevertheless, through the late 1990s, the thrust of Chinese technology promotion relied on government selection of "national champion" enterprises for nurturance and support. These national champions were often SOEs, which were instructed to develop into powerful enterprise groups, and helped to develop diverse capabilities, including R&D capability.[33] But at the end of the 1990s, this model collapsed. Part of the impetus for the collapse came from abroad. The prolonged stagnation of the economy in Japan and the crisis of the *chaebol* in Korea—the twin homelands of this development model—greatly diminished its attractiveness to Chinese policy-makers. Moreover, the dramatic explosion of the IT industry in the West significantly influenced how Chinese leaders think about innovation. Small smart-up companies—which often feature a prominent role for ethnically Chinese engineers and entrepreneurs—appear to have been the engine of this wave of innovation in the West, and Chinese leaders were anxious not to miss out on the benefits of rapid technological change, as they had in the 1960s, 1970s, and 1980s. Finally, China's leaders cannot have failed to notice that while their own technology policy was progressing reasonably well overall, their efforts to pick winners and designate specific firms as national champions had been remarkably unsuccessful.[34] The result was a shift in government policy designed to make it friendlier to innovation and new business creation.

First, and crucially, there has been a generous expansion of the type of enterprises that are deemed worthy of support. China now supports "national" enterprises, which include any technologically advanced enterprise, including small, private startups, and technology-intensive spin-offs from schools and research institutes. Instead of seeing private firms as rivals with publicly-owned enterprises, any domestic firm can become a national champion worthy of nurturance. Even foreign firms can benefit from the support of technology policy: while foreign investors have always been encouraged to bring advanced technologies, policy is changing in ways that seem to acknowledge that foreign companies will be part of China's long-term high technology community. In that sense, the "national treatment" promised by World Trade Organization (WTO) membership—lack of discrimination between domestic and foreign firms—has moved much closer to reality.

Second, the nature of support has changed. Government ministries have been reduced in manpower and mandate, and non-state firms were never subject to the same degree of government direction as SOEs were. Thus, the ability of the government to directly manage the process of selecting and importing technology has been substantially curtailed. Instead, the government provides a kind of across-the-board support for domestic enterprises designated "high technology." This support can take the form of tax relief, access to low-interest credit lines, preference in procurement decisions, or other kinds of regulatory preference or relief. This new reality is quite evident in the IC industry. A programmatic document on the IC industry was issued on June 24, 2000 (State Council Document No. 18). The policies put forward in Document 18 provide substantial support for the domestic IC industry. Value-added taxes, normally levied at 17 percent are lowered to 3 percent for domestic sales (technically, they are rebated). Since value-added taxes are still imposed on imported ICs, this amounts to significant protection of the domestic industry. Production machinery for IC fabs can generally be imported tariff free. These tax concessions are quite significant in the IC industry: because the industry is highly capital intensive, and all the main production machinery is imported, lower taxes mean lower capital costs. Combined with slightly higher sales margins, this adds up to a significant economic incentive.[35] Moreover, as an advanced technology industry, IC fabrication also qualifies for exemption of tax on profit for 3–5 years after start-up, and reduced rates of profit tax for a further 5 years after that. The Chinese government is thus providing very substantial tax advantages for the IC industry. But foreign-invested firms, even 100 percent foreign-owned firms, are able to take advantage of this preferential treatment to virtually the same extent as domestic firms.

China also supports the IC industry through the investment of government money in procurement and funded research. The national government has ordered a national "smart card" ID system, with an imbedded chip, the initial contract for which was placed with the Huahong-NEC (Project 909) IC fab. China has also commissioned the design of successive generations of CPUs, which it claims are being completed entirely by domestic design houses, and which are being fabricated by Huahong-NEC.[36] More generally, the Chinese government is pumping significant resources into IC design, creating an additional revenue source for domestic IC manufacturers.

The initiatives taking place in the IC industry are quite consistent with the general shift in China's technology policies. China has gradually begun encouraging the less tangible forms of technology transfer (i.e. licenses, consultancy, etc.) rather than "hardware" in the form of equipment imports. The IC industry policy of 2000 followed directly in the wake of a late 1999 decision that set forward a whole series of concrete, practical policies to foster domestic technology development.[37] These include changes in accounting and taxation rules, such that enterprise R&D expenditures can generate tax deductions, new technology transfers can be tax exempt, and profit tax rates are lowered for "advanced technology" enterprises. Technologically advanced equipment—so long as it is not available in China—can often be imported without import duties. In addition, rules on ownership stakes and the equity value of intangible technology contributions were significantly liberalized to permit entrepreneurs and venture capitalists to profit from successful start-up businesses. Finally, the domestic software industry qualifies for a range of concessionary measures, which are quite similar in scope and effect to those applied to the IC industry. Clearly, the Chinese government has no intention to take a "hands off" attitude toward technological development: they will continue to aggressively support favored firms and industries.

The Chinese government has also made extensive efforts to create a friendly environment for returning engineers and entrepreneurs. China's technology policy-makers are acutely aware of two factors: first, that China has experienced extensive "brain drain" over the past two decades, and also that Taiwan's IT industry really began to take off when it began to attract back to Taiwan technical personnel who had left the island and received training and entrepreneurial experience abroad. Many Chinese engineers have now begun to return to China. Moreover, the top levels of expertise at China's new IC fabs are coming from Taiwan, with individuals originally from Taiwan in some cases having achieved significant experience in U.S. industry as well. Most of the new fabs have senior Taiwan management. SMIC has Jowei Dun, senior director of fab operations and a former engineer at TSMC, and a Chief Technical Officer (CTO) from Intel. Grace's CTO is also from Intel. The president of Central Semiconductor Manufacturing Corp., considered China's first successful foundry, is Robert Lee, a Taiwan businessman.[38] In addition, returning entrepreneurs are founding startups: by one count, 166 firms specializing in chip and software development have been started by recent returnees.[39]

A particularly interesting development has been the emergence of government-supported efforts to define Chinese technology standards—in opposition to global technology standards—in order to give Chinese firms a competitive advantage. There are two dimensions to these efforts: by defining technical standards that have some "Chinese characteristics," the Chinese government imposes modest delays on foreign technology-holders: given their technological prowess, they can easily master the Chinese standards, but their product development is delayed by several months. This gives a breathing space to Chinese firms. The other dimension is pecuniary. Promotion of Chinese standards gives Chinese firms bargaining power with foreign suppliers over technology licensing rates. Chinese firms can resist paying—claiming their standards are different—and they can suggest swaps in which each side gains permission to use the other's technologies.

China seems to have first learned the potential in this effort with the development of the video CD (VCD). VCD is a relatively low-tech digital technology that became popular in the Chinese market—and virtually nowhere else—as a cheap alternative to videotape. Given the singularity of the Chinese market, Chinese companies naturally developed a dominant position—the first significant distinctive Chinese technological standard. But Chinese companies then leveraged their bargaining power by developing the Super VCD (SVCD) format, with enough differences that it could be used as a bargaining chip with Philips, Sony and the other companies holding the patents on CD technology. They have succeeded in largely evading royalties. They are now attempting to repeat this success with DVDs—a more sophisticated technology now spreading in the increasingly demanding Chinese market. A China consortium has developed the Advanced Versatile Disc (AVD) for sale only in Greater China. The move is widely seen as a gambit to evade or reduce the total $15–20 royalties on a DVD player, the production costs of which have fallen below $100. China, producers of over half the world's DVD players, has so far largely avoided paying royalties. Currently, Taiwan's largest research group, the quasi-governmental Industrial Technology Research Institute (ITRI) is leading the effort to develop a further generation of AVD technology.[40]

A similar example is unfolding with respect to mobile phone standards. Globally, two digital telecommunications standards have been in competition since the mid-1990s. Worldwide, the European Global System for Mobile Communication (GSM) has maintained a lead over the U.S.-favored Code Division Multiple Access (CDMA). Proponents of the U.S. standard argue that it is technologically superior to GSM, but because GSM was first to market, and has been supported by a steady stream of consumer-friendly product innovations, it has achieved a far larger world market share than has CDMA. GSM is also well established in China, while CDMA is only now beginning to break into the Chinese market through its alliance with Unicom, the start-up, but state-owned, competitor to the old state monopoly.[41] Chinese policy-makers may have intentionally slowed down the introduction of CDMA because they were unwilling to support the emergence of still another globally dominant U.S.-based technological standard. In this interpretation, Chinese policy-makers were willing to delay China's adoption of so-called "second generation" digital wireless standards in order to increase their influence over the configuration of the subsequent "third generation" (3G) digital wireless standards, which began a (difficult and delayed) roll-out in 2002. While all 3G standards mix elements of GSM and CDMA, there is still competition between 3G standards that are backward compatible with existing GSM operations (so-called wideband CDMA or WCDMA) and those that are backward compatible with existing CDMA operations (cdma2000), supported by European and U.S. firms, respectively. China's determination to play a role became clear when it announced its own 3G standard, called "time-division synchronous code-division multiple-access" (TD-SCDMA), which was approved by the International Telecommunications Union (ITU) in

August 2000.[42] The standard was developed by a Chinese SOE, Datang Telecom, in conjunction with a research institute of the Ministry of Information Industry, with technical assistance from Siemens. Not surprisingly, the standard is closer to WCDMA than to cdma2000, and promises backward compatibility with GSM operations. Its Chinese proponents argue that it is more efficient and cheaper in a dense urban environment. The standard is, in fact, a kind of joint maneuver between Datang and the MII Industry, on the one hand, and Siemens and Nokia on the other. The purpose is to increase the attractiveness of a GSM-compatible technology, and put China in a better position for the pecuniary bargain with the holder of the key CDMA patents, Qualcomm Corp., which are incorporated into all 3G technologies. The story gained added drama in October 2002, when the Chinese government allocated 55 MHz of core spectrum to TD-SCDMA (and 60 MHz each to WCDMA and cdma2000). This is apparently a contest that will continue to be vigorously waged.[43]

These examples thus give us a good sense about how Chinese technology policy is evolving in the decade of the 2000s. The resources put into technology and the claims on the attention of policy-makers have increased. But those resources are spread around in a much more diverse and competitive environment. Technologies are in open competition, domestically—as in the four competing broadband connections—and internationally. Moreover, more of policy reflects pecuniary concerns. There is less show-case, prestige-value-only technology development—or rather, to be more accurate, show-case technologies are still common, but they are developed as strategic cards in an ongoing poker game over licensing and royalty revenues.

Taiwan's Policy: Restructuring and Restrictions on Technology

Chinese government policy does not unfold in a vacuum, and the IT industry is among the most globalized of all sectors. The governments of both the United States and Taiwan have sought to restrict the flow of advanced IT to China, particularly in areas with potential military applications. The IC fab industry is a key focus of attention. For the United States, the motivation seems to be predominantly security-related, while for Taiwan the motivation is predominantly economic. Because the world frontier in IC fabrication is continuously advancing (figure 7.2), technology restrictions cannot be static and are, in a sense, perpetually being "relaxed" as the frontier advances. In fact, in a dynamic context, the United States seems to have maintained an objective of keeping the Chinese industry two generations behind the world frontier (thus, that China would be moving into 250 nm when the world frontier is adopting 130 nm would be consistent with this objective).[44] However, there is enormous scope for interpretation of what "two generations behind" might mean in practice. Until recently, Taiwan had forbidden all large investments in the IC fabrication industry.

The Taiwan government is in a particularly difficult position. After an initial economic rapprochement between Taiwan and mainland China, Taiwan policy-makers stepped hard on the brakes in late 1996, with the adoption of the "Go Slow, Be Patient" policy. This policy—championed by then President Li Denghui—limited all investment on the mainland to a maximum size of U.S.$50 million, and placed additional restrictions on investment in infrastructure or high-technology activities. The March 2000 election brought a new president, Chen Shuibian to power, but with only 39 percent of the vote. Although Chen was the candidate of the Democratic Progressive Party—which has traditionally been suspicious of mainland China and favored greater political independence for Taiwan—since he was elected without a majority, and lacked one in the legislature, he was under enormous political pressure to put together a workable set of compromise economic policies. Chen quickly signaled that he would be open to relaxing restrictions on economic interaction with mainland China. In this, he seems to have been guided by three considerations. First, despite government restrictions, the actual level of integration between Taiwan and the mainland had been steadily increasing, particularly in the electronics industry. Second, the rise of democracy and the erosion of traditional Guomindang power gave business interests a direct influence on policy-making that had eluded them previously, and Chen needed to respond to business concerns. Third, given the fact that Chen was unlikely to make concessions to China on political or security issues, economic flexibility seemed to offer an opportunity to avoid serious deterioration in the overall relationship between Taiwan and the mainland.[45]

Chen convened an "Economic Development Advisory Conference" to make recommendations and give him political cover for relaxing restrictions on China investment. In fact, on August 26, 2001, the Conference recommended that the "Go Slow, Be Patient" policy be replaced by one of "active opening and effective management." Chen embraced these recommendations, and began to dismantle the former restrictions in November. Just at this time, the WTO formally approved the accession of both China and Taiwan to the organization, a development which seemed to imply the eventual end of restrictions on commerce between the two sides. However, progress toward further liberalization has been extraordinarily slow and uneven. "Effective management" turned out to contain new regulations and significant obstacles to mainland operations. A new requirement was instituted that all mainland investments be fully declared—honestly this time!—by December 31, 2002. Most significantly, despite repeated tentative initiatives, little progress has been made in establishing direct transport links between Taiwan and the mainland.

The Taiwan government has been under enormous pressure from businesses eager to see easier economic relations with the mainland. A crucial milestone came in September 2001, when Morris Chang, the chairman of TSMC and undoubtedly the most influential technology executive in Taiwan, declared that the future of the world IC industry lay in China. Chang's was an important conversion, because he had long been a skeptic about conditions on the China mainland, and had argued against moves to the mainland by his own and other high-tech companies. Now Chang declared his support for a lowering of barriers to investments in mainland fabs, and joined with other prominent executives to criticize Taiwan government policy.[46] Influenced by the success that other firms with Taiwan roots were experiencing in China, Chang began to make plans for TSMC to take up a venture in the mainland.

In fact, the dilemmas that Taiwan faces are particularly acute with respect to the IC industry. On one hand, Taiwan's economy is more dependent on the electronics industry than any economy in the world, and Taiwan has achieved extraordinary success in continuously upgrading the sophistication of its industry and riding the global high-tech wave. The future profitability and competitiveness of all of Taiwan's IT industry depends precisely on its ability to take the lead in restructuring, and follow through on the creation of a highly integrated industry with the mainland. On the other hand, Taiwan is deeply worried that it will lose its existing competitive advantage, derived from its mastery of high technology competitive niches. IC fabrication, once an extremely high-tech operation that only the most advanced economies could master, has become more widely spread in the world, including, of course, to China. While it is still extremely difficult to operate fabs with low-defect rates near the technological frontier, and the technology is still beyond the reach of many economies, it is no longer clear that Taiwan will always be well positioned at the cutting edge. And if Taiwan loses that particular advantage, where exactly will it find its competitive edge? Part of the answer, of course, is that Taiwan will seek to maintain and leverage its design expertise. Taiwan has already developed successful IC fab *and* design industries, and early on established a competitive advantage in Application Specific Integrated Circuit (ASIC) design, and then developed a diverse design industry in tandem with its highly efficient and competitive IC fabs. But now the economics of both these industry segments is changing rapidly, and Taiwan faces great anxiety and economic pressure.

In March 2002, Taiwan announced a new policy that allowed investment in China in 200 mm fabs, but only by firms that had completed construction of new 300 mm fabs in Taiwan, and had undertaken to continuously upgrade their facilities and technology in Taiwan. Moreover, the government declared that it would approve only three 200 mm fabs, on a case-by-case basis, by 2005.[47] The new policy is a substantial relaxation of the earlier prohibition on IC investments, and the objective of the policy is to ensure that Taiwan's premiere IC firms continue to invest in Taiwan and maintain their cutting-edge capabilities in Taiwan—to prevent, in other words, the "hollowing out" of Taiwan's high tech industry. The government has displayed resolve in an attempt to enforce the policy. In January 2003, the Taiwan government announced fines of U.S.$57,000 on the chairman of Shanghai-based Grace Semiconductor, as well as fines of U.S.$30,000 on two venture capital firms, Prudence Capital and Universal Venture Capital Investment for investing in SMIC (even though both had withdrawn their investments before the fines were imposed).[48]

It is impossible to avoid the conclusion that Taiwan's policy toward the semiconductor industry is completely unrealistic. The requirement that Taiwan firms must first invest in 300 mm fabs in Taiwan before they can invest in China effectively limits approval to Taiwan's most technologically sophisticated firms, TSMC and United Microelectronics Corporation (UMC), since only they can plausibly afford the extraordinarily expensive 300 mm fabs. These firms are thus being restrained and rewarded at the same time, and both have already laid the groundwork for their first China fabs, so that they can move quickly once approval is forthcoming. In the meantime, a rush has begun to establish new unaffiliated ventures in China, with their Taiwan roots mildly disguised in order to circumvent ongoing restrictions.

The fact is that the global IC industry is fiercely competitive. Although TSMC and UMC are among the world's most efficient producers, their continued success is by no means assured. It is impossible to believe that a government that is *worried* about the competitiveness of one of its key industries is going to enhance the competitiveness of that industry by hobbling it with a series of restrictions. Taiwan's economy is extremely open and highly integrated with the world economy, and particularly with American firms. Taiwan's citizens are also extremely mobile, and the interchange of personnel and skills with Silicon Valley and other high-tech locales outside of Taiwan is large and ongoing.[49] People like Richard Chang—or Morris Chang—exemplify the complex "citizenship" (literal and figurative) of Taiwan's most important high-tech entrepreneurs. It is not likely that Taiwan government policy will be able to pen up such expertise within the physical boundaries of Taiwan.

The worldwide recession in the IT business has increased pressure on Taiwan and indirectly increased China's bargaining power. Since March 2000—when the US NASDAQ stock market hit its peak and the "tech bubble" began to deflate—the electronics industry everywhere has been under enormous economic pressure. Sales and profits have fallen everywhere, and Taiwan has been affected as much as any other region. The global downturn increases incentives for suppliers and technical personnel to evade restrictions and sell (or go) to China, which is one of the few rapidly growing markets. Indeed, it is hard to envision the success of SMIC without the economic downturn in Taiwan, which led many Taiwan engineers to opt for a career in China in the belief that opportunities in Taiwan were limited. In this incentive environment, controls have grown increasingly leaky.

Indeed, these market conditions affect policy outcomes everywhere. The governments in both Taipei and Washington seek to maintain limits on technology transfer to China, but the effectiveness of those policies is at least temporarily declining. Suppliers of equipment to produce semiconductors have endured 3 years of declining sales. Equipment suppliers outside of the United States—such as the rival suppliers of lithography equipment ASML (the Netherlands) and Nikon (Japan)—feel less constrained by vaguely worded international agreements, and creative solutions abound to get new projects moving.[50] Among chip manufacturers, Germany's Infineon has taken an aggressive posture in supporting the development of China's IC industry, and in particular of supporting SMIC.[51] Not coincidentally, the suppliers most actively supporting China's development—ASML and Infineon—have also been increasing market share in a difficult environment. With chip demand still growing slowly, and new capacity coming on stream in both China and Taiwan, these competitive pressures are unlikely to abate soon. Thus, despite Taiwan's anxieties and hesitations, the evidence is accumulating that current Taiwan policies will not be effective in preventing the further development of the IT industry in China, and the ever closer integration between Taiwan and China companies.

Conclusion

Powerful economic forces are driving Taiwan and China's IT industries together. In conclusion, it is worth briefly contrasting the situation in Taiwan with that in Hong Kong. Hong Kong has played an enormous role in linking China to the world economy, and its own labor-intensive manufacturing has been almost entirely relocated across the border. But Hong Kong is an also-ran in the key high-technology manufacturing areas. Indeed, Hong Kong has recently been reduced to competing with Shanghai in an attempt to attract outside investment in IC fabrication, including investment from mainland-based companies.[52] Instead, Hong Kong's comparative advantage lies in business services, particularly finance, information, and logistics. In addition, Hong Kong's companies leveraged their incomparable mastery of world marketing systems to maintain control of supply chains running in and out of China. Hong Kong's economic position thus depends to a certain extent on its ability to maintain control of these chains. As expertise develops in Shanghai and Beijing, Hong Kong's share of the business will decline. Hong Kong may well prosper in the future, but it will never be able to maintain the dominant position with respect to China's interactions with the world that it once had.

Taiwan's position is quite different. After Taiwan surrendered its low-technology, labor-intensive industries to the mainland, its remaining comparative advantage was highly concentrated in high-technology manufacturing. The comparative advantage can be transferred to the mainland, and Taiwan companies have in fact developed a huge stake in the emerging mainland industry, currently concentrated in Guangdong and the Shanghai region. This means that as expertise develops in Shanghai and Beijing, Taiwan's share of the business will not necessarily decline. Instead, Taiwan will be pulled into increasingly close involvement with mainland industries. This will have significant implications for economics, politics, and the development of new information technologies.

As of the beginning of 2003, then, we see dramatic, rapid development of the IT industry in China at nearly every stage of the industry. Downstream assembly, mid-stream fabrication of ICs, upstream design of ICs and systems, and product standard-setting all display accelerating involvement of Chinese firms. Moreover, in each of these areas, we see close involvement of Taiwan and China, and close cooperation among firms from the two sides. The pattern of simultaneous advance in several related areas would be noteworthy in any case. But since these sectors are closely related, increased capabilities in one sector are likely to spill over into increased efficiencies and cost savings in related sectors, so that we are likely to see reinforcement of capabilities and acceleration of growth. The speed of development will draw Taiwan and China closer together as both are pulled along in the wake of an accelerating vessel.

Notes

1. Chung, Chin, "The Electronics Industry in Taiwan and the China Circle," in *The China Circle: Economics and Technology in the PRC, Taiwan, and Hong Kong*, Barry Naughton (ed.) (Washington, DC: The Brookings Institution, 1997). (Chinese translation, Beijing: Xinhua, 1999.) See the other chapters in this volume as well.
2. *China Customs Statistic* (June 2002): 4–8.
3. "China Tops in High-tech Production," *The Nikkei Weekly* (August 26, 2002): 20.
4. Dieter Ernst and Kim, Linsu, "Global Production Networks, Knowledge Diffusion, and Local Capability Formation," *Research Policy*, 31, 8–9 (December 2002): 1417–1429.
5. Huang, Gai, "Guangdong 'Sanlai Yibu' Chanye Shengji" (Guangdong's Processing Industry is Upgrading) *21 Shiji Jingji Baodao* (September 2, 2002): 2.
6. Gordon Moore, the originator of "Moore's law," was one of the founders of the Intel Corporation. Intel pays homage to Moore's foresight and other achievements by keeping a copy of his original paper—from 1965—posted on their website. Gordon Moore, "Cramming More Components Onto Integrated Circuits," *Electronics*, 38, 8 (April 19, 1965), available online via: ftp://download.intel.com/research/silicon/moorespaper.pdf.
7. For example, Elpida (a 50–50 joint venture between NEC and Hitachi) produces 130 nanometer chips in Hiroshima, and will shift to 300 mm. wafers in early 2003; Infineon produces DRAMs in Dresden at 140 nm on 300 mm wafers. Anthony Cataldo, "Elpida Chief Eyes China for DRAM Manufacturing," *EETimes* (November 15, 2002); and "Hynix, Infineon Spar Over Number Three DRAM Spot," *EETimes* (November 18, 2002).
8. This is of course a highly schematic version of a complex reality. A minimally accurate account of the complex reality must include at least three additional facts. First, line widths are generally thinnest for dedicated memory chips, and then for logic chips. Application specific integrated circuits (ASICs) do not generally require the same extremes of line compression, but of course have their own demanding technical and competitive requirements. Second, it is difficult for fabs to fully "ramp up" high volume production. When fabs initiate a new generation, they typically have high defect rates, low yields, and high costs. As they gain experience with each new technology level, they bring defect rates down. This process takes place "in house," however, and it is difficult to get such information about defect rates and costs since these are closely guarded industry secrets. A generation is considered to be in production when a producer ships more than 10,000 ICs per month using production tooling, and is followed within three months by a second manufacturer. Third, companies often make overly ambitious announcements in order to position themselves with respect to competitors, customers, and governments. These announcements do not always correspond to the evolving reality. For more detail on all the earlier mentioned points, see Semiconductor Industry Association, *The International Technology Roadmap for Semiconductors: 2001*, available online via: public.itrs.net.

9. Barry Naughton, "The Emergence of the China Circle," in *The China Circle*, Naughton (ed.): 26.
10. Sunray Liu, "China's Chip Market Rebounds from 2001 Slowdown," *EETimes* (September 18, 2002); Yao, Gang, "China's Chipmaking Focuses on Yangtze River Delta," *Semiconductor International* (February 2003): 65–68.
11. Michael Pecht, Lee, Chung-Shing, Fu, Zongxiang, Lu, Jiangjun, and Wen, Wangyong, *The Chinese Electronics Industry* (Boca Raton: CRC Press, 1999): 113–115, 122.
12. Mike Clendenin, "China Fab Details Released as TSMC Seeks Permission," *EETimes* (September 9, 2002), "SMIC Steps Carefully Toward 90-nm Development," *EETimes* (October 28, 2002), and "Discussions of more China Fabs Reported," *EETimes* (October 31, 2002). Clendenin reports that SMIC forged an alliance with Chartered Semiconductor Pte. Ltd., with the latter transferring details of its 180 nm process flow, which will save several months of process tuning, in exchange for an equity stake. SMIC seems to be on schedule, says Clendenin.
13. George Leopold, "TI Deal Reignites China Exports Debate," *EETimes* (September 13, 2002).
14. Lan, Lijuan, "Zhang Rujing he tade Zhongxin Tuandui," (Richard Chang and his team at SMIC) *Cheers* (*Tianxia Zazhi: Kuaile Gongzuoren*) (April 2001), available online via: www.cheers.com.tw/content/009/009074-1.asp. I am indebted to Leng Tse-Kang for sharing this article with me.
15. Peggy Sito, "Shanghai Industrial Eyes Additional Chip Investment," *South China Morning Post* (September 30, 2002); Mike Clendenin, "China's Drive for IC Foundry Market Unnerves Taiwan," *EETimes* (October 5, 2001).
16. Mike Clendenin and Peter Clarke, "Infineon Empowers Asian Fabs," *EETimes* (March 31, 2003).
17. Market Intelligence Center, Institute for Information Industry, "Promotional Strategies and Movement to China to Boost Taiwanese LCD Monitor Production in 2H 2002" (Taipei, Taiwan: September 12, 2002), available online via: mic.iii.org.tw/english/pressroom/pressroom.asp?f = 4.
18. Tim Culpan, "IT Hardware Manufacturers Storm into Mainland," *South China Morning Post* (April 30, 2002).
19. It should be noted that this statement does not imply that the majority of the value-added in the industry is generated or earned in mainland China. Quite the contrary, much of the high value-added component production is still done in Taiwan, and virtually all of the high-value designing and R&D remains in Taiwan, or is shared with the United States and European companies. Even without attempting to account for the incomes earned by Taiwan citizens in mainland China, it is clear that Taiwan companies and residents still enjoy the lion's share of the income generated in the "Taiwan" electronics industry. Indeed, since the final assembly stage incorporates the value of all preceding activities, if all final assembly were moved to China, then by definition, the share of output in China would be more than half.
20. "Direct" investment means that the investing party has an ownership stake in the resulting business that gives it some measure of control (typically 10% or more). All Taiwan investment in China is also "indirect" in the sense that the Taiwan government forbids direct interactions across the Taiwan straits and require Taiwan businesses to go through intermediaries, typically in Hong Kong.
21. Chang, Peggy Pei-chen, and Cheng, Tun-jen, "The Rise of the Information Technology Industry in China: A Formidable Challenge to Taiwan's Economy," *The American Asian Review*, XX, 3 (Fall 2002): 149, 164, and 172.
22. Mobile phone subscribers increased by 60 million in each of 2001 and 2002. National Bureau of Statistics, "2002 Nian Guomin Jingji he Shehui Fazhan Tongji Gongbao" (Statistical Communiqué on National Economic and Social Development in 2002) (February 28, 2003), available online via: www.stats.gov.cn/tjgb/ndtjgb/qgndtjgb/1200302280214.htm.
23. Market Intelligence Center, Institute for Information Industry, "Domestic Makers to Provide Thrust for Chinese Mobile Phone Market Growth in 2002," Press release (Taipei, Taiwan: November 22, 2002).

24. The main competition is between Synchronous Optical Network (Sonet) solutions, and those that have been adapted for Resilient Packet Ring (RPR) technology. This competition is also going on in other countries, but on slightly different terms.

25. Sunray Liu, "China Stands at Broadband's Gate," *EETimes* (April 26, 2001).

26. Sunray Liu, "China's Chip Market Rebounds from 2001 Slowdown," *EETimes* (September 18, 2002).

27. See the discussion in Robert C. Leachman and Chien H. Leachman, "Globalization of Semiconductors: Do Real Men Have Fabs, or Virtual Fabs?," in *Locating Competitive Advantage*, Martin Kenney and Richard Florida (eds.) (Stanford: Stanford University Press, 2003).

28. Lucy Liang, "China's IC Swagger on Display in Shanghai," *EETimes* (April 3, 2002); Sunray Liu, "China Grooms Chengdu as Center of Growing Design Industry," *EETimes* (October 15, 2002).

29. Michael Liu, "IC Design House Survey 2002: China," at www.eetchina.com (2002).

30. "Zhonggong Zhongyang Guowuyuan Guanyu Jiaqiang Jishu Chuangxin Fazhan Gaokeji, Shixian Chanyehua de Jueding," (CCP Center and State Council Resolution on Strengthening Technological Creation, the Development of High Technology and its Implementation in the Economy) *Zhongguo Jingji Shibao* (August 26, 1999): 4.

31. State Statistical Bureau, "2001 Nian Quanguo Keji Jingfei Touru Tongji Gongbao" (Statistical Bulletin on National Science and Technology Inputs 2001) (November 13, 2003), available online via: www.stats.gov.cn/tjbg/rdpcgb/qgrdpcgb/200211130076.htm; and "2002 Nian Guomin Jingji he Shehui Fazhan Tongji Gongbao" (Statistical Bulletin on National Economic and Social Development 2002) (February 28, 2003), available online via: www.stats.gov.cn/tjgb/ndtjgb/qgndtjgb/1200302280214.htm for preliminary 2002 data. China Statistical Yearbook on Science and Technology, various years.

32. State Statistical Bureau, *China Statistical Yearbook 2001*, 654.

33. Barry Naughton and Adam Segal, "Technology Development in the New Millennium: China in Search of a Workable Model," in *Crisis and Innovation: Asian Technology After the Millennium*, William Keller and Richard Samuels (eds.) (New York: Cambridge University Press, 2002): 160–186.

34. Tomoo Marukawa, "WTO, Industrial Policy and China's Industrial Development," in *China Enters WTO: Pursuing Symbiosis with the Global Economy*, Ippei Yamazawa and Ken-ichi Imai (eds.) (Chiba: Institute of Developing Economies, 2001): 110–142.

35. One survey shows that tax advantages are the single most important factor influencing location decisions for IC producers. See Leachman and Leachman, "Globalization of Semiconductors."

36. "909 Gongcheng Shixian Jianshe Mubiao," (The 909 Project has Completed a Construction Target) *Huahong-NEC Press Release* (April 25, 2001).

37. The account in following pages is taken from the website of the State Council Development Research Center, available online via: http://www.drcnet.com.cn or from http://www.vcchina.com.cn.

38. Mike Clendenin, "China is Open for Business," *EETimes* (July 24, 2002), "Discussions of more China Fabs Reported," and "China's Drive for IC Foundry Market Unnerves Taiwan."

39. Sunray Liu, "Chinese EEs Return Home with Entrepreneurial Bent," *EETimes* (October 22, 2002).

40. Mike Clendenin and Junko Yoshida, "Taiwan Joins Chinese Effort on Proprietary DVD Format," *EETimes* (May 24, 2002).

41. Barry Naughton and John Norton, *Qualcomm in China: A Telecommunications Licensing Negotiation Exercise in Two Parts* (San Diego: University of California, San Diego Graduate School of International Relations and Pacific Studies, Revised Edition, 2000).

42. "International Telecom Union Adopts China's TD-SCDMA 3G Mobile Standard," *China Online* (August 15, 2000), reporting on *Caijing Zazhi* (Finance Magazine) report (August 11, 2000), available online via: www.chinaonline.com/topstories/000815/1/c00081107.

43. Mike Clendenin and Patrick Mannion, "China Puts 3G Spec on Speed Dial," *EETimes* (November 11, 2002); Reuters in Beijing, "China's Home-grown 3G Seen as Good Fit SCMP,"

South China Morning Post (November 6, 2002). David Pringle, "Mobile-Phone Suppliers Court China, Developing Countries," and "Chinese Developers Discuss 3G Patent with Qualcomm," *Wall Street Journal* (November 7, 2002): B10 (both articles).

44. There are no formal rules for, say, line-width, although governments coordinate guidelines through the Wassenaar agreement. US officials deny any intent to keep China two generations behind. George Leopold, "TI Deal Reignites China Exports Debate," *EETimes* (September 13, 2002).

45. See Scott Kastner, *Commerce in the Shadow of Conflict: A Domestic Politics and the Relationship between International Conflict and Economic Interdependence*, Doctoral Dissertation, Department of Political Science, University of California (San Diego: 2003).

46. Mark Landler, "From Taiwan, a Fear of China Technology," *New York Times* (October 3, 2001): B1, B7.

47. "Premier Yu Shyi-kun's Policy Statement on the Liberalization of Mainland-bound Investment in Silicon Wafer Plants" (March 29, 2002). Distributed by e-mail.

48. Economist Intelligence Unit, "Taiwan 2003," available online via: http://db.eiu.com/reports. asp?title = Country+Report+Taiwan&valname = CRTWD201&doc_id = 1165575.

49. Anna Lee Saxenian, *Silicon Valley's New Immigrant Entrepreneurs* (San Francisco: Public Policy Institute of California, 1999).

50. George Leopold, "U.S. Defends China Export Policy on Lithography Gear," *EETimes*, (September 26, 2002); Mike Clendenin, "China Shrugs off Import Restrictions, Plans 0.18 Micron Fabs," *EETimes* (August 27, 2001).

51. Clendenin and Clarke, "Infineon Empowers Asian Fabs."

52. Peggy Sito, "HK Beats Mainland Rivals to Hi-tech Venture," *South China Morning Post* (October 10, 2002).

CHAPTER EIGHT

Global Networking and the New Division of Labor Across the Taiwan Straits

TSE-KANG LENG

Introduction

Recent academic works of globalization indicate multiple driving forces of political and economic change at the current stage.[1] The first driving force realizes that non-state actors, such as multinational corporations and venture capital companies, form a "decentralization" force to transfer economic as well as political power away from nation-states. Dynamics of economic development is not vested on strong hands of a developmental state, but on global networking of international firms. Another school of thought argues that the state power does not "decline," but "transform." The state withdraws from traditional fields of direct intervention, but concentrates its power on infrastructures pivotal to the promotion of globalization. States also endeavor to attract advanced talents and improve social and political environments beneficial to global operation. At the same time, under the concern of economic security, the state still try to retain its political instruments of diverting economic affairs into political considerations. In brief, in the era of globalization, tensions between domestic political concerns and global economic benefits still exist.

The political economy in the information technology (IT) development across the Taiwan Straits reflects this tension. The new model of IT production between Taiwan and China is achieved collectively by multinational corporations (MNCs) and Taiwanese Original Design Manufacturing (ODM) companies. The expansion to mainland China as production bases is a natural choice based on global division of labor. Non-state, cross-boundary forces facilitate the process of integration and network formation. These forces include autonomous talent flows and globalized operation of venture capital (VC).

To cope with these new forces of globalization, the Taiwanese state faces a dilemma of protecting economic security and promoting economic integration with the other side of the Taiwan Straits. Many noneconomic factors intervene into the process of network formation and consolidation.

The purpose of this chapter is to analyze the tension between economic globalization and political forces governing cross-Taiwan Straits IT development. Based on first-hand data and personal interviews, this chapter first introduces the role of "hybrid" Taiwanese semiconductor company in forming a new global and local networks of IT production. The case of notebook PC will demonstrates the interaction of Taiwanese ODM firms and international brand-holders, and their collective efforts in developing the Chinese market. At the same time, interaction of human capital between Taiwan and China will be treated as driving forces of consolidating global IT networks across the Taiwan Straits.

The last two sections will discuss the political aspects of network formation. This chapter argues that the Taiwanese government intends to use both restrictive and encouraging policies to balance national security and economic globalization. This chapter indicates that political factors, such as Taiwan's struggle for national identity and the rejection of China's unification formula, lead to hesitation and contradiction in the policy-making process.

Formation of Taiwanese IT Networking

Taiwanese IT Manufacturers as Integrators

Taiwanese IT firms in China have become the major player in promoting the global network. Founded in April 2000, Semiconductor Manufacturing International Corporation (SMIC or *Zhongxin*), a U.S.$1.46 billion worth of Taiwanese semiconductor company located in Shanghai's Zhangjiang High-Tech Park, is a good example. Registered as an American company, SMIC is treated by the Chinese government as a leading indicator of domestic IC development. In addition to attracting talent from leading Taiwanese semiconductor firms, such as Taiwan Semiconductor Manufacturing Corp. (TSMC) and United Microelectronics Corp. (UMC) with which SMIC has a working relationship, SMIC's major human resources come from overseas Chinese and returning mainland Chinese students trained abroad. According to Zhang Rujing, Chief Executive Officer of SMIC, the firm's major recruitment target is returning Chinese students with graduate degrees. Zhang indicates that many mid-ranking Chinese managers formerly working at American companies have expressed their intention to join SMIC at half their US salary. In addition, SMIC has attracted at least 70 senior Taiwanese IC engineers from major U.S. IT firms, such as Intel, AT&T, Motorola, Texas Instrument (TI), Hewlett-Packard (HP), and Micron. Although most of these Taiwanese talents are now U.S. citizens, they have encountered the "glass ceiling" in terms of being promoted in the United States.[2]

The prospect of development of China's IT industry in general and that in Shanghai, in particular, provide strong incentives for overseas talent to have a new start in SMIC. According to current statistics, SMIC's technical team consists of 2,500 talented IC designers and managers.[3] Among them, 450 are from Taiwan, 130 from the United States, 70 from Singapore, Hong Kong, South Korea, and Japan, and 20 are from Europe. SMIC's international team is divided into: (1) the R&D sector, led by U.S. engineers; (2) the Operations sector, of which Taiwanese and Singaporean talents are in charge; and (3) the Logistics and finance sectors, led by managers from Hong Kong. Although it's founder and initial capital can be traced back to Taiwan, SMIC in Shanghai is operating like an international firm.

The hybrid SMIC's ultimate goal is not limited to its globalization drives; on the contrary, SMIC plans to localize its human resources policies and to attract and train local Chinese talents. SMIC, for instance, provides internship opportunities for local Chinese university students and graduates, especially in the field of IC design. Normally, these local "seeds," under the supervision of SMIC's international team, are given the opportunity to complete their master's thesis or PhD dissertations.[4] Chinese universities also produced 50,000 to 60,000 graduates with master's or doctoral degrees in engineering. This huge pool of brainpower is potentially the most important source of SMIC's human capital.

The SMIC case provides a sharp contrast to labor-intensive Taiwanese factories that hire cheap labor from China's remote countryside. This new semiconductor powerhouse has, from many perspectives, become an integrator to link international talent with that from Greater China.[5] The role of Taiwanese technology-oriented firms has been transformed from cheap-labor exploiter to high-tech broker and mediator. These firms also serve as a bridge to link global Chinese manpower to the huge Chinese market.

The SMIC case also demonstrates that Taiwanese IT firms are clever in establishing international and local networks. Since SMIC is registered as an American company, many Taiwanese regulations governing cross-straits investment are not applicable. To cope with the new Taiwanese laws regulating IT talent flows to China, SMIC plans to help Taiwanese engineers obtain passports from the third country.[6] In the year 2002, SMIC reached agreements with Toshiba and Chartered Semi-Conductor Manufacturing (CSM) of Singapore to improve its production capacity and introduce advanced technologies. Toshiba will transfer its 8-inch foundry, while CSM will transfer its 0.18 micron technology to SMIC. In exchange, Toshiba and CSM is each expected to hold 5 percent of SMIC's stock.[7] At the current stage, the Taiwanese government only allows 0.25 micron technology to be transferred to China.

This case demonstrates that even though Taiwan has established strict limitations with regard to talent and technology transformation to China, "hybrid" companies, such as SMIC, still have plenty of channels in which to grow. SMIC is carefully establishing its domestic networks. In addition to its power base in Shanghai, SMIC established its Beijing branch and manufacturing facilities and recruited Prof. Wang Yangyuan, the Head of the Institute of Microelectronics of Beijing University as Chairman. SMIC's Beijing project is to strengthen its political-business networks and utilize highly qualified and gifted talents from China's top universities in Beijing. The hidden agenda seems to balance two major IT bases in China, while ensuring their operations are politically correct. In other words, high-tech companies like SMIC play the game of balance of power to maximize benefits from competing local governments. It is obvious a part of SMIC's strategies of localization in the era of globalization.

Global Network and Taiwanese Notebook PC Industry

Taiwan's PC industry has developed an unique way to occupy a strategic place in the world market. Take Quanta Computer Inc. as an example. Quanta serves as the contract manufacturer to Dell, Compaq/HP, Gateway, Apple, IBM, Sony, Sharp and other brand-name owners. Quanta manufactures close to half of the notebooks sold by Dell, making it by far Dell's largest supplier. It will turn out more than five million notebooks in the year 2002, 30 percent of which will be manufactured in Taiwan.[8] Although almost unknown to PC consumers,

Quanta surpassed Toshiba as the world's No. 1 notebook computer manufacturer in 2001.

In the past decades, Quanta has evolved from a pure Original Equipment Manufacturing (OEM) vendor into a major ODM producer of the world's major PC brands. Quanta has developed an interdependent relationship with its major customer Dell. Dell, which accounts for half of Quanta's sales, is the global master of just-in-time manufacturing and has provided Quanta with the impetus to maintain its high standard. However, not until it started working with Quanta's design and manufacturing team, did Dell's mobile PC business really take off. Today, the Austin-based PC maker relies on the Taiwanese company to produce 55 percent of its notebook computers.[9]

Taiwan's entrepreneurs have been much more adaptable to the rapid change and short product cycles in the notebook computer industry than its competitors from Japan and South Korea. Normally, the U.S. brand holder may give a road map, such as product specifications and performance, while the Taiwan side tends to generate the ideas, creates the final product and delivers them to the customer. Taiwan finds one of its particular strengths in the time-consuming design of printed circuit boards, a customized system that is crucial to the overall speed and reliability of the finished computer. A highly interactive joint development process between the two sides, in fact, can come up with a new model in six to nine months. According to Quanta, its 500 design engineers did about half of the design work for Apple Computer's G4 notebook. For Dell, Quanta does about 60 percent to 70 percent of the design work.[10]

The enhancement of Taiwan's design capacity makes this international alliance a more interdependent one. To cite one example, in 1999, HP was on the verge of shutting down its notebook division when it decided to try Quanta. Now, the Taiwan company does just about everything for HP's notebook unit, from putting together hardware and installing software to testing the final product and shipping to customers—all in less than 48 hours.[11] In real terms, outsourcing to Quanta saved HP's business in mobile PCs.

Although Taiwanese ODM firms have become vital components of international PC networking, major notebook brand holder, like Dell, do not put all their eggs in one basket. Quanta is Dell's No. 1 ODM manufacturer, but at the same time, Dell has also established similar relationships with other Taiwanese firms—for example, Compal, Winstron, and Arima. In the year 2002, Dell transferred more orders from its Electronic Manufacturing Service (EMS) in the United States to Taiwanese ODM manufacturers. It is believed, however, that Dell will still keep minimum orders in the hands of its EMS partners.[12] As Fang Guojian, Dell's former Director of Procurement in the Asian Pacific, indicates, Dell's strategy is to adopt the strategy of "check and balance" and let its rival partners compete with each other.[13] Given this interdependent but precarious relationship, Taiwanese notebook producers have also been trying to reduce the risk of overdependence. Quanta, for example, currently serves nine of the ten major notebook manufacturers in the world.

In this unique patron–client relationship, multinational IT firms still maintain flexibility in manipulating the balance. In the summer of 2001, Dell decided to move its Asia-Pacific Procurement Center from Taipei to Hong Kong. According to Dell, its relocation was in response to both Taiwan's self-restraint cross-straits economic policy and its delay in establishing direct links with mainland China. Dell indicated that if direct transportation links between Taipei and Shanghai could not be realized for a long period of time, Taiwan's advantage in PC manufacturing will diminish quickly.[14] Since Taiwan does not allow direct links with China, Dell's international procurement officers in Taiwan could not effectively oversee manufacturing capacities in mainland China. That aside, mainland Chinese buyers are not able to participate in PC exhibitions in Taiwan, and even if they could, mainland Chinese talents face discrimination in entering Taiwan.

Dell's relocation obviously put pressure on the Taiwanese government to lift economic restrictions with China. Dell's strategists in the Greater China area, however, do not intend to lean on any side. On July 5, 2001, Dell declared to settle its first overseas R&D center in Shanghai. Dell is supposed to recruit 270 technical staffs at first, and the number will increase to 1,000 in several years.[15] One year later, Dell reorganized its China R&D capacities and strengthened its Taiwan Development Center (TDC). Dell's China Development Center (CDC) will be in charge of lower level, matured PC and software, whereas the TDC will concentrate on the development of notebook computers and Personal Digital Assistants (PDAs).[16] The ultimate goal of Dell is to fully utilize its human power in the region, and all the while, establish a network of PC production in the Greater China area.

Made in China, By Taiwan

The preceding analysis demonstrates the interdependent relationship between Taiwanese PC producers and international brand holders. In order to cut costs, enhance international competitiveness, and maintain their global production networks, Taiwanese PC firms have little choice but move their manufacturing capacities to mainland China, with decisions as to relocating/branching out in China being jointly made by international brand holders and Taiwanese contractors. Dell has pushed its ODM contractors, such as Quanta, Compal, and Winstron, to expand their production capacities to mainland China, including most PC parts suppliers in the supply chain.

On the other hand, Taiwanese firms had already arranged their mainland projects well before being requested to do so by their ODM hosts. The Taiwanese government did not lift its restrictions on notebook PC investments to China until November 2001. In reality, most major Taiwanese manufacturers had already established their networks of upstream suppliers of key parts one step ahead of governmental policies. The supply chain management is the key of success to eminent Taiwanese notebook PC producers. The innovative supply chain system allows major producers like Quanta to trace materials flow on a real-time basis and finish the products within 48 hours. Quanta has linked its database with the databases of more than 1,000 suppliers so they can easily coordinate with Quanta's order schedule.[17] In order to succeed, the complete supply chain must move with major contractors, hence creating clusters of Taiwanese notebook PC producers in mainland China.

The "mainland initiatives" on the part of Taiwanese PC manufacturers has created a new division of labor across the Taiwan Straits. This new type of business networking is dubbed as "Made in China, by Taiwan." In the past few years, Taiwanese firms have made substantial contribution to China's global share of the IT market. In 2001, output from mainland factories occupied about 5.5 percent of Taiwanese notebook PC production, and the figure is expected to soar up to around 40 percent in 2002.[18] The percentage of global market share of IT production in Taiwan and mainland China can be visually appreciated in table 8.1. At the current stage, the home bases of Taiwanese notebook PC firms are in charge of taking orders and performing R&D functions. Their production lines are being moved to China to reduce costs. To illustrate this, Compal maintains a work force of about 4,000 in Taiwan to tend to such matters as accounting and sales, R&D and the one factory it still has there. Compal's notebook PC factory in suburban Shanghai has accelerated production capacity from 150,000 to 250,000 units per month this year. With the enhancement of productivity in China, Compal will make 60 percent of its notebooks in China. Compal also realizes its "China Direct Shipping, CDS" model and attempts to complete the production process within 24 hours.[19] Quanta has also been

Table 8.1   Global market shares of Taiwanese IT products

Item (Year)	Bought from Taiwan Percentage of world output bought from Taiwan	. . . But Made in China Percentage of Taiwanese parts made in China
Scanner (2000)	93	80
Monitors (2000)	54	45
Disk Drivers (2000)	39	50
Note book (2002)	60	42

Sources: Yuanjian Zazhi (Global View Magazine) (November 16, 2002), available online
via: http://www.gvm.tw/cover-v.asp?wgvmno=946&orderno=1.

building up its Taiwan-based R&D team from 750 now to 2,000 by
2005 so that customers can outsource more of their design work to the
Taiwanese.[20] The new division of labor in the notebook PC sector
benefits both sides of the Taiwan Straits. To retain its competitive advantage in the global networking, Taiwan needs to enhance its R&D caliber
and global logistics capacities.

Venture Capital and Global Networking

Taiwanese VC firms play crucial roles in connecting Greater China
economies with global capital, know how, and highly skilled talent. For
many Chinese startups around the world, Taiwanese venture capitalists
are becoming "king-makers" of fueling dynamics well known for establishing incubators as one key base for investing in high-tech startups.
Typically, founders of Taiwanese incubators are themselves successful
entrepreneurs and have practical experience in establishing high-tech
firms in the United States. Taiwanese-run incubators are also fast becoming centers for fostering young ethnic Chinese entrepreneurs. Acorn
Campus, established by Chen Wu-fu and four other Taiwanese engineers
turned entrepreneurs, is a case in point in that it has established a successful business incubator in Silicon Valley. Acorn has plans to introduce
the Acorn model and establish start-up incubators in major Chinese
cities, like Shanghai. Chen, who plans to lead a new team in Shanghai
himself, has indicated that Acorn's focus is on China's advanced talent,
rather than China's market.[21] The case of Acorn Campus provides a potential model of networking cooperation among talent from Taiwan, China,
and the United States. A cross-border golden triangle—comprising
Taiwanese capital, a Silicon Valley-style of innovative spirit, and the ethnic Chinese advanced work force—does, in fact, seem to be emerging.

Within this "golden triangle," ethnic Chinese talent is the core and need-less to say, the United States provides an ideal ground for innovative train-ing for Chinese talent from both sides of the Taiwan Strait.[22] The US experience enhances the understanding of these people by exposing them to cutting-edge technologies and, more importantly, providing them with the confidence to start up their own businesses back on domestic soil. These US-trained advanced work forces, therefore, become a catalyst for manpower integration across the Taiwan Strait. Instead of bilateral interaction, this integrative mechanism is global oriented.

In the past decade, Taiwanese VC has added fuel and helped create global networks for mainland Chinese and Taiwanese firms. Taiwanese professional managers have become fundamental pillars in the develop-ment of the Chinese market for international VC firms. The common practice of these firms is to register as an American or Hong Kong VC company and attract capital from the Greater China region and interna-tional sources. For instance, the Taiwan-based H&Q Asia-Pacific is among the first foreign VC pioneers in China. With a total U.S.$1.6 bil-lion fund, H&Q Asia-Pacific has invested more than U.S.$200 million in China. Major targets of investment include the two largest Taiwanese semiconductor manufacturers in Shanghai—Zhang Rujing's SMIC and Winston Wong's Grace Semiconductor Manufacturing Corp (GSMC). In the past 10 years, H&Q has introduced American VC experiences as well as sophisticated, well-trained and gifted experts from Taiwan to mainland China. Not only capital but also human resources are undeni-ably the two necessary pillars of the scaffolding in the building of global networks of IT production.

Another case is WI Harper (in Chinese, Zhong Jing He). Registered as an American VC company, WI Harper plans to invest 20 percent of its new funds in Taiwan, 30 percent in China and 50 percent in the United States. Beginning in 1996, WI Harper and Silicon Valley entrepreneurs have invested in a state-supported telecommunications company, Navini Networks, to develop "third generation" (3G) mobile telecommunica-tions technologies in China. WI Harper, together with Qinghua University and the Beijing city government, has also created the Beijing Technology Development Fund (BTDF), the first state-supported over-seas VC, to invest in start-up high-tech companies in northern China. Further plans include the establishment of start-up incubators with China's major universities. In 2001, WI Harper and the Suzhou and Shenzhen city governments collectively invested $60 million in 3G wireless and Thin Film Transistor and Liquid Crystal Display (TFT-LCD) industries in China.[23]

The common characteristic of Taiwanese VC companies is in the globalization of their funding and management. In many cases, capital from mainland Chinese sources constitutes half of the total. In the global visions of such VC firms, one criterion for selecting Taiwanese start-up investment projects is their potential to expand and prosper in China. At the same time, these Taiwanese VC firms have established branches in major Chinese cities and trained first-generation VC managers there. American venture capitalists are becoming bridges to link Taiwanese and Chinese companies. Warburg Pincus, an American VC company, has established strategic alliances with Taiwanese Venture Capitalists to develop the Chinese market. One crucial goal of Warburg Pincus is to help to promote the cooperation among high-tech firms across the Taiwan Strait.

Taiwanese VC investment could also closely link up with China's drives for globalization and capital-market reform. In the initial stage, China's VC companies were organized by local governments, but these companies, for the most part, lacked professional, personnel, and marketing capacity. Recently China has begun to acknowledge the importance of attracting foreign VC to link Chinese start-up companies with international talent, sales routes, and capital markets,[24] and as a consequence, state-backed VC firms are being restructured like those in the West in order to compete in the market. For one, Shanghai Venture Capital Corporation (SVCC), a Shanghai city-owned VC firm, enjoys considerable autonomy in operating in accordance with market mechanisms, and SVCC has begun establishing strategic links with other Chinese VC firms, such as Shanghai New Margin Venture Capital (SNMVC), controlled by Chinese President Jiang Zemin's son, Jiang Mianheng. In order to introduce international management experience, SVCC and the Singaporean government-supported Venture TDF Company in 2000 jointly established a $50 million fund. In an attempt to tap a global network of contacts, the Shanghai government eventually agreed to let the Singaporeans control the fund.[25] If the trend of globalizing VC management continues, Taiwanese VC firms will have plenty of opportunities to become leaders in cutting-edge professionalism. The complex networking with local and international technology centers gives Taiwan a unique advantage to compete with other Asian nations in the VC market in China. Furthermore, allying with China's state-backed VC companies creates favorable conditions for integration with China's domestic networking operations.

Taiwanese VC companies also play an important role of helping to enhance state-business relationships across the Taiwan Straits. SMIC and GSMC have gradually built up their personal and institutional networks and obtained funding from China's domestic banking system and VCs, including SVCC and SNMVC. In the case of GSMC, the alliance between Winston Wong, son of the Taiwanese tycoon Wang Yung-ching, and Jiang Mianheng, son of PRC leader Jiang Zeming, demonstrates the foundation of GSMC's political networks in China. GSMC has, in the meantime, also succeeded in attracting supports from Crimson Asian Capital and Crimson Velocity, both of which belong to the Crimson Fund. Founder of Crimson Fund Gu Zhongliang is the son of Gu Liansong, head of Taiwan's prestigious China Trust Group. In addition to introducing global networks of manufacturing and management, Taiwanese VCs help strengthen local networks of relationships. In the era of globalization, this "localization" of networks is still the key of success in China.

Human Resources are the Foundation of Networking

The "mainland initiatives" of Taiwanese IT companies has accelerated the interaction of human resources across the Taiwan Straits. Before the rise of China's IT production centers such as Shanghai, the real brain drain from Taiwan to China was not observed, but that from the Greater China area to the United States. This drain is the result of the rational choices of talented individuals. The states on both sides of the Taiwan Strait have limited instruments to regulate this flow of talent, and as long as Silicon Valley, the high-tech capital of the world, continues to experience shortages in IT talent, this huge magnet will attract Chinese talent from both sides of the strait. Work experience in Chinese, Taiwanese or foreign firms provides a good springboard from which Chinese engineers can leap to their ideal work destinations. The "springboard effect" brings bright students and practitioners from both sides of the Taiwan Strait to the United States, thus reuniting and integrating Chinese talent outside the motherland.

The ascendance of Shanghai and the Yangtze River Delta area in the global IT arena facilitates the "reverse brain-drain" or "brain circulation" of ethnic Chinese talent back to the Greater China region. According to a survey conducted in Silicon Valley in 2001, 40 percent of the ethnic Chinese and Indian IT talents were considering returning to their home countries; 30 percent had even contacted official representatives from their home countries.[26] While the slow down in the new economy of the United States and new waves of lay offs in dot-com firms may account for part of the story, drastic changes in overseas talents' home countries provide another explanation. Since the 1980s, the "reverse brain drain" of ethnic Chinese IT talent from the United States to Taiwan helped establish Taiwan's burgeoning IT industry, but these firms have quickly matured and eventually been expanding into mainland China since the late 1990s, and this, in turn, has attracted more and more overseas and domestic talents to explore the new land of IT development. In some cases, Taiwanese talents have moved from Silicon Valley to Taiwan's Hsinchu Science-Based Industrial Park to start up new business. As their business in mainland China expand, they are doubling and even tripling their time in China to handle the huge, booming market and spending less time in Taiwan. Some of them fly back and forth between Shanghai, Hsinchu and Silicon Valley. More people choose to move their families to Shanghai as their business as well as family bases.

In addition to the global circulation of ethnic Chinese IT human resources, bilateral talent flowing between Taiwan and China has also increased in the past few years. The "brain drain" from Taiwan to China has recently become a major phenomenon owing to the decline in Taiwan's economic development and the expansion of Taiwanese firms to China. By contrast, very few mainland Chinese have come to Taiwan to work. According to a 2001 survey, 40.2 percent of male Taiwanese workers interested in working overseas choose China as their destination, surpassing all the other countries and regions. Table 8.2 demonstrates the ranking.

Among these mainland-oriented Taiwanese workers, 67 percent prefer Taiwanese companies, while 30 percent prefer other foreign companies in China. As to location, 52 percent choose Shanghai as the first priority.[27] Another survey shows that 27.3 percent of potential Taiwanese workers in China want to join IT-related industries, 20 percent want to join service sectors and another 22.3 percent prefer manufacturing industries.[28] However, as table 8.3 demonstrates, mainland Chinese

Table 8.2 Top choices of overseas assignment for the Taiwanese

	Male (%)	Female (%)
China	40.2	14.6
United States	23.1	25.9
Europe	16.1	24.2
Singapore	13.3	22.4
Other SE Asia	3.8	3.7
Hong Kong	3.4	9.1

Source: *Guojia Zhengce Luntan* (National Policy Forum) 1, 6 (August 2001): 67.

Table 8.3 Top choices of overseas assignment for the mainland Chinese

Country	Percentage
United States	21.6
Singapore	19.9
Canada	18.2
Hong Kong	15.6
European Union	15.0
New Zealand	5.7
Taiwan	1.7
Others	2.2

Source: Guojia Zhengce Luntan (National Policy Forum) 1, 6 (August 2001): 68.

Table 8.4 Average annual IT engineer's salaries across Asia

Year	2001 (U.S.$)	2002 (U.S.$)
China	7,033.0	8,135.55
South Asia	16,587.0	15,188.68
South Korea	20,516.0	21,492.91
Taiwan	22,092.0	18,539.71

Sources: "Experiences and Education Pays: literally," *Electronics Engineering Times* (October 1, 2002), available online via: http://www.eetasia.com/article_content_php3?article_id= 8800274877.

talents do not express strong interests in working in Taiwan. With the United States topping the list, only 1.7 percent of them choose Taiwan as the ideal location for employment.

As for salary levels, the gap between Taiwanese and mainland Chinese IT engineers is narrowing. In 2002, the average salary of Taiwanese IT engineers is U.S.$18,540, a decrease of 18 percent from 2001. The average salary of mainland engineers is U.S.$8,136, an increase of 16 percent from 2001.[29] Table 8.4 provides a comparison of the average salaries of Asian IT engineers.

In the past, Taiwanese engineers assigned to mainland China would enjoy double or triple paid benefits. Since 2002, according to various interview data, about half of Taiwanese engineers assigned to mainland China have received the same salary as in Taiwan; 20 percent of them are either under-paid or receive the same salary as their mainland counterparts. Only 30 percent of high-level managers enjoy higher salaries and stipends in China.

Policy and Political Interference of the Network

The preceding analysis demonstrates the three pillars of IT networking across the Taiwan Straits: the industry's division of labor, VC initiatives and the interaction of human resources. This section focuses on the noneconomic factors impeding deep integration between Taiwan and China in the IT sector.

Political Entangling and Globalization: The Case of 8-Inch Silicon Wafer

Taiwanese semiconductor companies, like the TSMC and UMC, are among the most cost efficient and globalized firms the world over. As the semiconductor industry also represents Taiwan's competitive advantage in the IT sector, it follows that the moving of semiconductor industries to China raises concerns when it comes to balancing economic benefits and economic security, two vital yet highly controversial issues in Taiwan's economic policies toward China. The long-delayed decision by the Taiwanese government to allow semiconductor industries to invest in mainland China was settled on April 2002 with the final decision being a compromise between the two national goals. Adopting a principle of "positive opening, effective management," Taiwan's Cabinet announced four guidelines in governing semiconductor industries:

(1) Before 2005, Taiwanese firms will be allowed to establish only three silicon wafer foundries on mainland China.
(2) The level of technology is limited to 8-inch wafers or bellow.
(3) Whoever invest in 8-inch wafers in mainland China must launch a new investment project on 12-inch wafers in Taiwan; and
(4) The production of key components and R&D capacities must be kept in Taiwan.[30]

The pro-open globalists in Taiwan argue that the mainland initiatives should be regarded as one crucial step in Taiwan's globalization strategy vis-à-vis of IT development. Since the size of the Chinese market and the lower costs of production there enhance China's competitive advantages, the expansion of Taiwanese IT firms to China seems to be a rational choice as far as strengthening Taiwan's competitiveness goes. There is little question that Chinese firms will learn or even "borrow" Taiwanese technology and know-how in IC production and design. To cope with such challenges from the mainland, Taiwan must upgrade its

R&D capacities instead of isolating itself from the global division of labor. Furthermore, since Taiwan does not control the key technologies in the global supply chain, China may obtain know-how from the United States, Japan and other advanced nations if it cannot be obtained from Taiwan firms. Once China establishes direct links with key component holders and excludes Taiwan's participation, Taiwan's strategy of globalization will, most assuredly, be put in jeopardy. At the current stage, the entry of the Taiwanese IC industry in the Chinese market will consolidate Taiwan's strategic role in global IC design and manufacturing.

The hard-core conservatives have made national security the first item of priority on the policy-making agenda. They claim that Taiwanese technology and know-how in silicon wafer manufacturing will be lost to China after the "cluster effects" are realized in major Chinese production centers. The "cluster effects" also refers to the moving out of the whole supply chain in the IT industry in general, and the silicon wafer production in particular. The mass movement of foundries to China will also cause serious unemployment problems in Taiwan. Given the fact that Taiwan does not control key technology in the production process, the cluster effect will facilitate the process for the Chinese to become the leading IC manufacturers in a short period of time. Once China becomes the dominant force in IC design and production, Taiwan's economy will be controlled and dependent on China, and Taiwan's national security will be in great danger. The "magnet attraction" of China will destroy Taiwan's grand strategy of globalization if Taiwan does not adopt balancing acts.

Negative Statecrafts

Following the lift of restrictions on 8-inches silicon wafer investments in China, the Taiwanese government drafted regulations "governing Taiwanese high tech personnel working in mainland China" (Gao keji rencai fu dalu renzhi xuke banfa). According to the new regulations, drafted by the National Science Council (NSC), high-tech personnel need official approval before working on mainland China. The draft was then revised by the Mainland Affairs Council (MAC) in October 2002, broadening the target of the regulation from just "high-tech personnel" to include "high-tech personnel, legal persons, groups, and other related institutions." In the NSC draft, a prohibited industry is only limited in specific sectors in IC design. The MAC draft expanded the restriction to "specific government-supported and sponsored institutions and personnel." The governing authority was also expanded from the NSC to "other related public sectors."[31]

The Taiwanese government has also expressed its intention to regulate mainland initiatives as they pertain to VC firms. The MAC asked that the Ministry of Economic Affairs (MOEA) strengthen its supervising mechanism concerning Taiwanese VC investments on China and deter mainland Chinese VC investments on Taiwan's high-tech industries.[32] The Taiwanese Cabinet also promulgated new regulations to prohibiting government sponsored VC firms from investing in mainland China. If governmental holdings exceeds 20 percent of the fund, any proposed project of the VC firm for the mainland will be blocked.[33]

Positive Promotion of Global Networks

In addition to restrictive policies which regulate capital and advanced human flow to China, the Taiwanese government has gradually been loosening various restrictive policies to allow for advanced talent inflows to Taiwan, including those from mainland China. In the beginning stage of cross-straits interactions with respect to advanced talented personnel in the 1990s, Taiwan only allowed mainland Chinese academics to conduct short-term research in Taiwanese academic institutions, and even then Taiwanese hosts had to go through a prolonged, complex review process and cope with extensive bureaucratic red tape. In 1998, the scope of such permission was expanded to include talented person-nel in the field of basic and applied technology. Mainland Chinese talent, therefore, is currently permitted to work in the R&D sectors of Taiwanese industries. According to regulations promulgated by the MOEA in 2001, individual Taiwanese firms can apply to bring over advanced workers from China in ten major high-tech fields for an extend period of up to 6 years from the previous three. There is no ceiling for total numbers of mainland Chinese talent, but the percentage must not exceed 10 percent of the total R&D staff of individual firms.[34] A new program to raise the percentage of mainland R&D staff up to 50 is currently being considered.[35]

The more liberal policy to attract mainland China talents is part of Taiwan's strategy to become a global IT development center. In the summer of 2002, the Taiwanese government unveiled plans to invest U.S.$ 5.1 billion in the next 6 years for Taiwan to boost innovation and development on a global scale. Detailed plans include support for oper-ations, special research loans for the private sector, tax breaks, and policies aimed at improving human resources.[36] International IT firms indicate that the strength of Taiwanese R&D capacity is "development" rather than "innovation." Major IT brand holders have decided to set up new development centers in Taiwan. HP, for instance, has closed its Product Development Center (PDC) in Singapore and China and established a new PDC in Taiwan.[37] In a similar vein, Intel also launched a new project dubbed "innovation alliance" to collaborate with Korean and Taiwanese ODM firms. According to Intel, it seeks a competitive advantage by working directly with manufacturers to define and develop products, thereby, playing a leading role in the development of new platforms and products.[38] These new cooperative mechanism between state, business, and MNCs clearly demonstrates the government's intentions to strengthen global networks in the high-tech and IT sectors.

Conclusion

This chapter indicates that the IT networking across the Taiwan Straits is the reflection of new forces of globalization and localization. The case of the semiconductor industry demonstrates that the "hybrid" type of IC firms play the role of integrating technology, know-how, and human resources in the global Chinese community. The ultimate goal of these global-oriented firms is to localize the human power and establish webs of state-business relationship in China. Companies like SMIC could not be classified as a pure "Taiwanese," "Chinese," or "American" firm. In the long run, strategies of localization will help sustain SMIC's power base on mainland China while pursuing global goals of networking.

Global networking also strengthens Taiwan's role in international division of labor in the notebook PC sector. Different from the OEM model of mass production in the traditional industry, Taiwanese ODM firms control key sectors of timely design and adaptation in the production process. These strategic advantages enhance Taiwan's bargaining chips in allying with international brand holders like Dell, HP, Apple, and so on. Taiwan's alliances with global VC firms also help reduce political risks and enhance international competitiveness. The "made in China, by Taiwan" model of IT production demonstrates the complex interdependence between MNCs, Taiwanese ODM firms, and production centers in China. The global networking enhances, rather than weakens, Taiwan's economic security with mainland China.

Rationality of the Taiwanese government to promote such global networking is handicapped by various political concerns. In coping with rising international competition in the IT sector, the Taiwanese government attempts to build Taiwan as a global talent, design, and logistics center. However, these globalization attempts are either slowed down or blocked by many political factors such as Taiwanese identity, political localization, and rejection toward China's unification momentum. The result is that the business community in Taiwan receives minimum supports from the state to expand their global networks to China. Taiwanese IT companies must adopt indirect ways to escape from governmental regulations and intervention.

Looking toward the future, this dual-track model of development may sustain for a period of time in Taiwan. However, the restrictive policies may deter Taiwan from developing into an international logistic and talent center in the IT industry. In the era of globalization, grasping the appropriate timing and policy instruments are keys to success. Facing a rising and globalizing China, Taiwan's competitive edge is rooted on its advantages in deepening international networking and incorporating China into a grand strategy of globalization.

Notes

1. For different aspects of globalization, please refer to David Held, Anthony McGrew, David Goldblatt, and Jonathan Perraton, *Global Transformation* (Stanford, CA: Stanford University Press, 1999); Susan Strange, *The Retreat of the State* (Cambridge: Cambridge University Press, 1996); Paul Hirst and Graham Thompson, *Globalization in Question* (Oxford: Polity Press, 1996); Harold James, *The End of Globalization: Lesson from the Great Depression* (Cambridge, MA: Harvard University Press, 2001); Manuel Castells, *The Rise of the Network Society* (Oxford, UK: Blackwell, 2000); Saskia Sassen, *Losing Control? Sovereignty in the Age of Globalization* (New York, NY: Columbia University Press, 1996); Saskia Sassen, *Globalization and Its Discontents* (New York, NY: The New Press, 1998); Ulrich Beck, *What is Globalization?* (Oxford, UK: Polity Press, 2000).
2. Visits to SMIC Shanghai, on September 14, 2001.
3. Leng, Tse-Kang, *Zixun Chanye Quanqiuhua de Zhengzhi Fenxi: Yi Shanghai Shi Fazhan Weili* (A Political Analysis of Information Technology Industries: Shanghai in Global Perspective) (Taipei: Ink, 2002): 246.
4. Ibid.: 247.
5. In this chapter "Greater China" refers to Taiwan, mainland China, and Hong Kong/Macau region.
6. *Lianhebao* (United Daily News) (July 24, 2002).
7. *Gongshang Shibao* (Commercial Times) (September 24, 2002); *Lianhebao* (July 24, 2002).
8. Mark Landler, "Taiwan Makers of Notebook PC Thrives Quietly," *New York Times* (March 25, 2002): C1.
9. Bruce Einhorn, "Quanta's Quantum Leap," *Business Week* (November 5, 2001): 79.
10. Andrew Tanzer, "Made in Taiwan," *Forbes* (April 2, 2001): 64–66.
11. Einhorn, "Quanta's Quantum Leap."
12. *Zhongguo Shibao* (China Times) (January 14, 2002), available online via: http://www.ctnews.yam.com/news/200202/14/225246.html.
13. Fang, Guojian, *Haikuo Tiankong: Wozai Daier de Suiyue* (Wide Sea and Sky: My Years in Dell) (Taipei: Tianxia Publishing Co., 2002).
14. *Jingji Ribao* (Economy Times) (July 29, 2001).
15. "Dell Settles First Overseas R&D Center in Shanghai," *Asiainfo Daily China News* (July 5, 2002).

16. Guan, Zhenxuan, " Waishang Xin yibo de Taiwanre," (A New Wave of Taiwan Fever of Foreign Business) *Tianxia Zazhi* (Commonwealth Magazine) (October 1, 2002): 112–116.

17. Faith Hung, "Quanta Holds Course in Turbulent Time," *EBN* (Electronic Buyers' News) (December 17, 2001): 48.

18. Xu, Jiahui, "Taiwan Jianchan, Dalu Liangchan," (Decreasing Production in Taiwan, Increasing Outputs in mainland China) *Yuanjian Zazhi* (Global View Magazine) (November 16, 2002), available online via: http://www.gvm.com.tw/cover-v.asp?wgvmno=946&orderno=1.

19. Cheng, Zhangyu, "Chen Ruicong Yao Renbao Na Diyi," (Chen Ruicong Urges Compal Becomes No. 1) *Yuanjian Zazhi* (Global View Magazine) (May 1, 2002): 104.

20. Einhorn, "Quanta's Quantum Leap," 80.

21. Zhuang, Suyu, "Chen Wufu: Xigu Zhu Youming de Huaren Chuangye zhi Shen," (Silicon Valley's God of Chinese Venture Capitalism Chen Wufu) *Yuanjian Zazhi* (Taiwan: April 2001): 120.

22. For a more complete discussion on the concept of "golden triangle," please refer to Leng, Tse-Kang, "Economic Globalization and IT Talent Flows Across the Taiwan Straits: The Taipei—Shanghai—Silicon Valley Triangle," *Asian Survey*, XLII, 2 (March/April 2002): 230–250.

23. "Ctech Channels," (special IT column) *Zhongguo Shibao* (Taipei: February 22, 2001), available online via: <http://news.chinatimes.com>.

24. Li, Kun, "Fengxian Touzi Ye Xuyao Liyong Waizi," (VC also needs foreign investment) *Renmin Ribao*, overseas edition (December 30, 2000).

25. Henny Sender, "China Flirts with Venture Capitalism," *Wall Street Journal* (January 3, 2001): A3.

26. Leng, Tse-Kang, "Economic Globalization and IT Talent Flows Across the Taiwan Straits," 244.

27. http://210.200.236.46/survey/china_q_1.htm#.

28. http://www.1111.com.tw.

29. *Gongshang Shibao* (October 11, 2002).

30. *Zhongguo Shibao* (March 9, 2002); *Lianhebao* (April 25, 2002).

31. *Lianhebao* (October 30, 2002).

32. *Zhongguo Shibao* (September 9, 2002).

33. *Zhongguo Shibao* (October 28, 2002).

34. *Jingji Ribao* (Taipei: February 20, 2001); *Zhongyang Ribao* (Central Daily News) (Taipei: October 13, 2001).

35. *Gongshang Shibao* (October 7, 2002).

36. Background Information from MOEA, ROC.

37. Guan, "Waishang Xin yibo de Taiwanre," 108.

38. Faith Hung, "Intel Inks Collaborative Deals with Top Asian Manufacturers," *EBN* (October 21, 2002), available online via: http://www.ebnonline.com.

CHAPTER NINE

Informational Capitalism and the Remaking of "Greater China": Strategies of Siliconization

NGAI-LING SUM

Introduction

The Asian Crisis has resulted in profound changes in the East Asian region. It can be argued that, while the Japan-led production network (otherwise known as the "flying geese" model) has been weakened, the "Greater China"[1] network is rising. Important aspects of this new regional dynamic are the many high-tech connections with the United States and the desire to emulate the success of the American model. More specifically, this takes the form of key economic and political actors in the region imagining "Greater China" becoming the home of the "next Silicon Valley." This "Silicon Wave" vision is very influential among public and private institutions/actors (e.g. policy-makers, state technocrats, think tanks, and business journalists) in the region. They imagine their economic future in terms of the "Silicon Valley model"[2] and, indeed, draw on and promote high-tech linkages with the Californian archetype to this end. They produce discourses, strategies, policies, and material practices that seek to promote, complement, extend, and embed this high-tech hegemonic paradigm in regional, national, and trans-local frameworks. For example, Taiwan is being reimagined as a "Green Silicon Island," Hong Kong has developed a self-image as an "Internet-hub" with a "Cyberport," and Shenzhen, Shanghai, and Beijing are profiling themselves as "China's Silicon Valley." They are all trying to move toward broader-based, more solidly rooted high-tech futures by emulating the original model in California—or at least what they understand as the Silicon Valley experience and the reasons for its success. This provides the basis for local or national accumulation strategies based on the "Siliconization" of economic and extra-economic institutions, organizations, and subjectivities to produce a coherent mode of informational capitalism[3] and to promote a favorable insertion of the emerging Silicon spaces into the global division of labor.

As it is unfolding in "Greater China," this Siliconization strategy involves three elements: (a) privileging the "Silicon Valley" model in particular and "high-tech development" discourses promoted by diverse private and public actors; (b) using these discourses to reconfigure techno-economic subjectivities in the hope of stabilizing emerging economic practices favorable to their particular insertions into the global informational capitalism; and (c) consolidating and mediating this regional mode of growth via the co-presence of cooperation–competition and integration–fragmentation (fragmegration). This strategy of localizing the global "Silicon Wave" encounters dilemmas and challenges rooted in the more general dynamics of political economy of integration and fragmentation.

The Strategy of Siliconization and the Reordering of Trans-Border Economic Space in "Greater China"

The strategy of Siliconization emerged first in official and corporate discourses. In the 1990s, there was no lack of discourses concerned to reinvent local and national economies around "high-tech," "knowledge-based" and "ICT"/"biotech" accumulation. Various economic and political actors have been using the symbolism of "Silicon Valley," "knowledge-based economy," and "biotechnology" in the effort to establish a new techno-economic vision to guide economic strategy. The Taiwanese government was a pioneer of this approach. The "Silicon Valley" imagination emerged in Taiwan in the late 1970s. The then economic visionary and Minister of Economic Affairs—Li Kuo-ting—visited the first Silicon Valley and advised his government to build the Hsinchu Science-Based Industrial Park in its image. Narrated as a nation-building project, the Park became a test bed for integrating Taiwan into the global circuit of capital and production. Silicon Valley "returnees," who provided the key transnational linkages, were attracted back to Taiwan through tax breaks and other economic incentives through organizations such as Monte Jade.[4] Almost half of the companies in the Park in 1997 had been started by U.S.-educated engineers. Entering the trans-Pacific division of labor with Silicon Valley in California, these companies concentrated on Original Equipment Manufacturing (OEM) of electronic hardware.

With American proposals in the early 1990s to build a "Global Information Infrastructure"[5] and Taiwan's westward extension of its own Silicon production chain to mainland China, the National Science Council (NSC) proposed to deepen the Siliconization strategy in its first Keji yu Zhengce Baipishu (*White Paper on Science and Technology*) in December 1997. It recommended that Taiwan should build on the Hsinchu model to become a "technologically advanced nation" during the first decade of the twenty-first century. Deploying the image of Silicon-Valley type "clustering," it envisioned the building of a "National Information Infrastructure," starting with the establishment of a suitable "core" and "satellite science-based industrial parks/clusters" throughout Taiwan. These would become nuclei for building "science cities," to be linked by major infrastructural networks that would turn Taiwan into a "science island."[6] This scientific-technological construction of Taiwan's economic future was translated into more concrete measures and a specific timetable in the form of *Dazao keji jingbu guo xingdong fangan* (Action Plan for Building a Technologically Advanced Nation), which appeared in April 1998. Regarding the establishment of high-tech clusters, this recommended the building of new satellite industrial parks at Chunan and Tungluo as well as software parks at Nankang and other locations.[7]

This imagination of Taiwan as a "science island" has been reinforced and deepened by the coming to office of President Chen Shuibian in May 2000. During a visit to London in December 1999, when he was the pro-independence Democratic Progressive Party's (DPP) presidential candidate, Chen had already made a speech that discussed United Kingdom Prime Minister Tony Blair's ideology of the "Third Way" in which he identified the "New Middle Way" as Taiwan's future path in the context of "globalization." It was also in this speech that Chen proposed his vision of Taiwan as a "Green Silicon Island."

> Over the years, I have had a vision of developing Taiwan into a Green Valley. I believe that human beings are entitled to enjoy a beautiful natural environment as well as the convenience of advanced technology; I cannot imagine an essential conflict

between the two . . . My blueprint for Green Valley must be extended to the entire island, based on the current successes and resources of Taiwan's silicon and computer high-tech industry. I hope that Taiwan in the next millennium will indeed become the Green Silicon Island.[8]

Chen was quick to return to this theme when he gave his inaugural speech as Taiwan's new President on May 20, 2000. He envisioned the development of a "sustainable green silicon island" that provides a "balance between ecological preservation and economic development."[9] Since then, the idea has found more concrete expression in the "Plan to Develop a Knowledge-based Economy in Taiwan," produced in September 2000. This claims to be "one of the driving forces for Taiwan's transformation into a 'Green Silicon Island,' " a project that is to be implemented in six ways:

(1) Set up mechanisms to encourage innovation and foster new ventures.
(2) Expand the use of information technology (IT) and the Internet in production as well as daily life.
(3) Lay the groundwork for an environment supportive to Internet use.
(4) Consider due modification of the education system in a drive to meet the development of personnel needs by training and importing a sufficient pool of knowledge workers.
(5) Establish service-oriented government.
(6) Formulate precautionary measures against social problems that arise from the transformation of the economy.[10]

While Taiwan was a keen supporter of the "Silicon Wave" at an early stage, Hong Kong and China's economic and political elites were less susceptible to its appeal as a model until the Asian Crisis in 1997.[11] The Hong Kong government tried to jump onto the Silicon bandwagon after the Asian Crisis. In March 1998, Hong Kong Chief Executive Tung Chee-Hwa set up the Commission on Innovation and Technology to examine the possibility of turning Hong Kong into a center of innovation and technology, its first report provided the background for him to link "high-tech" with the "Asian Crisis." In his first policy speech, delivered in October 1998, Tung thus remarked:

To help our economy respond to the changes I have described [Asian Crisis], our strategy will be to focus on increasing the

diversity of the economy by creating conditions for growth in
sectors with a high value-added element, in particular in those
industries which place importance on high technology and multimedia applications.[12]

Hong Kong Financial Secretary, Donald Tsang, translated this push for
high technology into more concrete projects when he delivered his
budget speech the following year. According to Tsang:

> There is no question that, for Hong Kong to meet the challenges
> of the 21st Century, it must adapt to the new forces of the
> Information Age. Technological advances such as digitalisation and
> broadband networks are introducing new ways of doing business,
> transforming traditional markets and altering existing competitive
> advantages . . .
> To respond to these mega trends . . . the Government proposes
> to develop a "Cyberport" in Hong Kong. The Cyberport will pro-
> vide the essential infrastructure for the formation of a strategic clus-
> ter of information services companies. These companies would
> specialize in the development of services and multi-media content
> to support businesses and industries . . .[13]

These "high-tech-Silicon Valley" discourses in Taiwan and Hong
Kong resonated with those in mainland China. The Mayor of Shenzhen,
Li Zibin, speaking in the Guangdong Technological Innovation
Symposium in March 2000, announced that his city would focus on
the "high and new technology sector, especially information products
based on the Internet and a digital Valley." At an Information Technology
Working Conference in Shenzhen, Li again specifically stressed
his ambition for the information industry to form a solid foundation
for Shenzhen to become "China's Silicon Valley," with an IT output
value expected to reach U.S.$16.9 billion by the end of the year 2000.[14]
Although the bursting of the "technology bubble" in May 2001
sent shock waves through the region, it has not fundamentally under-
mined the support for this paradigm. Indeed, Beijing and Shanghai
also emphasize their identities as key players in the development of
"China's Silicon Valley." Nonetheless the paradigm has been inflected in
many cases away from a temporary fascination with "dot-coms" and
"e-commerce" and back toward more solid forms of high-tech industries such as "integrated circuits," (IC) "software," "biotechnology," and
"biomedicines."

It is not surprising that these kinds of official-level high-tech discourses in Taiwan, Hong Kong, and mainland China, and their imagined IT and/or biotech futures, strongly resonated with those that are promoted by private actors. It can even be argued that there is a global-regional-local epistemic community that promotes the "Silicon Wave" in the region. The community comprises: (a) state officials and government departments (such as city mayors, chief executives, and politicians and officials from key economic ministries); (b) university academics (such as professors from science and business faculties); (c) Silicon-Valley returnees; (d) business journalists; (e) industrial and trade associations; (f) local-regional capitalists (such as Hong Kong's Richard Li of Pacific Century CyberWorks, Taiwan's Stan Shih of Acer and China's Simon Jiang of CyberCity Shenzhen); and (g) global capitalists with major regional interests (such as Microsoft's Bill Gates, Yahoo!'s Jerry Yang, and IBM's Craig Barrett). This latter group of "cyber-gods" even flew into the region to attain high-profiled conferences and exhibitions. They publicly endorsed the "Silicon Wave" as the way forward, and high-lighted their own role as tenants of science parks and/or partners with local projects. The individuals and organizations within this epistemic community expressed a common high-tech voice that contributes to the (re-)making of new techno-economic identities and practices in the trans-border space of "Greater China."

These techno-economic identities were constructed in and through high-tech symbols such as "Silicon Valley," "clustering," "entrepreneurship," "information technology," "knowledge-based economy," and "biotechnology." They circulate not only within the epistemic community but also in the wider society as new subjectivities of the Information Age. Techno-economic subjectivities of these kinds are influencing the building of new economic practices across different sites in "Greater China." They include the following:

(a) Developing flagship "incubators" that profile themselves as "the next Silicon Valley" and are promoted by private–public partnerships.
(b) Building and strengthening regional–global networks with Silicon Valley in California and with analogous clusters elsewhere.
(c) Extending the Silicon production chain to cheaper (trans-)local sites.
(d) Forming alliances between "old" and "new economy" as well as deepening into "biotechnology."
(e) Developing new sources of networking (such as industry–university co-operation) and finances for high-tech ventures.

(f) Tapping overseas/Chinese IT experts through schemes like the "Admission of Talent Scheme" in Hong Kong and new "visa wars," in which countries in the region issue visas to compete for the limited pool of high-tech workers.

(g) Developing and deepening intellectual property right (IPR) laws.

This chapter now discusses these practices and the way they are assembled into a possible informational regime both within and across borders. It should be noted that such assemblage takes place not in accordance with the will of the government or individuals, but by the articulation and concurrent development of practices with diverse trajectories in Taiwan, Hong Kong, and mainland China. The resulting contingent assemblages can be analyzed in terms of the co-presence of cooperation with competition/challenges in the building of informational capitalism in the region.

Taiwan's Siliconization Strategy and Practices: Building on a Successful Pathway

Taiwan can be seen as a pioneer of the Siliconization strategy. It started with a vision elaborated by Li Kuo-ting when he was a minister without portfolio as well as convener of the Applied Technology Committee. He brought different sectors together to formulate the *Kexue gongye yuan qu shezhi guanli tiaoli* (Statute for the Establishment and Administration of Science-Based Industrial Parks) in 1979. This statute became the policy basis for the building of the Hsinchu Science-Based Industrial Park. Narrated as "the Silicon Valley of the Orient," the Park became a locality for networking into the global Silicon production chain since 1980. More generally, mediated by state support and a diasporic network of Taiwanese engineers and venture capitalists who had studied and worked in California's Silicon Valley for at least a decade, Taiwan became the OEM center for electronics production. The mantra has been "Silicon Valley creates it, Taiwan makes it." Since the 1980s, many Silicon-Valley "returnees" brought back with them technical skill, organizational and managerial know-how, entrepreneurial experience, and connections to ICT markets in the United States. This group that can be seen as part of the reverse "brain drain," is slowly developing into a process of "brain circulation" in which the diasporic networks of scientists and engineers are continually transferring technology and know-how between California's Silicon Valley and Hsinchu.[15]

Given their role in mediating trans-Pacific linkages, this group of knowledge workers frequently travel (at least once a month) between Silicon Valley and Hsinchu. They are known as "astronauts" who spend much of the time on aeroplanes and work for long and flexible hours in different sites. Their work involves demands of time and speed in transferring information between Silicon Valley and Hsinchu about investment and partnership opportunities as well as about markets and technology. Some of these workers are not only mobile across borders, they are also mobile between the public and private sectors, between universities and private sectors, and between the manufacturing sector and the venture capital (VC) industry. For example, Morris Chang was the President of the Industrial Technology Research Institute—a government-founded organization—before he became chairman of the Taiwan Semiconductor Manufacturing Company (TSMC).

Mediated by these diasporic networks, California's Silicon Valley concentrates on R&D, new product definition, and leading-edge innovation. The IT-related cluster of firms in Hsinchu specialized mainly in OEM of desktop computers, notebooks, and other information appliances (such as memory ICs, motherboards, monitors, scanners, printers, etc.); at the same time they were also shifting their activities toward a growing volume of original design manufacture (ODM) and logistics. This can be seen as a system of vertically disintegrated firms that cross cut national boundaries. They were involved in intense competition as well as cooperation in dense networks of consortia, joint ventures and partnerships in the two trans-local sites.

This earlier system of cross-border division of labor between California and Hsinchu was challenged by the following factors in the 1990s. These include: (a) rapid wage increases in Taiwan; (b) appreciation of the Taiwanese dollar against the U.S. dollar; (c) the adoption of tougher environmental regulations in Taiwan; and (d) the challenges and opportunities that have followed from the opening of China to inward investment. Some specialized production in the Hsinchu cluster was moved to China to take advantage of its cheap (non-)skilled labor, preferential tax terms, flexible rules, steady supply of products and huge market potential. During the 1990s, for example, production of lower-end, commoditized products such as keyboards, mice, monitors and the assembly of desktop PCs moved to local sites such as Dongguan and Shenzhen areas in southern China. At the mid-1990s, Taiwan manufacturers began to shift their focus to Yangtze River Delta because of its better transportation infrastructure and favorable tax incentives offered by local municipalities. Higher value-added products such as motherboards, scanners, video cards, notebooks, and integrated circuits (IC) are transferred to sites around Shanghai area such as Suzhou and Kunshan. This stretching of Silicon production chain to the Shanghai-Suzhou and the Shenzhen-Dongguan areas are consolidating as cross-border OEM centers for IT/electronics production.

In most cases, Taiwanese firms in mainland China dispatch numerous company cadres to oversee the subsidiaries. The first-generation of expatriate workers were offered preferential terms (e.g. higher salaries) to work in China. With the increase in unemployment in Taiwan, such preferential terms start to diminish from 80 percent higher than Taiwan's salary to 30 percent or less.[16] In fact, migrating to China has become a popular option for the unemployed younger generation that sees working and living in "Shanghai" as being "cool" and offering plentiful opportunities on and off the job. According to *Xinmin Weekly*, the number of Taiwanese working and living permanently in the greater Shanghai area has reached 300,000.[17] As more and more of them settling down in the region, they begin to call themselves "Shang-Tai-nese" (*Shang Tai ren*)—a new trans-border identity that encompasses a double meaning: "Taiwanese in Shanghai" and "powerful Taiwanese people." Apart from the expatriate workers settled in the Shanghai area, it has been estimated that about 10,000 move between Taiwan and Shanghai every month.

With this westward migration of its Silicon production chain and labor to southern and eastern China, Taiwan is enhancing its insertion into global informational capitalism by rebuilding its R&D capacity. This is achieved by promoting other Silicon-Valley type clusters in Tainan, Chunan, Tunglu as well as a software park at Nankang in the 1997 White Paper and its associated Action Plan. The plan to build the flagship software park in Nankang was actualized when the then President Li Denghui inaugurated its opening in Taipei County in October 1999 (table 9.1). This "milestone-type" public-private project was commissioned by the Ministry of Economic Affairs (MOEA) and developed by Shizheng kaifa gongsi (Century Development Company), a joint venture of 19 domestic and foreign companies. The International Software Development Centre was established on 2,000 ping (1 ping = 11 sq. meters) of floor space purchased by the Ministry, and operates to encourage the grounding of global–local links between multinational software companies and indigenous Taiwanese firms. In addition, the Ministry will spend NTD995 million to procure 3,100 ping of floor space to set up an incubator programme for around 60 start-up companies. The park thus aims to provide software companies with infrastructure facilities, networking services, training programmes, and market information. Software

Table 9.1 Nankang software park

Cost:	NTD 12.8 billion (U.S.$402.5 million)
Size:	8.2 hectares
Location:	Nankang, Taipei County
Completion date:	1999 (first stage); 2003 (second stage)
Partners:	Century Development Corp.
Cluster:	Home to global and local software companies
	Proximity to the Academia Sinica's Institute of
	Information Sciences and projected Nankang
	Economic and Trade Park
Signed-up tenants:	15 (including IBM, HP, Compaq, Intel)
Terms:	Foreign companies have to sign cooperative
	documents with Taiwan companies
Expected return:	U.S.$14 billion by 2005

Source: Author's compilation from various issues of Central News Agency, Taiwan.

companies that locate there may also take advantage of tax incentives and subsidies for developing strategic technology.

Nankang Software Park does not exist in isolation; it is part of a larger plan to deepen Taiwan as a "Green Silicon Island" according to the Six-Year Development Plan published in May 2002. This Plan, entitled *Taozhan er ling ling ba* (Challenge 2008), creates a number of other high-tech centers that are intended to host clusters of domestic and international businesses and research institutes (see table 9.2). Priority areas include biotechnology, nanotechnology, system-on-chip design and telecommunication. These core centers and the technologies they promote aim to further reconfigure Taiwan into Asia's R&D base.

From a political perspective, this kind of diversification into "biotechnology" is less controversial than the practice of extending the Silicon production chain to cheaper trans-local sites in mainland China, a process that began with low-tech products such as umbrellas and footwear in 1987.[18] The present round involves IT-related products, such as keyboards, mouse technology and switching power supplies. Production sites spread from an initial concentration in Guangdong and Fujian provinces to Shanghai-Suzhou area. This trend of relocation to the mainland has become increasingly controversial as it has coincided with the global recession in high-tech production and the decline in political confidence that has accompanied the political transition from Guomindang (GMD) to DPP rule in spring 2000.

Given that Taiwan has a longer history than other parts of "Greater China" in pursuing the strategy of siliconization, it has consolidated a "Silicon coalition" of powerful industrial capitalists, exemplified by

Table 9.2   Taiwan's new high-tech centers in the Six-Year Development Plan 2002

Name of high-tech/research institution	Nature of high-tech project
Nankang Software Park	Specializing as a software design center
Academia Sinica	Building a genome research center
Chung-Shan Institute of Science and Technology	Building a mobile communications-engineering center
Industrial Technology Research Institute in Hsinchu	Building a research center for the application of nanotechnlogy

Source: The Six-Year Development Plan 2002, Taiwan, http://www.washingtonstate.org.tw/English/taiwan-trade-economy/6-year-plan/international-r&d-base.htm.

figures like Acer's Stan Shih and Matthew Miao of the Mitac-Synnex Group. Taking advantage of China's cheaper production costs[19] and its large potential markets, this group has expanded production in mainland China in the same way as industrial capitalists such as Wang Yung-ching of Formosa Plastics Group have. For example, the Acer Group invested U.S.$50 million in late 1999 in a manufacturing plant in Zhongshan, Guangdong Province, to produce computers and DVD players. In 2001, the company produced about 122,000 mainboards per month, 250,000 CD-ROM drives and 50,000 bare-bones systems in its Zhongshan plant. It has been estimated that 30 percent of Taiwan's total IT production was made in mainland China in 2000.[20]

This extension of Taiwan's Silicon production chain "westward" has sparked new power struggles in Taiwan. In order to add credibility to its cross-straits activities, a "Silicon coalition," with the support of other capitalists and the political opposition alliance, deploys a "China-as-partner" discourse that narrates "China" as an "external economic boost for Taiwan." By mapping Taiwan's economic future with that of China, this "Silicon (plus) coalition" calls for the Taiwan government to relax its *Jieji yongren* ("no haste, be patient") policy[21] toward the mainland by lifting curbs on investment across the Strait. Wang Yung-ching of Formosa Plastics even suggests that Taiwan should accept Beijing's "one-China" principle. The "win-win" discourse of this "Silicon (plus) coalition" is also articulated by a plethora of commercial books that mediate the negotiation of China's identity in Taiwan. Deploying titles such as *The Winning Commercial Potential of 1.3 Billion Chinese, Dipping into the Golden Bowl of Shanghai*, and *Thirty-Five Gold-Panning Measures for the mainland Stock Market*, such works construct an image of mainland China as a "gold mine" and Shanghai as a "cool city" in which Taiwanese capitalists and professional people can "live, work and play."[22]

Such positive constructions of China coexist with new political and economic practices that are promoted by the "Silicon (plus) coalition." For example, the government is subject to lobbying to abandon restrictions on IC industries, especially the 8-inch wafer lab, from moving to China. Supporters for easing such restrictions argued that the great potential of China's markets made it essential that Taiwanese companies staked their claim early and, if Taiwanese firms would not make investments, other countries would. This "go-west" imagination and its associated practices have raised considerable economic and political concerns in Taiwan. More specifically, there were growing fears over rising unemployment and the outflows of capital and manpower to China, with some 300,000 person-nel, mostly managers, reported to have moved across the Taiwan Strait.[23] Such trends sharpened Taiwan's dilemma between protecting its security concerns and promoting its geo-economic interests. This dilemma was grounded not only in the fear of loosing "sensitive high-tech technology" to mainland China, but also in the international and domestic implications of an imminent challenge to Taiwan's position as the major nodal point in the Silicon production chain.

Under the pressure of the "Silicon (plus) coalition," the DPP govern-ment adopted a "de-Li Denghui" policy to relax Li's restraints on invest-ing in mainland China. Chen's first initiative was to create "mini-three-links" through the offshore islands of Kinmen, Matzu and Penghu. By September 2001, the Economic Development Advisory Committee, an influential group of Taiwan business, academic and government leaders recommended the loosening of Li's *Jieji yongren* ("no haste, be patient") policy in favor of the policy of *Jiji kaifang youxiao guangli* ("active opening and effective management"). The latter includes: (a) opening direct investment with no need for enterprises to set up a subsidiary company in a third place; (b) relaxing the ceiling of cumulative total investment made in the mainland by individuals and small- and medium-sized enterprises, with NT$60 million being raised to NT$80 million; (c) abolishing the regulation to the ceiling of cumu-lative total investment amount to U.S.$50 million for individual case. Chen endorsed these recommendations in August 2001. Under contin-uous pressure from the "Silicon (plus) coalition" and Taiwan's entry into the World Trade Organization (WTO) in January 2002, the MOEA in March 2003 permitted the Taiwan Semiconductor Manufacturing Corporation (TSMC) to start preparations for the construction of an 8-inch wafer plant in Shanghai on condition that it helps to upgrade technology at home by starting new plants to produce 12-inch chips in Taiwan.

Hong Kong's Siliconization Strategy and Practices: Searching
for a "Suitable" Pathway

Hong Kong's Siliconization strategy started much later than that of Taiwan. Hong Kong moved its labor-intensive industries to southern China following the opening of the mainland China in 1978. When the partial vacuum created by this "hollowing out" process was filled by Hong Kong's acquisition of functions that made it into a global–regional gateway city, the result was a heavy dependence on the service sector— especially real estate and finance. A major debate on "service versus industry" thus raged from 1993 onward,[24] which became even more pressing when the Asian financial crisis demonstrated the vulnerabilities of the real estate and financial sectors in Hong Kong. It was in this context of the post-financial crisis desperate search for new object(s) of economic growth that Tung Chee-Hwa made his 1998 Policy Speech emphasizing "high-tech," using it as an economic symbol that might be capable of expanding the boundaries of the debate on Hong Kong's future trajectory. It was not long after, in March 1999, that his technological mode of calculation was taken up and articulated as the idea of building a Cyberport by Pacific Century's Richard Li.

Li's Cyberport is premised on possibilities for expanding and upgrading the service cluster(s) for informational capitalism. He thus describes it as providing "a comprehensive facility designed to foster the development of Hong Kong's information services sector and to enhance Hong Kong's position as the premier information and telecommunications hub in Asia."[25] Using "Silicon Valley" and its "social density" as metaphors, it is alleged that the Cyberport will be able to "attract, nurture and retain the relevant innovative talent necessary to build a cyber-culture critical mass in Hong Kong."[26] Within this narrative, the Cyberport is re-presented as a new type of service-based node for connecting Hong Kong to the fast time of "information flows." More specifically, it is a project that reimagines the territory's competitive advantages in terms of capturing global "information flows" and managing them within the service-space of Hong Kong and its broader regional scale through, for example, the formation of a multimedia and information services hub. In addition, Hong Kong's services are to be connected to fast cyber-time and the knowledge-based economy. Finally, a localized social space is to be consolidated within which to build a "cyber culture critical mass" that links the global, the regional, and the local to consolidate a "pool of talents" in the shortest possible time.

This vision of expanding and upgrading Hong Kong's service cluster(s) has clearly been appropriated by the government to symbolize and spearhead its post-financial crisis politics of "technological optimism." In his 1999 Budget Speech, Financial Secretary Donald Tsang thus earmarked the "Cyberport" as a flagship project, involving a private–public partnership in which the government provides land worth HKD6 billion, while Pacific CyberWork pools capital to construct the buildings. This project is then supposed to provide "incubator" services to create a "critical mass of firms" that will be nurtured by a physical form modeled on "Silicon Valley" (table 9.3).

Not surprisingly, this emerging discourse and its private–public practice has encountered resistance from within the service sector and political

Table 9.3   A new economic object of "Growth": cyberport

Cost:	HK$13 billion (U.S.$1.68 billion)
Size:	64 acres (25.6 hectares)
Location:	Telegraph Bay, Pokfulam
Aims:	"To create a world class location for the conduct of a variety of activities which through the use of in-formation technologies, can leverage Hong Kong existing strengths in the service sector (e.g., in financial, media, retail, transportation, education, and tourism services)."[27]
Built environment I:	Cyber facilities (2/3 of the site) • fiber optic wiring • satellite signal senders • built-in high-speed modems • cyberlibrary • media laboratories and studio facilities
Built environment II:	Real estate (1/3 of the site) • houses and apartments • hotel • retail
Completion Date:	2007 (commencing from 2002)
Job Creation:	4,000 during construction 12,000 professional jobs on completion (10% from outside Hong Kong)
Partners:	Pacific Century CyberWorks (HK$7 billion equity capital) Government (land worth HK$6 billion)
Cluster of Tenants:	Multinationals (Microsoft, IBM, Oracles, HP, Softbank, Yahoo!, Hua Wei, Sybas) Local tenants of small to medium-size IT companies
Metaphors/images used:	Silicon Valley, "catching up," and "clustering"

Source: Author's compilation from various issues of *South China Morning Post.*

groups. Seven property developers publicly denounced the project, and were later joined by three more, angry that they had been excluded from the high-profile project by the government's decision to provide free land for the Cyberport without any public tendering process. In response, the Financial Secretary argued that the Cyberport was a "technology" and not a "residential project," explaining:

> We have not tried to exclude anybody in the process . . . The whole emphasis is Cyberport. The whole emphasis is technological project. It is not residential development as such. Even if you use all the money that we have from selling the residential portion, we will not have sufficient capital to develop the Cyberport. So the way we are approaching the issue is the most economic, most efficient way, from a taxpayer's point of view . . . You must realize of course the Cyberport, at the end of the day, will be owned by the public, will not be owned by any private developer. We will be determining the leasing requirements. We will be determining who will be our tenants, and we will be determining the rental value as well. So for someone who has expertise, who has the connection, and is able to put up with the business risk for this matter, and is a technology firm, it is a very rare find. I think we have got the right thing, and we've got the right deal for the Hong Kong public.[28]

This narration of the Cyberport as a "technology project" did not entirely pacify the discontented developers, who still saw it as a "residential project." They even came up with an alternative proposal, according to which the government could auction off the ancillary residential property and receive U.S.$1.08 billion in cash up front, of which U.S.$640 million could be used to construct the Cyberport. The government rejected this by appealing to the commercial logic of "risk calculation," according to which the private–public partnership would mean less "risk" for the government.

It was not only property developers who saw the Cyberport as constituting a "residential" project. Some financial market analysts also criticized the project for amounting to little more than "Cyber villas by sea," claiming that it was "no 'Silicon Valley'." [29] The Hong Kong Democratic Foundation, moreover, adopted an even harsher tone, responding to the 1999/2000 Budget by remarking that:

> . . . We do not believe that a property-based development is a meaningful way to promote high technology industrial development.

The clustering of technology-related industry does not depend on property; there are already small scale clusters in areas of Hong Kong that have received no special favor, for example, the Wellington Street area.[30]

The Democratic Foundation's report also criticized the granting of the Cyberport land to a well-connected company without any tendering procedures for raising the spectre of cronyism and damaging Hong Kong's reputation. Members of the Democratic Party echoed this charge, and challenged the government's lack of transparency, pointing out that Richard Li is the son of Li Ka-Shing, a good friend of the Chief Executive. The Financial Secretary responded as follows:

I do not want to comment on what other people say, but I will be very patient in explaining to them this is a very important infra-structure, and we have been doing it very fairly. But the require-ments for selection of a developer are very strict because it is not a property development project. And I would be very careful in explaining cronyism is never, never in Hong Kong's dictionary. We pride on being transparent, we pride on playing on a completely level playing field. There is not (sic) question whatsoever of Hong Kong Government, the SAR Government, engaging in cronyism.[31]

Despite these challenges to the government's plan for a private–public partnership, the emerging techno-economic discourse has generated other new economic practices within the service sector. Up to the bursting of the technology bubble, one notable case was the way in which large prop-erty and commercial conglomerates in Hong Kong began to combine the so-called "old" and "new" economies with varying degrees of success. For example, in August 1999, Sun Hung Kai Properties (SHKP) transformed its empty properties in Tsuen Wan to establish a "Cyberincubator" project in partnership with the Hong Kong Industrial Technology Centre. Under this scheme, SHKP would provide rent-free space for new "infopreneurs" for 3 years in return for 15 percent stakes in their respective businesses. The response to this initiative was poor, however, due to the terms involved, with start-up firms believing that the value of their equity stake was much higher than the rental that could be saved from receiving the free indus-trial space being offered by SHKP. In May 2001, the Hong Kong Industrial Technology Centre abandoned this rent-for-equity model.

Tung Chee-Hwa's July 1999 visit to Silicon Valley also fed into the creation of new practices by building new linkages between local informational communities and the Chinese diaspora. The Hong Kong–Silicon Valley Association and a new website (SV-Hong Kong.com) were formed in late 1999 to enhance possible global–local flows of knowledge, expertise, and manpower. The Hong Kong Stock Exchange also began to experiment with new initiatives, such as the launching of the Growth Enterprise Market (GEM)[32] in 1999, the territory's version of Nasdaq, offering an alternative listing choice for incubating start-up technology companies and raising VC in the "Greater China" region. Up to the bursting of the bubble, 13 firms were listed, with 7 from Hong Kong, 4 from China and 1 from Taiwan. One of the high-profiled listings was Tom.com, an Internet arm of Li Ka-Shing's Cheung Kong-Hutchinson Whampoa empire. Li, identified as the "superman" of property, telecommunications, and port facilities, managed to re-ignite the dizzying pre-crisis speculation craze. Five-hundred thousand investors mobbed local branches of the Hongkong and Shanghai Banking Corporation to deposit applications for Tom.com's initial public offering (IPO) in February 2000. The IPO was oversubscribed 2,000 times due to an "Internet fever" that was largely related to people seeking to earn "a quick buck" in the same way that they had once overinvested in the property market. In this regard, the "Cyberport," "Silicon Valley," "Richard Li," and "Tom.com" became short-term economic icons just before the bursting of the "technology bubble."

When the burst did finally come, it not only brought falling share prices and retrenchment in the high-profile corporations, it also revealed the conflictual nature of the assemblages of techno-economic practices that had developed in Hong Kong. First of all, the use of the Cyberport as a symbol to trigger the expansion of the "old" economy into the "new" failed to bring about the intended expansion of existing economic boundaries to embrace "technology." Instead, it became evident that it had spurred Hong Kong's embedded property-finance interests to react in a short-term euphoric manner. Second, the short-term "high-tech" fanfare, if not spec-fare, ignited by the service-finance sectors and the subsequent bursting of the technology bubble actually stimulated a good deal of public adversity toward "technology." In a paradoxical way, therefore, a project aimed at promoting "technology" ended up doing the opposite. "Technology," largely understood in speculative terms, is neither facilitating Hong Kong's catching up process nor bridging the service-industry divide. Third, global competition to capture the fast time of informational capitalism in Hong Kong has changed the temporalities of its decision-making process, most notably by speeding up the building of the Cyberport. Such speeding up, however, came into direct conflict with the routine procedures of the public tendering process upon which public confidence of the system depends.

However, this does not mean that the strategy of Siliconization (as opposed to Cyberport) has had little impact in Hong Kong. Its more long-term impact has both path-dependent and path-shaping aspects.[33] In the post-dotcom-bubble period, the political regime and its economic allies are searching for new objects around to reconstruct its insertion into the global–regional economic processes. Building on Hong Kong's finance-service developmental path, they seek to reshape it in a more high-tech direction. Key actors such as the Chinese government, the SAR government as well as trade and service organizations (e.g. Hong Kong General Chamber of Commerce, Hong Kong Coalition of Service Industries) are supporting Hong Kong as a knowledge-based city with a special role as a "logistic, financial and business hub" that links the Pearl River Delta with the global economy. This emphasis on Hong Kong as a hub providing high-tech services for a transnational/trans-local space is evident in the setting up of the Logistics Council in December 2001. The Council called for: (a) the development of Hong Kong's infrastructure to take advantage of opportunities in "virtual logistics" (e.g. using virtual reality of software, logistic system such as automated warehouses, intelligent material handling system); and (b) the provision of logistic services under the demand and supply chain that operates through or from Hong Kong. The Chinese government also supports infrastructural and administrative initiatives, including 24-hour border crossings, streamlined visit procedures, and plans for the construction of a Hong Kong-Macau-Zhuhai bridge.

These logistic services and facilities are complemented by financial and business ones (e.g. syndicated loans, professional, and managerial services) that can supply "non-research" framework such as accounting, banking, legal, intellectual property, and patent services that can support China's and the region's attempts to develop biotechnology ventures. For example, Hong Kong's property conglomerates are seeking to enter the biotechnology field. For example, Cheung Kong (Holdings) invested HKD10 billion in its biotech division of CK Life Sciences International Inc. working on fertilizer products. The New World Group, along with other investors such as Compaq Computer, Chengdu University of Traditional Chinese Medicine, Sichuan Internet, etc., invested U.S.$3 million to establish a Chinese medicine portal called TCM1.com in 2001. It includes laws and regulations, trade consultation, and research and study of Chinese medicine. It also provides a platform for B2B distribution of Chinese raw medicines. In addition, New World Group, along with six other investors, has invested around U.S.$2 million for a stake in ChipScreen BioScience, a bioinformatics, and chemoinformatics joint venture with Qinghua University based in Shenzhen.

Southern China's Siliconization Strategy and Practices:
Shaping the National Development Pathway

The area of the Pearl River Delta and Guangdong Province, bordering Hong Kong, has seen numerous projects to remake the region for informational capitalism. Attempting to ride the "Silicon Wave," central government organs like the Ministry of Science and Technology, as well as municipal authorities promote the building of high-tech industrial development zones in the cities/towns of Guangzhou, Shenzhen, Zhuhai, Huizhou, Zhongshan, and Foshan. Most of these projects offer preferential terms for global capital and local firms to enter the zones. In Guangzhou, the government has the ambition to capture global flows of technology, knowledge and manpower via the development of the Guangzhou Science City, the Guangzhou Tianhe Software Park, and the Guangzhou International Bio-Island. The Science City, which profiles itself as "the Rising Silicon Valley in Guangzhou," offers tax exemptions for global and local capital for the initial 2 years and unlimited sales in Guangdong for high-tech electronics, computer communication and aerospace engineering products. The Guangzhou Tianhe Software Park will concentrate on the R&D of software as well as the incubation of software R&D. Apart from promoting IT production, the Guangzhou Municipal Government is also planning the development of biotechnology and bio-industry. It has established the Guangzhou International Bio-Island that focuses on "modernization of traditional Chinese medicine," that is, applying modern science and technology to Chinese medicine. Locally, the Bio-Island can draw on the biomedicine R&D from more than 30 relevant institutes (e.g. Life Science Academy in Zhongshan University, Zhongshan University of Medical Sciences, and Guangzhou Bio-engineering Centre). Regionally, this project echoes with the Traditional Chinese Medicine Harbour Plan in Hong Kong and the Traditional Chinese Medicine Valley in Shenzhen. The grand imagination is a Guangzhou-Shenzhen-Hong Kong trans-local cluster concentrating on traditional Chinese medicine with linkages to their counterparts in Shanghai and Beijing.

Apart from the repositioning of Guangzhou, Shenzhen Municipal Government is pressing ahead with its development of the Shenzhen

Hi-Tech Industrial Park since 1996. It has promoted a number of high-tech projects with domestic and overseas institutions, for example, Shenzhen Qinghua University Research Institute, Shenzhen-Hong Kong Industry, and the Shenzhen International Institute for Technology Innovation with Harbin University. In promoting the development of more high-tech clusters, the municipal government founded a "Virtual University Park" in 1999 with the intention of building a Silicon-Valley type cluster in the region. Since it began operations in September 2001, the virtual park has attracted 34 Chinese universities (e.g. Shanghai Jiaotong University, Nanjing University, and Chinese Academy of Engineering), including three from Hong Kong (e.g. City University of Hong Kong, Baptist University, and Hong Kong University of Science and Technology), and 17 overseas universities (e.g. University of Leeds, University of Western Sydney, and Simon Fraser University). The project is constructed in the image of the so-called triple-helix model, that is, the increasing interdependent and cooperation among universities, industry, and government in a range of innovative public–private frameworks that is conducive to collective learning and advancing structural competitiveness.[34] In the case of the Shenzhen Virtual University Park, collective learning is alleged to be enhanced through the building of a conglomerate of research and teaching centers that can commercialize IT/biotechnology research in the region, provide a high-level training base, and promote cooperation and communication among academia and business. At the time of writing, there are a number of universities setting up research centers and projects in the park (see table 9.4). Apart from attracting universities, the government is also offering favorable terms to enhance global–local linkages in the building of informational capitalism in the region. In October 2002, Oracle announced the establishment of Oracle Research and Development Center in the high-tech park to work on application solutions with the China-based Legend.

Seeking to distinguish itself in the "Silicon Wave" in the region, Zhuhai profiles itself as a high-tech site located in the "scenic Tangjia Bay" with "nice sea views" and "quality leisure facilities" such as golf clubs. Its Zhuhai Southern Software Park is a high-profile project in promoting R&D on Internet application (table 9.5). Phase I of this project came into operation in October 2000 and has since attracted a cluster of local and multinational firms (e.g. Ericsson) as well as City University of Hong Kong to set up research centers in the Park. In August 2001, the State Development and Planning Commission of PRC and the Ministry of Information Industry jointly approved it as a State Software Industry Base.

Table 9.4 Examples of universities and research projects based in the Shenzhen Virtual University Park

Name of university	Research center name	Research project
City University of Hong Kong	Biotech & Health Centre	● Biotechnology and health sciences ● Mangrove replanting technology
	Industrial Technologies Centre	● Smart dispensing control system ● Smart batch production
Hong Kong University of Science and Technology and Beijing University	Shenzhen Industrial, Education and Research Centre	● Education training ● Translation software
	Medical Centre	● Biotechnology
Qinghua University (Beijing)	Shenzhen Qinghua University Research Institute	● Education training
Baptist University of Hong Kong	International Network	● Education training ● Technological development

Source: Author's own compilation.

Table 9.5 The Zhuhai Southern Software Park

Size:	340,000 sq. m.
Location:	Tangjia Bay of Zhuhai city
Aims:	To attract software companies and talents
	To develop as a world-class software training base
	To promote software production outsourcing and subcontracting among the world
Completion:	2000 (first stage); 2003 (second stage)
Facilities:	Broadband communication
	Business services
	Living accommodation
Cluster:	Global and local software companies
	Promixity to Sun Yat-Sen University
Tenants:	Ericsson, City University of Hong Kong,
	Motorola, Microsoft, local start-up firms (nearly 100 companies)

Source: Author's own compilation from information on the Southern Software Park website, http://www.china-ssp.com/English1/index.htm (accessed: March 22, 2002).

These Siliconized projects in the Pearl River Delta and Guangzhou area are typical of a huge number of projects in China. In general, the attempt to build the "next Silicon Valley" is narrated in China as being part of its national development project. Given that most of these projects offer preferential terms for global and regional capital to enter the zones, they can also be seen as Silicon sweatshops in which foreign capital uses this time not only the low-cost unskilled labor but also cheap brain power of knowledge-based workers trained in Chinese universities.

The question is whether the Siliconization strategies in different sites can consolidate a new regional division of labor in the trans-border space of "Greater China." In respect of Taiwan, it can be argued that the relocation of industries to mainland China and the upgrading of its own technological base enables the island to concentrate more on R&D, the global connections of its computer and IT companies and possibly on the supply of Internet content as well. In the case of Hong Kong, its role as a traditional entrepôt city is declining with the emergence of other ports in the Pearl River Delta and the Asian "Crisis" has also exposed an overdependence on property and financial markets. The territory is thus repositioning itself as a "logistic, financial and business hub" with hard and soft infrastructure for Internet services (broadband networks, e-commerce, business consultancy, data centers, content distribution, marketing skills, GEM) and project finance for biotechnology. Given that Taiwan is relaxing restrictions on investments in mainland China, where the demand for investment and VC is only likely to increase with WTO accession, Hong Kong is strategically positioned to act as a gateway and fund-raising center for the whole "Greater China" region. Likewise, Shenzhen, the Pearl River Delta, and Shanghai-Kunshan area are well placed to provide cheap labor/brains for electronics/IT products and offshore software sites for developing Chinese-language and multilingual products.

Despite these possibilities for cooperation in the building of informational capitalism in "Greater China," however, trans-local competition also exists among the various incubators that are being developed. As shown earlier, the number of self-professed high-tech/software/biotech parks in the region is growing, and their similarity may well lead to mutual competition. This can be seen in a number of areas, such as the provision of facilities to house software and biotechnology companies specializing in, for example, Chinese-language applications and pharmaceutical products, or the incubation of local small start-up firms for joint ventures and market listings. The same can be said of the shared regional aim of attracting global capital such as Microsoft, IBM, and Oracle to use their parks as "hubs," in the hope that other local and (trans-)local technology firms and universities will be drawn along in their wake. There will also be intense competition to lure talented personnel from other provinces within China, from among the diasporic entrepreneurs, and overseas-Chinese student community to work in the parks or elsewhere in the economy. As Shenzhen mayor Li Zibin put it in a May 2000 interview in *Asian Affairs*, "[Hong Kong] needs to attract talents from overseas and it is targeting the same sort of people as Shenzhen."[35]

Apart from warning about the competition for talent, Li also remarked on the poor coordination between Hong Kong and Shenzhen when it comes to "high-tech" development, noting:

> . . . in the high-tech industry, I have personally appealed two or three years ago for both sides to develop Research & Development on a common basis. It is really important to put our strength together and work for a common human resources development scheme. But it is not the case. In the financial sector as well. The two cities can work closer, but Shenzhen is much more willing to move on this topic too.

Even more significant for the emerging power dispensation within "Greater China" is the way that Li Zibin then went on to interpret the Hong Kong–Shenzhen relationship in terms of a "colonial" hierarchy, in which Hong Kong is seen to be better than Shenzhen and doesn't need Shenzhen, while Shenzhen needs Hong Kong, explaining:

> . . . some people at some level who deal with these questions in Hong Kong do not adhere to the view that to develop a closer relationship with Shenzhen and harmonize the build-up of high value industries will be beneficial to both. They look down on Shenzhen, and although we repeatedly emphasized the opportunities for each side to benefit from each other, they really believe that they will do well on their own. In this way, they are just keeping an old colonial mentality. They still ignore the fact that Shenzhen can develop without Hong Kong.[36]

Whether or not Li Zibin's interpretation of the relationship between Hong Kong and Shenzhen is correct, if such views are widely held then they could weaken the possibilities for interurban cooperation in southern China by encouraging a search for alternative partners. That would only further intensify competition in the "Greater China" region.

Apart from the trans-local cooperation and competition inherent in this mode of growth, these clusters of Silicon Valleys in "Greater China" are part of the longer Silicon production chain that stretches to the heartland of informational capitalism in the United States. Together they form the backbone of the hardware industry. America's high-tech industry is becoming increasingly reliant on production in Taiwan and mainland China, thus heightening the economic stakes of any cross-straits hostilities. Any disruption of this Silicon production chain could reverberate through the U.S. economy via a slump in the technology sector. The *New York Times* reported in July 2001 that representatives of Dell Computer, one of the largest buyers of laptop computers from Taiwan companies, have been pressuring Taiwan officials to establish direct trade and transportation ties with the mainland.[37] China and Taiwan's accession to the WTO and the expected expansion of economic linkages between the two might make the U.S. economy more vested in peaceful cross-straits relations. One could even argue that there is an emerging "transnational silicon coalition" that cuts across the trans-Pacific region.

This transnational Silicon coalition and its claim to superprofits from "innovation" and "invention" are protected by an IPR regime under informational capitalism. This legal regime that is put in place by state agencies (e.g. the United States Trade Representatives), international organizations (e.g. WTO and World Intellectual Property Organization), and representatives of transnational corporations (e.g. the U.S.-based Information Technology Industry Council),[38] is transferred to the region in the form of IPR laws (see table 9.6). The latter is deepened to include informational products and electronics circuits in recent years. However, this regime is under constant challenges by piracy as a "way of life" in the region.[39]

Piracy of software and media products (e.g. VCDs and DVDs) is a "way of life" (on the piracy rates see table 9.6). It is practiced by consumers (businesses, non-profit organizations, high school and college students,

Table 9.6 IPR laws in "Greater China"

IPR Laws	Hong Kong	Taiwan	Mainland China
Trade Marks Ordinance	•	•	•
Patents Ordinance	•	•	•
Registered Designs Ordinance	•		
Copyright Ordinance	•	•	
Prevention of Copyright Piracy Ordinance	•		
Lay-out Design of Integrated Circuits Ordinance	•	•	

Source: Author's own compilation.

etc.) and by producers (especially petty capitalists). Their activities are based on "counter-truths" that subvert the global-legal regime. They range from the ethical stance that IPR should only apply to tangible goods and not intangibles, such as information, to the more commercial argument that multinationals ask consumers in developing countries too much for their software. The ethical justification rests on the claim that information- and knowledge-based products are part of a "global intellectual commons" that depends on sharing, common access, or cooperative production. It is further argued that the rhetoric of "protecting rights of creators" is hypo-critical because ownership benefits accrue to the corporations rather than to the true creators (e.g. programmers and artists), who are just paid employees. The commercial justification sees IPR protection as "unfair"/"unaffordable" for low- income consumers in some Asian coun-tries (e.g. China) who cannot pay the full price for the software—especially as the latter is often priced around 20 percent higher than the same or equivalent software in the United States. As for the producers, there is "a feeling among some people that the pirate software dealers are simply engaged in competitive business practices against companies who are charging too much for their products."[40] Some even credit them with "Robin Hood" status (like the famous English outlaw, who "robbed the rich and gave to the poor").[41] In between these extremes, there are oth-ers who are puzzled by the concept of IPR and see its infringement as at most a "victimless crime." They argue that the success of the "Greater China" economy is based on "flexible imitation," regard IPR as an "alien concept" that originates from a "rights-based" society, or claim that much of U.S.-based IPR is itself based on past or present acts of "piracy" (e.g. "biopiracy" of food crops). This wide range of counter-IPR narratives and practices has generated a battleground for piracy in the region (table 9.7).

Piracy, especially when pursued by noncommercial players, involves consumers challenging the IPR regime through the use of tactics. Their

Table 9.7 Piracy rates in "Greater China" in 1995 and 2000

	1995 %	2000 %
China	96	94
Hong Kong	62	57
Taiwan	70	53

Source: Sixth Annual BSA Global Software Piracy Study 2000.

tactics, which may be linked to their "freeware" identities, include demanding "fair" prices for software through anti-IPR campaigns; passing on to friends or colleagues copies of licensed software; swapping master disks among friends and colleagues; exchanging information on access to new unlicensed software; uploading and downloading unlicensed software from bulletin boards or the Internet; frequent switching of third-party storage sites for illicit software (e.g. college students putting them on campus servers); copying a handful of licensed software products to all other computers in an organization; transferring licensed software from office to home computers; and obtaining unlicensed software from shopping malls, night markets, and mobile hawker stalls at "fair" prices.

As for the producers of pirated goods, they are petty capitalists who undertake piracy for profit. They operate on three levels: production, distribution, and retail. In the PRC, for example, a substantial amount of pirated goods is produced in the coastal areas of Guangdong and Fujian Provinces, sometimes with financing from Hong Kong and Taiwan. Production occurs in scattered, unorganized, and small-scale operations with workers from other provinces. State-owned factories in China have also been involved, especially during times of poor domestic demand for legal products. While manufacturing pirated products tends to be scattered, distribution is much more organized. From production sites in China's coastal provinces, pirated goods are smuggled across border to Hong Kong.

Petty capitalists in mainland China, Hong Kong, and Taiwan sell the goods openly in sites such as shopping malls, where it is well known that pirated software is for sale. Such traders expect occasional raids and treat fines as a calculable business cost. More covert sales practices involve the sale of coupons and software covers that enable buyers to pick up the pirated software at another time or in less centrally located areas. Pirated software is also sold in temporary outlets (e.g. shops that have short leases), mobile sales points (e.g. hawker stalls and out of suitcases), and over the ether (e.g. pagers and the Internet). This makes it very hard for the authorities to trace sellers and gather hard evidence. Pirates have recently begun to employ juveniles and illegal immigrants to sell software. The former are too young to be imprisoned and the latter can only be deported.

Concluding Remarks

This chapter has examined ways in which globalized idea of "Silicon Valley" as a "model of development" allows private and public actors to deploy the symbolism of "high-technology," "clustering," and "information technology" to redefine the economic future within "Greater China," especially since the Asian financial crisis. The resulting strategy of "siliconization" involves actors constructing and seeking to develop modes of co-ordination and governance around informational capitalism. This can be manifested in a number of ways in local sites, such as the emergence of "Silicon Valley" discourses to reconfigure subjectivities and to consolidate economic practices favorable to informational capitalism. Discourses such as "innovation," "entrepreneurship," "incubation," "knowledge-based economy," and "ICT/biotechnology" circulate among an epistemic community of private and public actor at global, regional, and local level. These discourses mediate the building of new economic practices which include the introduction of the GEM in Hong Kong as a fund-raising avenue for high-tech startups, the extension of diasporic silicon networking to sites in California and China, attempts by leading "old-economy" firms in the region to form strategic alliances or joint ventures in the hope of turning "Greater China" into an e-production and biotechnological space, the emergence of public–private partnerships to build the "next Silicon Valley," and the deepening of IPR laws to include informational products.

These practices of localizing the global development model are inherent in the strategy of Siliconization. The various "Silicon Valley" constructions can be seen as global projects that encounter dilemmas and challenges rooted in the more general dynamics of political economy of integration and fragmentation (fragmegration). This chapter has identified three instances of fragmegration in the building of informational capitalism in the "Greater China" region. First, the Siliconization strategy consolidates intensified integration that may create a deepening division of labor. For example, the westward move of the Silicon production chain may lead Taiwan to turn into a R&D base for Asia, while OEM manufacturing will take place in southern and eastern China. Hong Kong will become a "logistic and financial center" with hard and soft infrastructure for project finance, while Shenzhen focuses on OEM of electronics products, as well as offshore software sites for Chinese-language products and traditional Chinese medicine. This tendency toward integration is also accompanied by fragmentation in that the different "Silicon Valleys" compete with each other for global capital, technology transfer, and knowledge-based workers.

Second, the westward extension of the Silicon production chain is encouraging economic integration between Taiwan and mainland China. This is reflected in the emergence of China-friendly discourses in Taiwan and new hybrid identities such as "Shang-Tai-nese." Supported by the "Silicon (plus) coalition," the resulting "China Fever" may weaken the process of nation-building in Taiwan. This can be seen in DPP's adoption of the "de-Li Denghui" policy of "active opening and effective management." Currently, it can be argued that Taiwan is caught in a frag-megration dilemma in which the push for further economic integration is accompanied by some fragmentation of identities premised on the building of an "independent" Taiwan.

Third, the Siliconization strategy is related to the economic practices of localizing global IPR laws to the various sites in "Greater China." This global–local integration of IPR laws, which aims to protect "innovation" and "invention" in the Information Age, is constantly challenged by piracy as a "way of life." The latter can be seen in the form of counter-truths and piracy tactics of commercial and noncommercial actors. Together they fragment and even subvert the domination of this global IPR regime and its associated informational interests. This coexistence of integration and fragmentation is made more complex depending on the location in the Silicon production chain. Currently, Taiwan is both a challenger and a sup-porter of this regime. In relation to multinational informational interests (e.g. Microsoft, IBM) and their protection of their software and hardware products, certain quarters in Taiwan, especially among everyday users, are promoting an anti-anti-piracy position. In relation to China and Taiwan's transfer of applied technology to its various sites, Taiwan capital insists on the importance of IPR as an important method to protect its competitive advantages as the Silicon chain is extended into China. This is one of sev-eral paradoxes that affect Taiwanese interests and policies as it upgrades its position within the global division of labor.

Notes

1. Although I recognize that Greater China is a controversial term, I use it here as a convenient shorthand to indicate the cross-border urban economic space of Hong Kong, Pearl River Delta, Taiwan, and Yangtze Delta. To remind readers that it is controversial, it has been demarcated with inverted commas.
2. On the Silicon Valley model, see Lee, Chong-moon, "The Silicon Valley Habitat," in *The Silicon Valley Edge*, W. Miller, M. Hancock, and H. Rowen (eds.) (Stanford: Stanford University Press, 2000): 1–15. The model is associated with the following techno-economic regime of truth: (a) a faith in entrepreneurialism; (b) a vital role for venture capital; (c) the critical role of research uni-versities; (d) a healthy supply of highly qualified researchers; (e) benefits from firms co-locating and incubating (agglomeration economies); and (f) its embedding in a free market environment.
3. Informational capitalism is one among several labels for the current stage of capitalism. Castells in his book entitled *Network Society* (Oxford: Blackwell, 2000) distinguishes it from earlier stages in terms of the dominance of technologies for knowledge generation, information pro-cessing, and symbolic communication and argues that the action of knowledge on knowledge itself serves as the main source of productivity.

4. On the Chinese and Taiwanese professional associations in Silicon Valley, see Annelise Saxenian, "Networks of Immigrant Entrepreneurs," in *The Silicon Valley Edge*, 248–275.

5. See Ngai-Ling Sum, "Informational Capitalism and U.S. Economic Hegemony: Resistance and Adaptations in East Asia," *Critical Asian Studies*, 35(3): 373–398.

6. Executive Yuan, NSC, *White Paper on Science and Technology* (Taipei: NSC, ROC, December 1997): 5–6.

7. Executive Yuan, NSC, *Action Plan for Building a Technologically Advanced Nation* (Taipei: NSC, ROC, April 1998): 10.

8. Chen, Shui-bian, "The Third Way for Taiwan: A New Political Perspective," (December 6, 1999), available online via: http://www.president.gov.tw/1_president/e_subject-04a.html (accessed: January 27, 2000).

9. See Chen, Shui-bian "President Chen Shui-bian's Inauguration Speech," (May 20, 2000): 4, available online via: http://members.tripod.com/Ken_Davies/inaugural.html (accessed: February 27, 2002).

10. Executive Yuan, Council for Economic Planning and Development, *Plan to Develop Knowledge-based Development in Taiwan* (Taipei: Council for Economic Planning and Development, ROC, September 2000): 8.

11. See Ngai-Ling Sum, "(Post-) Asian 'Crisis' and 'Greater China': On the Bursting of the 'Bubbles' and Hi-Tech (Re) Imaginations," in *China in the 21st Century*, P. Preston (ed.) (London: Curzon, 2003): 190–220.

12. Tung, Chee-hwa, "From Adversity to Opportunity," Policy Speech Delivered by the Chief Executive in the Legislative Council Meeting (Hong Kong: Hong Kong SAR Government, October 7, 1998): 8.

13. Donald Yam-keung Tsang, "Onward with New Strength," Budget Speech delivered by the Financial Secretary in the Legislative Council Meeting (Hong Kong: Hong Kong SAR Government, March 3, 1999): 15.

14. See, "Shenzhen Plans to Become 'China's Silicon Valley'," *China Online* (April 3, 2000), available online via: http://www.chinaonline.com/industry/infotech/NewsArchive/cs-protected/2000/april/B200032411.asp (accessed: April 4, 2001).

15. See Annelise Saxenian, "Transnational Communities and the Evolution of Global Production Networks: The Cases of Taiwan, China and India" (2002), available online via: http://www.sims.berkeley.edu/~anno/papers/INDUSTRY &INNOCATION.pdf (accessed: March 3, 2003).

16. On the source of the information, see "Economic Exchanges Across the Taiwan Straits," *Shanghai Flash*, 12 (December 2001), available online via: http://www.sinoptic.ch/shanghaiflash/2001/2001.12.htm (accessed: November 22, 2002).

17. On the source of the information, Ibid.

18. Ngai-Ling Sum, "Rethinking Globalization: Rearticulating the Spatial Scale and Temporal Horizons of Trans-Border Spaces," in *Globalization and Asia-Pacific: Contested Territories*, K. Olds, P. Dickens, P. Kelly, L. Kong, and H. Yeung (eds.) (London: Routledge, 1999): 140.

19. According to an AsiaBizTech report entitled "Taiwan Firms Shift R&D to China," available online via: http://neasia.nikkeibp.com/nea/200204/srep_178978.html (accessed: March 2, 2003). Computer engineers in the mainland cost a quarter of those of their counterpart in Taiwan.

20. On Acer's investment in Zhongshan, see D. Baldwin, "Acer Opens Biggest Mainboard Plant in Zhongshan," *Nikkei Electronics Asia* (April 2000), available online via: http://www.nikkeibp.asiabiztech.com/nea/200004/cocn_98652.html (accessed: March 29, 2002).

21. Up to 2001, the MOEA and Securities and Futures Commission restricted China-bound investment to 40 percent of a company's capitalization and 20 percent of its net worth. The government limits individual investments to NTD 50 million.

22. For a discussion of this Taiwanese literature, see Tsai, Ting-I, "Media Ignore China Investment Risks" (July 23, 2001), available online via: http://www.taipeitimes.com/news/2001/07/23/story/0000095302 (accessed: December 22, 2001).

234   *Ngai-Ling Sum*

     Ngai-Ling Sum

23. On the outflow of Taiwanese manpower to China, see M. Forney, "Taipei's Tech-Talent Exodus" (May 21, 2001), available online via: http://www.time.com/time/asia/news/printout/0,9788,109642,00.html (accessed: December 5, 2001).
24. On the industry versus service debate in Hong Kong, see Bob Jessop and Ngai-Ling Sum, "An Entrepreneurial City in Action: Hong Kong's Emerging Strategies in and for (Inter-)Urban Competition," *Urban Studies*, 33, 3 (2000): 2287–2313. Special Issue on Asia's Global Cities.
25. See Hong Kong Cyber-Port, "What is Cyber-Port?," 1, available online via: http://www.cyber-port.com/whatis.html (accessed: June 9, 1999). Information on the Hong Kong's Cyber-Port is no longer available when the author sought to reaccess this site on April 18, 2002 but a copy is available from the author. However, the domain name still exists and is up for sale. New information on the Cyber-Port is now posted on a new site, available online via: http://www.cyberport-management.com/ (accessed: April 18, 2002).
26. See Ibid., 1.
27. See Ibid., 1.
28. Donald Yam-keung Tsang, "Financial Secretary's Transcript on Cyberport" (Hong Kong: Hong Kong SAR Government, March 17, 1999), available online via: http://www.info.gov.hk/gia/general/199903/17/0317146.htm (accessed: December 6, 1999).
29. David Webb, "Cyber Villas by Sea" (March 22, 1999), available online via: http://www.webb-site.com/articles/cybervillas.htm (accessed: December 12, 1999).
30. Hong Kong Democratic Foundation, "Policy Paper: Response to 1999/2000 Budget" (December 5, 1999), available online via: http://www.hkdf.org/papers/990512budget.htm (accessed: December 6, 2000).
31. Tsang, "Financial Secretary's Transcript on Cyberport."
32. The GEM began operating on October 25, 1999 in Hong Kong. It was created to develop Hong Kong's IT industry and is one of several Asian attempts to emulate the United States' Nasdaq. The GEM is expected to serve the "Greater China" market, whereas Singapore's Sesdaq and Malaysia's Mesdaq are to serve the south Asian markets and Kosdaq serves the Korean market. Some competition could come from China, where Shanghai and Shenzhen are reported to want second boards to compete with Hong Kong and Nasdaq. However, Beijing currently prefers mainland non-state enterprises to seek flotation in Shenzhen and the GEM. The biggest competitor is Nasdaq, which has attracted a number of initial public offerings (IPO) from the region. Many VCs are far more comfortable with the 28-year-old Nasdaq. Given its liquidity and stable regulatory environment. Fearful of losing its edge, Hong Kong Stock Exchange has eased its requirement for a lock-in period, during which management were unable to sell their shares, from two years to six months.
33. Path-dependency implies that an economic system's prior development shapes current and future trajectories. But this does not justify fatalism. For social forces could intervene in current conjunctures in the hope of reorienting paths so that new trajectories become possible.
34. On the triple-helix model, see H. Etzkowitz and L. Leydesdorff (eds.), *Universities and Global Knowledge Economy: A Triple Helix of University-Industry-Government Relations* (London: Cassell Academic, 1997).
35. L. Malvezin, "Hong Kong Needs Shenzhen, Shenzhen Does Not Need Hong Kong," *Asian Affairs* (Spring 2000 Issue): 4, available online via: http://www.asian-affairs.com/China/lizibin.html (accessed: March 21, 2001). Interview with Li Zibin, Former Mayor of Shenzhen—Vice-Minister.
36. Ibid., 4.
37. See Mark Landler, "China Feud Has New Risks for Taiwan," *New York Times* (July 28, 2001): C1.
38. On the international and national support for the Silicon coalition through the intellectual property regime, see Sum, "Informational Capitalism."
39. On a theoretical understanding of "way of life," see M. de Certeau, *The Practice of Everyday Life* (Minneapolis, MN: University of Minnesota Press, 1998).

40. See Y. Cohen, "Software Pirates Pile Up Profits in Afflicted Asia," *The Christian Science Monitor* (December 29, 1997), available online via: http://www.csmonitor.com/durable/1997/12/29/intl1.html (accessed: October 30, 2001).
41. See D. Swartze, "The Intellectual Property Battle," *Bangkok Post* (October 29, 2001), available online via: http://www.bangkokpost.net/breakfast/a291200.html (accessed: November 2, 2001).

CHAPTER TEN

Urban Assemblages: An Ecological Sense of the Knowledge Economy

AIHWA ONG

Introduction

Scholarship on the Asia-Pacific has always been sensitive to the implications of geopolitical configurations. Besides the usual concerns with old civilizations, new cultures and nation-states, we have talked about the region in terms of ecological niches, civilizational hubs, and economic performance. Themes about entrenched sociospatial spaces have included highland versus lowland, insular versus mainland, cultural centers versus barbarian peripheries.[1] More recently, a sense of new geography has proliferated, and we have come to think of the region as the home of Asian tiger nations, of the U.S.-dominated Pacific Rim,[2] or as a space crisscrossed by resurgent Chinese business networks.[3] Indeed, analysts of economic globalization focus on how business networks create regions that cut across the global system of nation-states. Kenichi Ohmae[4] uses the term "region state" to refer to the rise of areas linked by economic activity but not confined by national boundaries. A related idea is the global city-region, or regional networks of cities that operate as "territorial platforms from which concentrated groups or networks of firms contest global markets."[5] Clearly, a greater sensitivity to spatial practices has become part of our analysis of how global economic forces are reconfiguring the Asian region, and how Asian actors are reconfiguring spaces of mobility, capital, and modernity.

Networks, Scales, or Assemblages?

The rise of information economy calls for a refinement of the global network idea. Manuel Castells maintains that communications technology occupies a central but not determinant position within the information society, allowing networks to achieve a scale beyond the nation-state and to operate in real global time. He argues that networks are structured by nodes and hubs that play strategic functions in the communicative process.[6] In "this [networked] space of flows," managerial elites are the major social actors who conceive, decide, and implement networks, who are in the position to exclude, segment, and disorganize the masses. This space of flows and power, he concludes, supersedes "the logic of any specific place," because "the logic of global power escapes the socio-political control of historically specific local/national societies."[7]

In recent years, geographers have deployed a language of scales in order to describe the economic implications of globalization.[8] The narrative holds that the effects of global forces are not uniform, but are distributed across different scales—the personal, the local, the urban, the national, and the regional.[9] From the vantage point of state action, scale strategy may cross cut national borders, as in the creation of growth triangles or economic zones, thus rearranging conventional economic spaces that cut across national borders.[10] Often, the discourse of regionalism is an attempt to specify the scales of significant or distinctive economic action that crisscrosses countries, shaping for instance the region called Greater China. The focus on scale politics has directed analysts to study the tensions that emerge between the two kinds of social orders—the political order of nation-states, and the economic order of economic scales, leading to the formation of new rivalry and cooperation, stratification and fragmentation.[11]

Both the network model and the focus on scalar processes are highly economistic and structural in orientation. When it comes to the actual forging of networks, Castells gives primacy to managerial elites and their capacity to transcend the scale of the nation-state, thus slighting the possibility that technocrats also design and put into play multiple networks and the spaces of their intersections. Second, the notion of scale as a metric for sociospatial structuration under capitalism is mainly concerned about how scalar configurations are linked to "global networks" of market action. But we do not learn how new sociopolitical spaces are being produced through global networks.[12] The network and scale approaches thus maintain that elite managers organize global networks that participate

in the scaling of economic activities worldwide. The global logic of the
space of flows and the scaling processes create new hierarchies of sociopolitical spaces that challenge the system of nation-states.

I see at least three problems with the current formulation of the
network-scaling technologies.

(1) First, elite managers are considered key agents in organizing flows
    and networks, and through their decisions in shaping multiscalar
    configurations, thus gaining both spatial and temporary autonomy
    beyond the state. Political or technocratic actors are ignored or
    minimized as producers of networking or scaling activities, or in
    shaping transnational spaces through the deployment of informa-
    tional networks.

(2) The economistic reading of scalar configuration ignores vital eco-
    nomic, geopolitical, and sociocultural interests that inform the
    shaping of new informational spaces. These emerging zones are
    not merely technical in nature; they play a role in shaping our
    ideas of what it means to be human.[13] Technological zones often
    smuggle in nationalist aspirations and entail the construction or
    naturalization of racial, ethnic, and gender differences, as well as
    the orchestration of the migrant circulations that are put into
    interaction with each other.

(3) Third, the discourses of networks and scales suggest relationships
    that are already forged, and assumed to be stabilized. This structural
    view of networks and scales does not give enough attention to the
    instability and contingency of trans-local interactions and prac-
    tices. Emergent spaces of networks are subject to contestation,[14]
    and the sociopolitical spaces are both stabilized as well as under-
    mined by the crisscrossing networks that sustain them.

In short, too much attention has been focused on global networks and
their economic and scaling processes, and not enough to the disparate
actors and institutions that have come together in space-making activities. Castells has argued that in the Asia-Pacific region, Chinese "entrepreneurial familism" has allowed for the kind of "network flexibility"
that fosters the growth of the information economy,[15] but the emergent
informational landscape—growth triangles, high tech corridors,
biotechnology centers—has been dependent more upon state actors in
partnership with new kinds of networks than on old ethnic networks.[16]
Indeed, a new term—cluster-development—is used to describe the
clusters of state-foreign partnerships that plug into regional and global

networks in a differentiated way. This emerging informational space has relied on technocrats to forge relations with foreign institutions and actors in order to bring about nodes of informational expertise.

I use the Deleuzian term "assemblage"[17] to describe this analytical problem-space that is an intersection of disparate elements, of the old and the new, and of territorialization and deterritorialization. Assemblage allows us to think about power not as homogeneous but as "defined by the particular points through which it passes."[18]

An assemblage allows us to designate an emerging cluster of relationships, activities and values, that may disintegrate or stabilize over time. It captures the contingent way different components—the state, institutions, actors—are brought into interaction, and how their polyvalent cultural associations and values are shaped in these unfolding relationships.[19] The Asian financial crisis, and the rapid changing domains in East and Southeast Asia beg for the kind of analytical entry that captures the ways various elements—administrative rationality, enterprises, entrepreneurs and experts—are brought into play in volatile conditions, engendering new social spaces and citizen subjects of Asian globalization.

Urban Assemblages

Our analytical entry point thus requires that we go beyond the structural notion of the "developmental state"[20] and its implicit assumptions that there can be a singularity and uniformity in state action. Elsewhere I have argued that since the 1980s, Asian states have shifted away from a focus on the technical aspects of development toward the problematization of the population as the key factor in achieving wealth. I use the term "postdevelopmental strategy" to denote this tendency to manage the economy indirectly through the micro-management of the population. Countries such as Malaysia and Singapore for instance have adopted neoliberal reasoning, in seeking to improve its populations in relation to the global marketplace, and in letting social rights be increasingly coordinated by market calculations.[21] Partnerships between states and global companies created spaces of "graduated sovereignty" whereby social rights for different segments of the population depend to a large extent on their capacity to engage global market forces.[22] I thus draw attention to a mode of accumulation that focuses on the management of different groups—both local and transnational—in terms of their possession of a variety of human capital and skills.

Since the so-called Asian financial crisis of 1997–98, "the knowledge-based" economy has emerged as the answer to the global fears, dreams, and ambition of the more agile states in Asia. In the new transition, Asian technocrats themselves approach the fast-changing capitalism by assembling crucial elements—venture capital (VC), foreign expertise, global companies—in order to move up the global "value-added chain" from manufacturing to knowledge industries. Technocrats have collaborated with global managers to reconfigure their national territories into heterogeneous sites—free-trade zones, science parks, cyber-hubs—that are differently plugged into global networks of capital, knowledge, and expertise. For instance, the Taipei Hsinchu Science Park, which has been connected to Silicon Valley through the exchange of personnel, technology, and capital, is increasingly linked to the Chinese mainland, with its vast pool of cheap labor and engineering experts. We see a merging of software and information systems located in Taiwan and China, leading to what promises to be the biggest informational technology development in Asia, with Taipei and Shanghai leading the way. The Indian informational technology scene is rather different. Cyberhubs in Hyderabad and Bangalore, appear destined not to be major centers of high-tech development, but rather providers of software and informational services to the world, with links to the Silicon Valley,[23] and to the Multimedia Super Corridor in Malaysia.[24] These sites are thus urban assemblages that put together disparate networks and actors in order to forge connections to other nodes in the global hierarchy of information networks.

The recent entry of Hong Kong SAR (Special Administrative Region), Singapore and Malaysia to the information age provides some telling details of how such assemblages come about. Hong Kong views itself as a gateway to China, and being an information hub adds a new dimension to this relationship. Singapore has recast itself as an Asian oasis for nurturing global talent in biotechnologies. Kuala Lumpur has built a digital corridor to attract software companies and to sell multimedia products and services. In all three cases, technocrats in varying degrees put into play venture capital, global companies, and foreign talent. Such urban assemblages are held by specific mechanisms, in particular immigrant practices, and are articulated by emerging spatial forms and effects. By looking at changes in terms of urban assemblages, we gain a richer sense of the spatial scales that are produced, and the biopolitical calculations that privilege certain kinds of actors over others.

Opening Borders to Brains

The Asian financial crisis of 1997–98 stimulated neoliberal thinking and calculation about human skills and capital in their respective labor markets. In Hong Kong SAR, Singapore, and Kuala Lumpur, a response to the crisis has been to assemble the disparate elements that will convert Asian cities into bastions of knowledge workers and sites for the creation of intellectual property and services.

The neoliberal thinking is that in the new information economy, a city without a high proportion of global managers and knowledge workers risks losing its competitive edge. There is concern to build up human resources through programs for life-long education at home, while attracting talented people from abroad. All three cities suffer from a lack of skilled workers and of entrepreneurial risk takers in the knowledge economy. The new administrative rationality for engaging foreign institutions and skills—glosses as globalizing moves—involves two sets of activities: the active recruitment of external networks of expertise on the one hand, and the space-making activities that extend the critical technological space on the other. These technocratic activities seem most explicable in ecological terms. Indeed, the quest for global city status depends on a policy of "opening borders to brains," to encourage the "leveraging [of] managers and knowledge workers across industries, regions, and cultures."[25] More specifically, what is ecological about the recruitment of foreign experts and students is the creation of an extended space of circulation whereby foreign experts are induced to pass through, work or settle down in the city, thus contributing to the skills mix of the urban population. Second, by channeling the flows of foreign human capital and encouraging their interactions with the domestic population, the goal is to engender a higher level of productivity, creativity, and diversity than would otherwise be the case. Hong Kong SAR, Singapore and Kuala Lumpur increasingly see themselves as the hubs of new "ecologies of expertise"[26] whereby the traffic of a more diverse population of experts whose knowledge and interactions with the local working populations will help generate greater wealth-making capacities.

In Hong Kong SAR, the stress is now on risk-taking cultural brokers who can facilitate the flow of technical knowledge into China, or who can mediate the interface between global technical competencies and Chinese cultural rules of operation. There are two major sources from which Hong Kong SAR expects to get the entrepreneurial and cultural expertise to strengthen its role as the corporate and information conduit to China, a function increasingly being replaced by Shanghai. There is now a new breed of Western expatriates—less rich and upper-class than the old colonial officials—who find jobs in corporations, university teaching, and the financial sector. At the same time universities and companies are recruiting mainland Chinese professionals and students for the engineering and medical sciences. The Chinese University of Hong Kong SAR for instance trains many mainland students in a variety of fields. The new Cybercity expects to have many of its research facilities be filled by mainland Chinese engineers. However, given its resolutely commercial character, the influx of knowledge workers into Hong Kong SAR is still very limited, and many of the immigrants from China are in business. There is no official program to recruit mainlanders, given the limited and contested residential politics of Hong Kong SAR, but the tendency is to favor the well educated and the well heeled from the mainland (and other countries) who can feed the growth of networks spanning Hong Kong SAR and the mainland, especially Guangzhou industrial zones and other cities. Hong Kong SAR positions itself as a knowledge broker—offering Chinese cultural knowledge to foreign business, and foreign technical knowledge to China—but it is increasingly fearful that Shanghai is becoming a competing synapse, a new transfer-point that is more effective in sparking China's informational industry.

In Kuala Lumpur, a multibillion Multimedia Super Corridor dwarfs the Hong Kong SAR Cybercity. Technocrats hope this superhighway will pry the country out of low-cost manufacturing to make the "leapfrog into the Information Age."[27] Despite its impressive infrastructure, the corridor is "a testbed for trying out not just the technology but also the way of life in the age of instant and unlimited information."[28] Malaysia is severely restricted by a dearth of skilled workers, though universities are producing graduates by the thousands. At present, the digital corridor is relying on an influx of software engineers from Australia, South Africa, and mainly India. For Indian expatriates, Kuala Lumpur is viewed less as a capital of software experts—and more as a multilingual center that enables a small number of Indian software producers to penetrate into emerging Asian and third-world markets. By locating in the super corridor, Indian companies and experts hope to convert their software templates for use in a variety of Asian markets such as Thailand, Burma, and African countries.[29] The corridor is widely considered a second-level hub for producing cheap software services and products, and less promising than Singapore.

The city-state calls itself "a vibrant and effervescent enterprise ecosystem, where large and small enterprises can thrive by leveraging on innovation and intellectual property to create value."[30] The city-state has most successfully realized the goal of systematically recruiting foreign experts—mainly from China, India, and the United States—in order to transform itself into a hub of cutting-edge expertise in the sciences.[31] The Prime Minister notes that "gathering human talent is not like collecting different species of trees . . . to green up Singapore . . . . In the Informational Age, human talent, not physical resources or financial capital, is the key factor for economic competitiveness and success. We must therefore welcome the infusion of knowledge that foreign talent will bring. Singapore must become a cosmopolitan, global city, an open society . . . ."[32] An environment has to be created, a nursery of where the government provides the resources and environment for nurturing talent.

Stressing "technopreneurial practices," the state forms partnerships with world-class institutions such as MIT and Johns Hopkins, and global companies such as GlaxoSmithKline, to establish training programs that can train knowledge workers who will create new knowledge products. A new biopolis has been established to do research on Asian stem cells and produce individually tailored drug regimes. To staff its research farms, special university scholarships, immigration rules, and tax regimes have been altered to favor foreign university students and foreign experts who wish to come to train or work in Singapore, and perhaps consider eventually becoming citizens. The boast is that Singapore will become "the Boston of the East," leveraging business and science education into foreign talent who will arrive and help the nation-state move up the added-value chain in the high growth knowledge industries.

Singapore is an island nation of about 4 million people, the majority of whom are ethnic Chinese, the rest ethnic Indians and Malays. Already, there are half a million foreign workers, of whom one-fifth is highly skilled. Nevertheless, there is an on-going campaign to get Singaporeans to accept foreigners as a significant and permanent feature of a society that seeks to be part of the global business scene. Trade officials argue that the acceptance and welcoming of expatriates is an issue of national survival since their presence have staffed corporate offices and helped increase wealth. In the 1990s, it is claimed, 41 percent of the GDP was achieved on the back of the inflow of foreign human resources. With the low birth rate, brain drain, and a lack of direct substitution between the skill profiles of local and expatriates, the need to attract these foreign talents will be « a matter of life and death » for the nation. Thus the infusion of foreign expertise is vital for sustaining the social body and stabilizing the body politic.

Although the elite migrant stream includes professionals from Australia, Europe and the United States, increasingly headhunting programs recruit promising students from China and India for local universities and laboratories and companies. Without fanfare, it appears that there is a preference for students from China. I was told that initially educators assumed Indian students in the sciences would perform better because of their command of English. However, there has been great unevenness in the quality of Indian students, the tendency is to focus on scholars from the Chinese mainland. During a 2002 summer visit to the engineering department of the National University of Singapore, which has formed a program with MIT, I noticed that almost all the students were from China, speaking Mandarin that marked them off clearly from the Mandarin speech of Singaporean Chinese. There is the expectation that mainland Chinese students are more likely to consider settling down as citizens in Singapore and meld with the existing society dominated by ethnic Chinese from Southeast Asia. The smaller recruitment of Indian students seems proportionate to the ratio of ethnic Indians in Singapore society. Thus the recruitment of different ethnic streams of foreign students and experts is closely coordinated with social engineering of the knowledge and ethnic distribution in society. The infusion of foreign human capital is thus intended to sustain the social body, as well as to be incorporated into the intellectual and ethnic contours of the body politic.

Globalizing Asian cities are thus aggressively pursuing a cosmopolitan image and population in order to forge linkages between disparate populations and geographical points. Hong Kong seeks to exploit its role as a transfer point of commercial and high-tech knowledge to the Chinese mainland. Kuala Lumpur is positioning itself as a node in the global web of Indian software market. Singapore has recast itself as the emerging site for combining Western intellectual capital and Asian brains. Diverse expatriate actors are being corralled by attractive immigration packages in order to upgrade these cities and plug them into the value-added knowledge chain. These expatriate networks, mobilized by growing presence of global firms and world-class managerial institutions constitute emerging geographies of expertise that do not conform easily to the space of Greater China.

An Ecological Sense of Space

Partnerships and collaborations between Asian technocrats and foreign companies, and universities are indicative of a new ecological sense of technological space. For some time now, the term Greater China has been invoked to describe what is widely held to be a unifying ethno-economic space that embraces Hong Kong SAR, Taiwan, and sites in Southeast Asia. Hong Kong and Taiwan have indeed become more firmly integrated into Greater China, extending dense webs of economic, social, and cultural links to the southern provinces and beyond. Hong Kong's industrial investments and management have become more tightly interwoven with mainland Chinese labor.[33] In contrast, Kuala Lumpur and Singapore represent assemblages of diverse networks, institutions and actors that include but also bypass Greater China.

As mentioned earlier, the Multimedia Super Corridor in Malaysia can be considered a glamorous outpost for giant Indian companies such as Infosys Technologies. Indian companies consider the digital corridor as a platform for converting South Asian software solutions into multilingual packages suitable for diverse developing markets. Indian expatriate workers view Kuala Lumpur as a node in a second-tier informational network, a stepping stone to richer and more vibrant information hubs such as the Silicon Valley. While the super corridor is more closely connected to Indian rather than China's informational technologies, Malaysia is host to thousands of mainland Chinese enrolled in English and technical courses. Young mainland Chinese consider Malaysia a cheap Asian venue for obtaining certification for applying to universities in Australia and the West. Malaysia is thus a second-level high-tech crossroads, a kind of information switching station through which knowledge workers from India and China are in transit to major sites in Western countries. By coordinating the global flows of second-tier knowledge workers, the Malaysian knowledge hub is oriented toward South Asia and the United States.

Singapore, in contrast, sees itself as the center of "the wider Asian region of 2.8 billion people within a flight radius of seven hours,"[34] that is, an Asia-Pacific zone of market access as well as of Asian brains. This knowledge-driven trajectory spins further outward toward the United States and Western Europe whose world-class universities, companies, and scientists are induced to relocate in Singapore. Technocrats understand that the knowledge-driven economy must spiral outward, and that vectors of power are not determined by Asian geography, networks or culture. The goal is not to become a regional hub, a satellite of China, but a global player, to make Singapore as the Asian center for specialized knowledge industries such as biotechnology and the life sciences. This spiraling projection requires the state to forge specific connections between Western academic and scientific institutions and globally-competitive knowledge expatriate. Part of this new spatiality of development includes making Singapore into a "global schoolhouse," beginning with local programs established by MIT, Johns Hopkins, the University of Chicago, the Wharton School, Insead, and other centers of transnational managerial knowledge.[35] By making concrete connections between institutions, actors, techniques, and practices, Singaporean technocrats are defining a knowledge scale that follows an ecological logic of advantages, traffic, associations, and interrelations between global poles of knowledge power.

Urban assemblages in Kuala Lumpur and Singapore show that a new ecological sense of scale now dominates space-making activities as technocrats become more acutely sensitive to the alternatives for forging collaborations with multiple external institutions and actors who can be brought into interaction with domestic populations, in order to upgrade their human capital. Such ecological processes also put at stake the meanings of rooted as opposed to transient citizenship in these knowledge zones.

Intellectual Citizenship

Foucault[36] uses the term biopolitics to refer to the processes whereby individuals and populations become the explicit object of policies of government. The new ecologies of expertise in South East Asia must be examined in relation to graduated sovereignty or governing practices that coordinate the social and intellectual capacities of their populations in relation to neoliberal calculations. Regimes of valorization now read-just social rights in relation to skill profiles. Here, I will discuss only the social technologies that shape differential worth of citizens and expatriates, thus undermining the sociopolitical basis of citizenship.

For instance, the aim of Hong Kong to become "the Manhattan of Asia" is linked to technologies for progessively excluding working-class families long supported by massive public housing. While mainland professionals are welcome in Hong Kong, the mainland children of local workers are excluded. Under the right of abode law, the city authorities have limited the right of abode to only 5,000 of the estimated tens of thousands of children born to Hong Kong residents, a move supported by the People's Republic of China. The goal is to put a cap on the influx of poor working families, and to export them from Hong Kong: those who cannot afford to live in Hong Kong should consider living in nearby Shenzhen. The new cosmopolitan character of Hong Kong is to be finally officially "multicultural," to stress acceptance of diverse Asian as well as European expatriates, and to downplay ethnic Chinese chauvinism. There have been media exposures of racist discriminations against professionals from other Asian countries. The losers in this new intellectual game are poor, less-educated Chinese who have less of a claim to the city.

In Malaysia, the digital corridor is a test bed for a new kind of knowledge society that is yet to exist. An official justifying the new budget claims: "We shall all become citizens of the K-economy. . . . Survival in a borderless global economy based on knowledge requires everyone to be equipped with new skills and assimilate the culture of high technology and dynamic entrepreneurship. This is not wishful thinking. In fact, the Government has painstakingly endeavored to build a strong foundation, in particular through education and human resource development. I am confident that there is someone in every village who has acquired skills and knowledge in the field of technology from an institution of higher learning. I believe this was not possible five or ten years ago . . . To ensure success from the new economy, we need a pool of the best talent from at home and abroad. Efforts need to be taken to hire the best brains regardless of race or nationality, from Bangalore to California. This is a step toward creating a world-class workforce."[37]

Clearly, a new regime valorizing intellectual power is at play in a society still struggling to generalize high-tech knowledge across its population. It appears that the few thousand Indian software engineers working in the high-tech corridor have a symbolic purpose other than training Malaysians to adopt software solutions. Their presence show the road that is still to be traveled by Malaysian high-tech workers, and even more worrisome, the new regime of valorization that may replace pre-existing social ranking based on ethnicity. Bumiputera refers to the native-born Malay majority in neighboring Malaysia who get preferential treatment in all areas of the economy, political hierarchy, and education. The Prime Minister Mahathir Mohamed, himself has been a major architect of affirmative action for Malay bumiputera, recently charges them with lacking "the will to excel."[38] Bumiputera, he asserts, are "not equipping themselves with the necessary education and skills." He laments that affirmative action has become a "prosthesis" that Malays must discard rather than treat as the mark of a higher racial standing over non-Malays. The sense of security that comes from being coddled by affirmative action programs is hollow, Mahathir remarks, since it rests on the knowledge of others, and it can be swept away by global competition that depends on new skills and knowledge. But even some members of the educated

Malay class reject the new stress on a requisite mastery of science, mathematics, and English, and the need to be competitive with non-Malay citizens, much less with foreigners. There is the perception that the stress on intellectual advance in the sciences is a form of cybercolonization, of being discriminated against when the wealth of the country—from oil, gas, rubber, and timber—does not necessitate the rise of a knowledge society. The knowledge possessed by foreigners—who perform a kind of prosthetic function for the cyber corridor—need not be a requirement for Malays also because it undercuts their race-based privileges. The new valorization of intellectual capital is thus highly contested.

In Singapore, there is no such ambivalence over the new knowledge, but rather a sense of the raising of already exceptionally high stakes of intellectual excellence. Officials have stated that making a knowledge society is about "deciding whether talent flows in or out."[39] There are continuities with an older political rationality of controlling flows of people, resources, and substances while filtering out political problems and impurities. The current way to stay relevant to the world's big economies is to corral foreign experts in research farms as a way to attract global companies to base themselves in Singapore. "We are," an official told me, "focused on more skills, more privileges [at the top], and more control [at the bottom]." The immigration process for attracting expatriates makes very fine gradations. The top criteria are for foreigners with professional qualifications, university degrees, or specialist skills. They must either be entrepreneurs or investors, or hold professional or administrative positions. They should not have basic monthly salaries falling below U.S.$2,000 a month. A point system coding qualifications, skills, and income smooths the way for the individual expatriate to obtain permanent residency. Expatriates are not restricted from bringing their families, and buying condo properties. They are clearly treated as a special class of urban citizens regardless of their actual legal status. The goal to create a "cosmopolitan and creative" global city includes making it "an oasis of talent" that attracts the global business and professional classes, tourists, artists, and performers, while tightly controlling immigrant workers and all forms of vagrancy.[40]

While Singaporeans are among the most highly educated populations in the world (taking second places in global surveys of high school mathematics and sciences), there is a sense among lower class citizens of being left behind as the stakes of intellectual capital get higher. Students have become less certain about their career chances, and they believe that they have become less eligible for university scholarships. For instance, the Singapore-MIT program awards dozens of scholarships to foreign Asians who also receive fee waivers and other perks in education and employment. The welcoming carpet for foreign Chinese and Indian students and scientists incites fears that local subjects of the same ethnicity may be increasingly overlooked. For locals who do not aspire to be elite professionals or new economy managers, there is a sense of reverse bumiputera-ism or nativism. Singaporeans, who have long felt superior to Malays in Malaysia and in Singapore itself, now feel themselves to be second-class citizens in relation to Asian expatriates who seem to be preferred by the government-led corporations and private industry.

Local people refer to expatriates as "citizens without local roots," that is, figures who enjoy the benefits of citizenship without being citizens, and yet are free to come and go. Expatriates from Europe, North America, and Australia—mainly in the business, finance, and academic fields—tend to be on 5-year contracts, but many leave sooner, and few stay beyond 10 years. Expatriates most likely to apply for citizenship are mainland Chinese and Indian students who pass through the local universities on to jobs in the high-tech sector. Nevertheless, it is not clear either that these do not also constitute a "flow through" population. For instance, Wendy is a mainland Chinese who was trained in an Australian university. She recently left her lecturer husband in Melbourne with their baby to take up a 2-year contract with a bio-technology company based in Singapore. She intends to return to Australia. Some Chinese students view working in the Singapore research farms as a step in their career paths, which may eventually lead to better jobs back in China or in the United States. The very people upon whom are lavished educational and job benefits may plan to simply flow through Singapore on their way to other perhaps more advanced knowledge hubs.

Meanwhile, among those who are technically citizens, some are beginning to feel unrooted. A young man looking for a university scholarship pointed out that expatriate permanent residents do not have to perform national service. All native male Singaporeans must spend at least 2 years in military service, submitting to the ultimate measure of citizenship. Young men are put into the army during the 2–3 critical years when they are ready to launch themselves into high-powered careers. Thus the new regime valorizing knowledge has induced a sense of being re-nativized in the colonial sense, of becoming a reserve army to protect an island already set adrift in the ocean of the informational technology. In the new ecology of expertise, the economic coordination of rights and skills leaves open the question of moral identification with the city and the nation. Should foreign experts receive more social rights than citizens when the length of their residency remains an open question? Expatriates seem to enjoy a transnational intellectual citizenship that cuts across different political domains of social rights.

Conclusion

We need to rethink the assumption that informational technologies will follow the networks already shaped by trade and manufacturing in configuring Greater China. There is the implicit claim that given geography (propinquity to China) and ethnicity will shape as well the emerging informational landscape that will fit neatly into a Greater China container. I have suggested that instead of a structural focus we think about emerging social forms in terms of assemblage, a term that captures the emergent, mobile and contingent nature of interrelationships among disparate elements brought into play. In ambitious Asian cities, assemblages of multiple social logics, including neoliberal rationality, depend on space-making mechanisms that extend the technological space beyond the metropolis. I discussed how technocrats in partnership with managers shape ecological spheres of expertise, spaces of desired interactivity between mobile foreign experts and the domestic population, spinning networks that include but also extend beyond the space of Greater China. At the same time, such accumulation of expatriates and intellectual capital have engendered new regimes of valorization that put at stake the pre-existing ethnically marked notions of citizenship. Intensified interactions between a mobile knowledge population and rooted citizens raise in a rather stark way greater expectations of performance and consumption, and introduce a new moral economy of globalized intellectual citizenship.

Notes

1. The Wallerstenian center-periphery model has been modified by neoMarxists who now argue that there are multiple centers and peripheries, with for instance East Asian constituting its own complex of cores and peripheries. See G. Arrighi, "The Rise of East Asia: World Systemic and Regional Aspects," *International Journal of Sociology and Social Policy*, XVI, 7 (1996). Andre Gunder Frank (1998) has written a controversial book that describes China as the core of a multiple peripheries in the Asia-Pacific before the coming of the Europeans. Andre Gunder Frank, *Re-Orient: Global Economy in the Asian Age* (Berkeley: University of California Press, 1998).
2. A Dirlik, "The Asia-Pacific Idea: Reality and Representation in the Invention of a Regional Structure?" *Journal of World History*, 3 (1992): 55–79.
3. Aihwa Ong and Donald Nonini (eds.), *Ungrounded Empires: the Cultural Politics of Modern Chinese Transnationalism* (New York: Routledge, 1997).
4. Kenichi Ohmae, *The End of the Nation State: the Rise of Regional Economies* (New York: The Free Press, 1996).

5. A.J. Scott, J. Agnew, E.W. Soja, and M. Storper, "Global City-Regions," Global City-Regions Conference, 1999, available online via: http://www.sppsr.ucla.edu/globalcityregions/abstracts/abstracts.html.

6. Manuel Castells, *The Rise of Network Society* (Oxford: Blackwell, 1996): 413–414.

7. Ibid.: 416.

8. Peter Dicken, *Global Shift: Transforming the World Economy* (New York: Guilford, 1998).

9. Philip Kelly and Kris Olds, "Questions in a Crisis: The Contested Meanings of Globalization in the Asia-Pacific," in *Globalization and the Asia-Pacific: Contested Territories*, Olds, Kris, P. Dicken, P. F. Kelly, L. Kong, and H.W-C Yeung (eds.) (London: Routledge, 2000): 2.

10. For a discussion of growth triangles as a spatiosocial reconfiguration of sovereignty, see Aihwa Ong, "Graduated Sovereignty in Southeast Asia," *Theory, Culture and Society*, 17, 4 (August 2000): 55–75.

11. These are the points made in the general argument by Françoise Mengin, for conference on "New Information Technologies and the Reshaping of Power Relations: An Approach of Greater China's Political Economy," CERI, Paris, December 16–17, 2002.

12. Neil Brenner, "The Limits to Scale? Methodological Reflections on Scalar Structuration," *Progress in Human Geography*, 25, 4 (December 2001): 591–614.

13. Andrew Barry, *Political Machines: Governing a Technological Society* (London: The Athelone Press, 2001).

14. Brenner, "The Limits to Scale?": 592.

15. Manuel Castells, *The Rise of Network Society*, 179. For a perspective that problematizes discursive tropes of Chinese business networks and provides varied historical and contemporary accounts of their operations in the Asia-Pacific, see Ong, Aihwa, and Donald Nonini (eds.), *Ungrounded Empires*.

16. Annelise Saxenian, in *Regional Advantage: Culture and Competition in Silicon Valley and Route 128* (Cambridge: Harvard University Press, 1996): 2–3, argues that different high-tech sites gain "regional advantage" through distinctive patterns in the interlinked organization of infrastructures and firms. "Silicon Valley is a regional network-based industrial system that promotes collective learning and flexible adjustment among specialist producers of a complex of related technologies. The region's dense social networks and open labor markets encourage experimentation and entrepreneurship." This module of interlinked firms, industrial infrastructure and social technologies has informed Asian government-driven plans, but Saxenian is skeptical that there is any regional advantage in Asian high-tech hubs because there is a limited supply of skilled workers: Saxenian, *Silicon Valley's New Immigrant Entrepreneurs. San Francisco* (Public Policy Institute of California, 1999).

17. Gilles Deleuze and Félix Guattari, *A Thousand Plateaus: Capitalism and Schizophrenia* (Minneapolis: University of Minnesota Press, 1987): 3–4. (Translation: B. Massumi.)

18. Gilles Deleuze, *Foucault* (Minneapolis: University of Minnesota Press, 1988): 25. Trans. Sean Hand, Foreword by Paul Bove.

19. See Aiwha Ong and Stephen J. Collier (eds.), *Global Assemblages: Technology, Politics and Ethics as Anthropological Problems* (New York: Blackwell, 2005).

20. Manuel Castells, *The Rise of Network Society*.

21. Aihwa Ong, *Flexible Citizenship. The Cultural Logics of Transnationality* (Durham and London: Duke University Press, 1999): chapter 8.

22. Aihwa Ong, "Graduated Sovereignty in Southeast Asia,": 55–75.

23. Aihwa Ong, "Ecologies of Expertise: Governmentality in Asian Knowledge Societies," in *Global Assemblages*, Ong and Collier (eds.).

24. Ibid.

25. "The Tug of War for Asia's Best Brains," *Far Eastern Economic Review* (FEER) (November 9, 2000): 38–44.

26. Aihwa Ong, "Techno-migrants in the Network Economy," in *Global America? The Cultural Consequences of Globalization*, U. Beck, R. Winter, and N. Sznaider (eds.) (Liverpool, England: The University of Liverpool Press, 2003).

27. MDC (Multimedia Development Council) 2002, 1.
28. Mark Clifford, "Amid the Rubber Trees, a Multimedia Super Corridor?," *Business Week* (August 7, 1997).
29. See Aihwa Ong, "Ecologies of Expertise."
30. Economic Development Board (EDB), *Into the Fifth Decade* (Singapore: EDB, 2001): 9.
31. FEER, "The Tug of War for Asia's Best Brains."
32. Goh, Chong Tok, "Speech at the National Day Rally," *The Straits Times* (August 30, 1997).
33. For a view of other managerial networks plugging into China's labor markets, see Aihwa Ong, "Engineering Personalities and Guanxi in Shanghai," in *Frontiers of Capital: Ethnographic Reflections on the New Economy*, Melissa Fisher, and Gregory Downey (eds.) (forthcoming).
34. Economic Development Board (EDB), *Into the Fifth Decade*, 10.
35. Kris Olds and Nigel Thrift, "Cultures on the Brink: Re-Engineering the Soul of Capitalism on a Global Scale," in *Global Assemblages*, Ong and Collier (eds.).
36. James Faubion (ed.), "Governmentality," in *Essential Works of Foucault, 1954–1984*. Vol. 3 *Power* (New York: The New Press, 2000): 201–222.
37. "The Budget Speech: Strategies and Thrusts," *New Straits Times*, available online via: http://www.nstpi.com.my/z/Focus/copy_of_Budget/Two/20001028010916/wartrevamp (downloaded March 22, 2002).
38. *Star* (June 25, 2002).
39. "Good Governance," *Wall Street Journal* (January 1, 2000).
40. Brenda S.A. Yeoh and T.C. Chang, "Globalising Singapore: Debating Transnational Flows in the City," *Urban Studies*, 38, 1025 (June 2001).

NAME INDEX

Althusser, Louis   7, 85

Baker, James   71, 86
Barrett, Craig   210
Batto, Patricia   3, 5, 8
Bayart, Jean-François   12
Bentham, Jeremy   4, 31
Blair, Tony   207
Breslin, Shaun   74
Bush, George W.   141

Cai, Yingwen   97, 100
Castells, Manuel   59, 86, 109, 129, 238,
    239
Certeau, Michel de   11
Chang, Morris   177, 179, 212
Chang, Richard (see Zhang, Rujing)
Chen, Wu-fu   192
Chen, Shuibian   62, 85, 91, 92, 97, 100,
    103, 106, 107, 126, 131, 140, 176,
    192, 207, 208, 216
Chevrier, Yves   13
Chiang, Kai-shek   105
Clinton, Bill   71, 79

Damm, Jens   56
Deng, Xiaoping   56, 106
Dun, Jowei   173

Fang, Guojian   190
Ferdinand, Peter   144

Foucault, Michel   31, 56, 247
Frederick, H.H.   80

Gaspar, Roger   81
Gates, Bill   210
Giese, Karsten   3, 4, 7, 9
Granovetter, Mark   14, 52, 63
Gu, Liansong   195
Gu, Zhenfu   98
Gu, Zhongliang   195
Guiheux, Gilles   60, 63

Hu, Angang   130
Huang, Qi   31, 54, 88
Hughes, Christopher R.   5, 7, 8, 12, 13,
    54, 141
Hung, Chin-fu   3, 5

Jiang, Mianheng   13, 74, 162,
    194, 195
Jiang, Sheng   44
Jiang, Simon   210
Jiang, Zemin   13, 48, 74, 76, 85,
    105, 106, 126, 133, 162,
    194, 195

Kalathil, Shanti   142, 143
Kantor, Mark   73
Keller, Perry   79
Kluver, Alan R.   142
Krasner, Stephen D.   53

Lee, Ching Kwan   55
Leng, Tse-Kang   2, 3, 6, 8, 13, 58,
   60, 62
Lessig, Lawrence   86
Levin, Gerald   76
Li, Denghui   98, 103, 104, 126, 141,
   176, 213, 216, 232
Li, Gang   44
Li, Hongzhi   46, 48
Li, Ka-shing   64, 220, 221
Li, Kuo-ting   8, 206, 211
Li, Peng   106
Li, Richard   64, 210, 217,
   220, 221
Li, Zibin   209, 227
Lieberthal, Kenneth   140
Lin, Hai   53, 73, 86
Lindblom, Charles E.   59
Lonsdale, John   58, 59
Lu, Hsiu-lien   103

Mahathir, Mohamed   248
Mao, Zedong   106
Mathiesen, Thomas   81
Mengin, Françoise   5, 7, 13
Miao, Matthew   215
Moore, Gordon   158
Moses, Robert   88
Murdoch, James   76
Murdoch, Rupert   74, 75

Naughton, Barry   2, 6, 8,
   10, 13
Negroponte, Nicholas
   129, 132
Nolan, Peter   61
Norris, Pippa   136
Nye, Joseph S.   125

Ohmae, Kenichi   1, 57, 237
Ong, Aihwa   3, 7, 11, 12

Palmer, David A.   3, 4, 8, 10, 12
Pearson, Margaret   13

Qing, Xitai   44

Rocca, Jean-Louis   55, 59

Scalapino, Robert A.   57
Schneier, Bruce   80
Shambaugh, David   136
Shao, Yuming   104
Shih, Stan   210, 215
Suharto (President)   85
Sum, Ngai-Ling   2, 3, 6, 8,
   9, 11, 13
Swedberg, Richard   14, 52

Tak, Wing-Ngo   64
Tang, Jiaxuan   85
Toffler, Alvin and Heidi   132
Tsang, Donald   209, 218–220
Tung, Chee-Hwa   63, 64, 208,
   217, 220

Walton, Greg   77, 87, 88
Wang, Yangyuan   188
Wang, Yung-ching   13, 162,
   195, 215
Wank, David   61
Wong, Winston   13, 162,
   193, 195
Woods, Ngaire   128, 129

Xu, Guanchun   75

Yang, Jerry   210

Zeng, Li   88
Zhang, Rujing   161, 179
Zhu, Rongji   60, 106, 133
Zinnbauer, D.   86

SUBJECT INDEX

"Active opening and effective management" (*jiji kaifang, youxiao guanli*) policy 57, 176, 198, 216, 232

Asian crisis 6, 205, 208, 217–218, 231, 240, 241, 242

"assemblage" (Gilles Deleuze) 7, 211, 221, 240–241, 246–247, 251

bentuhua, see Taiwanization

biopolitics 11, 241, 247

biotechnology 9, 206, 209–210, 214, 222–226, 231, 239, 246

brain drain, *see* talent flows

Bulletin Board System (BBS) 4, 9, 20, 23, 25–34, 43

bureaucracy, bureaucratic, bureaucratized 9, 13, 39, 61, 63, 200

business (community) *see also* capitalists 8, 11, 60, 62–64, 74, 101, 105, 110–112, 114–115, 132, 135, 138, 162, 173, 176–177, 188, 192, 194, 201–202, 216, 224, 237, 243, 249, 250

capital:
  global capital 11, 53, 128–129, 192, 206, 223, 226, 231, 237, 241
  venture capital 185–186, 192, 212, 241

capitalism 6, 11, 55, 206, 211, 213, 217, 221, 223, 224, 226, 227, 228, 231, 238, 241

capitalists:
  global capitalists 13, 210
  local/regional capitalist 13, 210, 214–215
  petty capitalists 11, 229, 230
  venture capitalists 161, 172, 192, 194, 211

censorship, *see also* surveillance 21, 24–26, 31, 54, 56, 77–78, 86, 137

Chinese diaspora *see also* Overseas Chinese 102, 106, 114, 221

citizenship 11, 12, 179, 247, 250–251

civil society 49, 62

class (social class) *see also* working class 4, 12, 14, 23, 39, 55–56, 103, 109, 140, 243, 248, 249, 250

cluster (cluster development, cluster effect) 9, 158, 191, 199, 207, 209–210, 212–214, 217–218, 220, 223–225, 227, 230, 239–240

competitiveness 11, 135, 163, 168, 177–179, 190, 198, 201, 224, 244

Confucian, Confucianism 23, 40, 42, 136

Cultural Revolution 40, 141

Cyber-attacks, cyber-warfare, *see* warfare

danwei 4, 20, 21, 23
Daoism 4, 37, 38, 42–45
decision-making process 62, 63, 73, 130, 221
democracy 8, 31, 54, 55, 62, 73, 80, 81, 82, 86, 87, 88, 91, 103, 104, 109, 176
democratization 53, 55, 62–63
deterritorialization, *see* territorialization
developmental state 185, 240
dissident(s) (*see also* opposition) 31, 47, 54, 55, 86, 143

e-commerce 72, 78, 114, 129–135, 144, 209, 226
elite 13, 23, 29, 52, 61, 63, 64, 76, 208, 238, 239, 245, 250
entrepreneurial familism 239
entrepreneurship 9, 44, 210, 231, 248
environmental issues 31, 45, 55, 212
epistemic community 13, 210, 231
ethics, ethical 11, 72, 229
ethnic, sub-ethnic, ethnicity 1, 9, 12, 22, 23, 30, 54, 73, 85, 86, 141, 170, 192–193, 195–196, 239, 244–246, 248, 250–251
expatriate(s) 12, 213, 243–251

Falun Gong 4, 8, 31, 37, 40–41, 46–49, 73, 76, 86, 142, 143
"flying geese model" 205

gender 9, 23, 29–30, 32, 239
global intellectual commons 11, 229
global/local, globalization/localization 3, 6, 13, 134, 186–188, 194–195, 201–202, 206, 210, 213, 214, 217, 220–226, 229, 231–232, 238
global/regional, *see also* global/local 226, 239
governance 2, 7, 40, 79, 80, 87, 88, 129, 231

governmentality 14
Greater China 1, 2, 3, 5, 6, 9, 11, 28, 58, 113, 114, 126, 127, 136, 138, 144, 174, 187, 190, 192, 193, 195, 205, 206, 210, 214, 221, 226, 227, 229, 231, 232, 238, 245, 246, 251

hacker, hacking 5, 54, 84, 116, 141–143
Human Right (s) 8, 31, 48, 54, 55, 77–79, 83, 87–88

identification 1, 4, 20–22, 26, 33–34, 250
identity 4, 9, 14, 19–23, 26–33, 39, 40, 55, 85, 93, 128, 136, 186, 202, 209, 210, 213, 215, 230–232
ideological apparatus (of the state) 2, 7, 85
illegal, *see* legal
independence (of Taiwan) 98, 106, 108, 111, 176, 207, 232
individualism, individualistic, individualization 10, 20–22, 27, 39, 44, 45, 53
Intellectual Property Right (IPR) 11, 211, 228–232
Internet café 25, 26, 54, 137
Islamic (movement, region) 73, 82

labor 55–56, *see also* talent flow, and also:
  cheap labor 187, 188, 226, 241
  division of labor 6, 11, 57, 186, 191–192, 198, 199, 201, 206, 207, 212, 226, 232
  labor-intensive 6, 134, 155, 156, 158, 167, 180, 187, 217
  skilled labor 6, 167, 192, 242, 243, 244
  unskilled labor 212, 226
legal and illegal 11, 14, 53, 73, 85, 97, 101, 143, 228–230, 249
leisure 4, 22, 56, 224
lifestyle 4, 21, 27–29, 32–33, 55

local/global, localization/globalization, *see* global/local, globalization/localization

local government (s)   57, 61–62, 74, 77, 131, 188, 194

middle class   4, 23, 56, 140
modernity   5, 9, 10, 19, 38, 40, 59, 92, 237
modernization   9, 10, 38, 54, 59, 144, 223,
moral economy   11, 251
multicultural   248
multinational firm(s)   134, 142, 157, 160, 164, 185, 190, 201, 213, 218, 224, 229, 232

nationalism, nationalist projects, nationalist movements   54, 55, 84–86, 116, 141–143, 239
nation-state   1, 52, 53, 58, 125, 136, 139, 185, 237, 238, 239, 244
neoliberal   240, 242, 247, 251
"No haste, be patient" (*jieji yongren*) policy   57, 176, 215, 216
nongovernmental   49, 93, 113, 139
norm (s), normative   9, 10, 28, 56, 86

One China (principle)   108, 140, 215
"One country, two systems" formula   99, 108, 128
opposition (political opposition) *see also* dissident   31, 91, 137, 215
Overseas Chinese, *see also* Chinese diaspora   3, 4, 9, 28, 38, 49, 75, 85, 93, 102, 114, 136, 137, 143, 187, 195, 196, 211, 227

panopticon   4, 9, 20, 24, 26–27, 31–32, 37, 49, 56
"peaceful evolution" (of China)   53, 56
piracy   11, 228–230, 232

pluralization   53
pop culture   27, 136
power   2, 3, 5, 10–12, 14, 19, 29, 31, 33, 37, 48, 51, 56, 58–59, 61, 62, 64, 129, 144, 238, 240, 246
private/public, *see* public/private
privatization   20, 22, 61
propaganda   20–21, 47, 83, 84, 93, 104, 108, 110, 115, 116, 136
public/private   2, 5, 6, 13–14, 60–61, 73–74, 205–206, 210, 212–213, 218–220, 224, 230–231
public discourse   4, 20, 23, 28
public interest   7, 72, 73
public opinion   28, 97–100, 103–104, 109, 116, 136, 140–141
public space   9, 22–23, 33, 40, 49

qigong   40–41, 43, 46–47

regionalism   238
religion   4, 5, 8, 10, 37–49, 73, 85, 142
religiosity   10, 13, 38, 40–41, 44, 49
research and development (R&D)   58, 76, 77, 168–170, 172, 187, 190–192, 198–200, 212–214, 223–224, 226, 231
rule of law   53

sacred et profane   39
sectarianism   40
security:
    economic security   185–186, 198, 201
    international security   87, 88
    national security   5, 6, 7, 52, 53, 56, 57, 62, 72, 73, 76, 79, 80, 83, 139, 186, 199
sexual (freedom, relationships, sexuality)   9, 23, 27, 29–30, 32
siliconization   6, 11, 206, 207, 211, 214, 217, 222, 223, 226, 231, 232

small- and medium-sized
   enterprise (s)   114, 216
social interaction   30–31
social right(s)   11, 12, 240, 247, 250, 251
sociology:
   economic sociology   14
   historical sociology   14
   sociology of international
      relations   57
sovereignty   1, 5, 52, 53, 54, **55**, 57, 58,
   80, 126, 127, 128, 132, 139, 140, 142,
   143, 240, 247
spiritual, spirituality   4, 13, 39, 41, 43, 48,
   49
standardization   79, 166
State-owned enterprise (SOE)   60, 62,
   74, 75, 169, 170, 171, 175, 230
surveillance, *see also* censorship   7, 9,
   25–27, 34, 56, 76–78, 81–82, 86, 88,
   109

taiwanization   140
talent flow(s)   58, 62, 186, 188,
   196, 249

Taoism, *see* Daoism
territorialization/deterritorialization   7,
   39, 240
terrorism, terrorist   45, 80–82,
   86, 103
third generation (3G)   174–175, 193
Tibet (issue)   56, 73, 82, 85, 143
tradition, traditional   4, 10, 11, 20, 21, 23,
   28–30, 32, 38–44, 46, 49, 142, 223,
   231
transnational   2, 9, 12–14, 53, 55, 57–59,
   83, 207, 222, 228, 239, 240,
   247, 251

warfare (cyber-, electronic,
   information)   5, 76, 83, 84, 116
"way of life" (Michel de Certeau)   11,
   228, 232, 243
Weberian (state)   5, 59
working class   11, 55, 247
World Trade Organization (WTO)   7,
   54, 57, 61, 71, 72, 73, 74, 76, 79, 126,
   135, 171, 176, 216, 226, 228

FRANÇOISE MENGIN, political scientist, is Senior Research Fellow at the Centre for International Studies and Research (Sciences Po, Paris). Her most recent works focus on the re-mapping of the Greater China space in the context of globalization. She is the author of *Trajectoires Chinoises: Taiwan, Hong Kong et Pékin* (Paris, Karthala, 1998), and has co-edited with Jean-Louis Rocca, *Politics in China: Moving Frontiers* (New York, Palgrave, 2002).

GPSR Compliance
The European Union's (EU) General Product Safety Regulation (GPSR) is a set
of rules that requires consumer products to be safe and our obligations to
ensure this.

If you have any concerns about our products, you can contact us on

ProductSafety@springernature.com

In case Publisher is established outside the EU, the EU authorized
representative is:

Springer Nature Customer Service Center GmbH
Europaplatz 3
69115 Heidelberg, Germany